Ruminations
on
C++

Ruminations

on

C++

*A decade of programming
insight and experience*

Andrew Koenig

compiled & edited by
Barbara E. Moo

AT&T  Laboratories

▲▲ **ADDISON-WESLEY**

An imprint of Addison Wesley Longman, Inc.

Reading, Massachusetts • Menlo Park, California • New York • Harlow, England
Don Mills, Ontario • Sydney • Mexico City • Madrid • Amsterdam

Library of Congress Cataloging-in-Publication Data

Koenig, Andrew.
   Ruminations on C++ : a decade of programming insight and
experience / Andrew Koenig, Barbaba E. Moo.
      p.   cm.
   Includes index.
   ISBN 0–201–42339–1
   1. C++ (Computer program language)   I. Moo, Barbara E.
II. Title.
QA76.73.C153K68   1996
005.13'3––dc20   96–20161
                                                                          CIP

ru•min•ate *v.* **1.** To chew cud. **2.** To meditate at length; muse.

—*American Heritage Dictionary, second college edition* (Houghton Mifflin, 1985)

Cover design by Barbara T. Atkinson, with kibitzing by Andrew Koenig
Back cover photograph by Dag Brück
Cover illustration by Leslie Evans

Many of the designations used by the manufacturers and sellers to distinguish their products are claimed as trademarks. Where those designations appear in this book, and Addison-Wesley was aware of a trademark claim, the designations have been printed in initial caps or all caps.

The authors typeset this book (`pic|eqn|troff -mpm|dpost`) in Palatino, Helvetica and Courier, with assorted Sun Sparcstations and Hewlett-Packard laser printers, and two helper cats.

1 2 3 4 5 6 7 8 9 10-MA-99989796

*In recognition
of seventy years of research
at Bell Labs*

Preface

Origins

Early in 1988, about when I had finished writing *C Traps and Pitfalls*, Bjarne Stroustrup told me that he had just been invited to join the editorial board of a new magazine called the *Journal of Object-Oriented Programming* (JOOP). The magazine was intended to fit between the conventional academic journals and the magazines that are mostly product reviews and advertising. They were seeking a C++ columnist; was I interested?

C++ was just beginning to become an important influence on the programming community. Usenix had recently held its first C++ workshop, in Santa Fe, New Mexico. They had expected 50 people; more than 200 showed up. Many more would hop on the C++ bandwagon, which meant that the community would need an articulate, reasoned voice to speak against the torrent of hype that was sure to come. It would need someone who could make clear the difference between hype and substance and keep a cool head in all the turmoil. I took the offer anyway.

I am writing these words while thinking about my sixty-third column for *JOOP*. The column has appeared in every issue but two, during which time I badly needed a break and was lucky enough to be able to get Jonathan Shopiro to take my place. On a third occasion, I wrote only the introduction to the column, stepping aside for the distinguished Danish computer scientist Bjørn Stavtrup. In addition, Livleen Singh talked me into writing a column for the quarterly *C++ Journal*, which lasted six issues before folding, and Stan Lippman cajoled me into doing a column for the *C++ Report* when it changed from a newsletter into a full-fledged magazine. Adding my 29 *C++ Report* columns to the others brings the total to 98.

That's a lot of stuff to be scattered in periodicals all over the place. If the articles are useful individually, they should be even more useful when collected. In consequence, Barbara and I (mostly Barbara) have gone back over the columns, selected the best, and added to or rewritten them as needed for coherence and continuity.

Just what the world needs—another C++ book

Now that you know why the book exists, let me tell you why you should read it instead of some other C++ book. Goodness knows, there are enough of them; why pick this one?

The first reason is that I think you'll enjoy it. Most C++ books don't have that in mind: They are curriculum-based. Enjoyment is secondary at best.

Magazine columns are different. I suppose there must be some people out there who thumb through a copy of *JOOP* in a bookstore and skim my column before deciding whether to buy the magazine, but it would be arrogant to think that there are more than a few. Most readers will be seeing my column after they've already paid for it, which means that they have a completely free choice about whether to read it or not. So each column has to be worth reading on its own.

This book contains no long, boring discussions of obscure details. Beginners are not intended to be able to learn C++ from this book alone. A few people, who already know several programming languages thoroughly, and who have fig-ured out how to infer the rules for a new language by reading code, will be able to use this book to get an overview of C++. Most readers starting from scratch would do well to read *The C++ Programming Language* (Addison-Wesley 1991) by Bjarne Stroustrup, or Stan Lippman's *C++ Primer* (Addison-Wesley 1991), and then read this book.

This is a book about ideas and techniques, not details. If you want to find out how to make virtual base classes do double reverse backflips, you will have to turn elsewhere. What you will find here is lots of code to read. Try the examples for yourself. Classroom experience indicates that getting these programs to run and then modifying them is a good way to cement your understanding. For those who prefer to start with working code, we have made available selected examples from the book by anonymous FTP from `ftp.aw.com` in directory `cseng/authors/koenig/ruminations`.

If you know some C++ already, I think that this book will not only entertain but also enlighten you. This is the second reason to read it. My intent isn't to teach C++ per se. Instead, I want to show you how to think about programming in C++, and how to look at problems and express a solution in C++. Knowledge can be acquired systematically; wisdom cannot.

Organization

Although I intended each column to stand alone, I believe that the collection will be easier and more enjoyable to read when grouped by concept. The book is therefore divided into six parts.

Part I is an extended introduction to themes that will pervade the rest of the book. You won't find much code, but the ideas of abstraction and pragmatism explored there underlie both this book and, more important, the design of C++ and strategies for its effective use.

Part II looks at inheritance and object-oriented programming, which most people think are the most important ideas in C++. You will learn why inheritance is important and what it can do. You will also learn why it can be useful to conceal inheritance from its users and when to avoid inheritance altogether.

Part III explores templates, which *I* think constitute the most important idea in C++. The reason I think templates are so important is that they provide a particularly powerful kind of abstraction. Not only do templates allow the construction of containers that know almost nothing about the types of what they will contain, but they make it possible to abstract away things far more general than just types.

One reason that inheritance and templates are important is that they are ways of extending C++ without waiting (or paying) for people to produce new languages and compilers. The way to organize such extensions is through class libraries. Part IV talks about libraries—both their design and use.

With the basics well understood, we can look at some specialized programming techniques in Part V. Here you will find ways to tie classes inextricably together, as well as ways to keep them as far apart as possible.

Finally, in Part VI, we turn back for a last look at the terrain we have covered.

Compilation and editing

One artifact of these papers having been written over a number of years is that they do not always use all the current features of the language. This raises a problem: Do we rewrite the columns as if full-fledged ISO C++ were the norm when the standard hasn't been approved yet? Or do we deliberately write in an archaic style?

As with so much else in C++, we compromised. Where the original column was simply incorrect—either in light of how the language has changed since the column was written or because of a change in our understanding of how things should be—we've fixed it. A particularly pervasive example is our use of `const`, the importance of which has steadily grown in our understanding since `const` entered the language.

On the other hand, for instance, lots of examples here use `int` to represent true or false values, even though the standards committee has accepted `bool` as a built-in data type. The reasoning is that the columns were written that way originally, using `int` for such values will still work, and it will be years before most compilers support `bool`.

Acknowledgments

In addition to publishing our ideas in *JOOP*, the *C++ Report*, and the *C++ Journal*, we refined them through giving talks (and listening to students) in many places. Particularly noteworthy were the conferences organized by the Usenix Association and by SIGS Publications, publishers of *JOOP* and the *C++ Report*. In addition, there are the weeklong courses that the two of us have taught at Stanford

University under the auspices of the Western Institute in Computer Science, and at Bell Labs for members of the Acoustics Research Laboratory and Network Services Research Laboratory, as well as several courses and lectures that Dag Brück, then at the Department of Automatic Control at the Lund Institute of Technology and now at Dynasim AB, organized in Sweden.

We are also grateful to the people who read and commented on drafts of the book and the columns that it comprises: Dag Brück, Jim Coplien, Tony Hansen, Bill Hopkins, Brian Kernighan (who gets extra credit for reading the entire book twice carefully with pen in hand), Stan Lippman, Rob Murray, George Otto, and Bjarne Stroustrup.

The columns would never have become a book without the help of Deborah Lafferty, Loren Stevens, and Tom Stone at Addison-Wesley, and the copy editing of Lyn Dupré.

We are particularly grateful to the enlightened managers at AT&T who made it possible to write these columns and to compile this book, including Dave Belanger, Ron Brachman, Jim Finucane, Sandy Fraser, Wayne Hunt, Brian Kernighan, Rob Murray, Ravi Sethi, Bjarne Stroustrup, and Eric Sumner.

Andrew Koenig
Barbara Moo

Gillette, New Jersey
April, 1996

Contents

0

Prelude

Once upon a time, I met someone who had worked in many programming languages, but had never written a C or C++ program. He asked a question that made me think: "Can you convince me that I should learn C++ instead of C?" I've given talks about C++ to quite a number of people, but it suddenly dawned on me that these people had all been C programmers. How could I explain C++ to someone who had never used C?

I started by asking him what languages he had used that were similar to C. I knew he had programmed a lot in Ada—but that didn't help, because I didn't know Ada. He did know Pascal, though, as did I. I wanted to find an example that would rest on the limited basis of our common understanding.

Here is how I tried to explain to him what C++ can do well that C can't.

0.1 First try

The central concept of C++ is the class, so I started by defining a class. I wanted to write a complete class definition that was small enough to explain and might still be useful. Moreover, I wanted it to have public and private data, because I wanted to work data hiding into the example. After a few minutes of head scratching, I came up with something like this:

```
#include <stdio.h>

class Trace {
public:
        void print(char* s) { printf("%s", s); }
};
```

I explained how this defined a new type called Trace, and how to use Trace objects to print output messages:

```
int main()
{
        Trace t;
        t.print("begin main()\n");
        // the body of main goes here
        t.print("end main()\n");
}
```

So far, what I have done looks much like it would in other languages. In fact, even in C++, it might have made sense to use printf directly, rather than going through the extra step of defining a class and then creating an object of that class, in order to print these messages. However, as I went on explaining how the definition of class Trace worked, I realized that even this simple example had touched on some of the important things that make C++ so flexible.

0.1.1 A refinement

For instance, as soon as I had used the Trace class, I realized that it might be useful to be able to turn off the trace output on occasion. No problem; just change the class definition:

```
#include <stdio.h>

class Trace {
public:
        Trace() { noisy = 0; }
        void print(char* s) { if (noisy) printf("%s", s); }
        void on() { noisy = 1; }
        void off() { noisy = 0; }

private:
        int noisy;
};
```

Now the class definition includes two new public member functions called on and off, which affect the state of a private member named noisy. Printing occurs only if noisy is on (nonzero). Thus, saying

```
t.off();
```

will suspend printing on t until we later resume printing by saying

```
t.on();
```

I also pointed out that, because these member functions were part of the Trace class definition itself, the C++ implementation would expand them inline, thus making it inexpensive to keep the Trace objects in the program even when no tracing was being done. It occurred to me that I could effectively turn off all Trace objects at once simply by defining print to do nothing and recompiling the program.

0.1.2 Another refinement

The real insight didn't hit me until I asked, "How would users be likely to want to modify a class like this one?"

Users always ask for changes to programs. Often, these changes are generalizations, such as "Can you make it shut up when you want?" or "Can you make it print on something other than the standard output?" I had just answered the first question. The second question caught my attention next, and turned out to be trivial to answer in C++, but not in C.

I might have used inheritance to create a new species of the `Trace` class. Instead, I decided to keep the demonstration simple, and to avoid introducing a new concept. Accordingly, I changed the `Trace` class to remember the identity of an output file in its private data, and to provide a constructor to let the user nominate an output file:

```
#include <stdio.h>

class Trace {
public:
        Trace() { noisy = 0; f = stdout; }
        Trace(FILE* ff) { noisy = 0; f = ff; }
        void print(char* s)
                { if (noisy) fprintf(f, "%s", s); }
        void on() { noisy = 1; }
        void off() { noisy = 0; }

private:
        int noisy;
        FILE* f;
};
```

This change relies on the fact that

```
printf(args);
```

is equivalent to

```
fprintf(stdout, args);
```

Creating a `Trace` object without special pleading causes that object's f member to be `stdout`. Thus, the call to `fprintf` does what the call to `printf` did in the previous versions.

The `Trace` class now has two constructors: The one without arguments sends the output to `stdout` exactly as before, and the other one allows an output file to be specified explicitly. Thus, the previous sample program that used the `Trace` class would continue to work, but it could also be changed to write on, say, `stderr`:

```
int main()
{
        Trace t(stderr);
        t.print("begin main()\n");
        //  the body of main goes here
        t.print("end main()\n");
}
```

In short, the particular way I had used C++ classes made it trivial to change the program in useful ways, without breaking any of the code that used those classes.

0.2 Doing it without classes

At this point, I started thinking about a typical C solution to this problem. It would probably start with a trace function (instead of a class) something like this:

```
#include <stdio.h>

void trace(char *s)
{
        printf("%s\n", s);
}
```

It might then allow me to suppress the output like this:

```
#include <stdio.h>

static int noisy = 1;

void trace(char *s)
{
        if (noisy)
                printf("%s\n", s);
}

void trace_on() { noisy = 1; }
void trace_off() { noisy = 0; }
```

This solution would work, but it would have three distinct disadvantages when compared with the C++ solution.

First, the trace function here is not inline, so it involves function-call overhead even when tracing is turned off.* This overhead can be substantial in many C implementations.

---

* Dag Brück pointed out that putting efficiency first is a trademark of the C/C++ culture. It is a sign of how much that culture has influenced my thinking that I mentioned efficiency first without even noticing that I had done so.

Second, the C version introduces three global names: `trace`, `trace_on`, and `trace_off`, where the C++ version introduces only one.

Third, and most important, it is hard to generalize this example to write on more than one file. To see why, consider how we might use this `trace` function:

```
int main()
{
        trace("begin main()\n");
        //  the body of main goes here
        trace("end main()\n");
}
```

In the C++ version, it was possible to mention the file to be used just once, at the creation of a `Trace` object. In the C version, in contrast, there is no convenient place to supply a file name. The obvious place is as an additional argument to the `trace` function, but that requires finding every call to `trace` and inserting the extra argument. An alternative would be to introduce a fourth function, called something like `trace_out`, that would switch trace output to some other file. This would have the same problems as keeping track of whether tracing is on or off. Consider, for example, the effect of `main` calling some function that happens to use `trace_out` to write on a different file. When is the output switched back? Clearly, getting it right would take considerable vigilance.

0.3 Why was it easier in C++?

The difficulty in extending the C solution comes from the lack of a convenient place to store auxiliary state information—in this case, the file name and "noisy" flag. This problem was particularly annoying here, because its first solution did not need any state information at all; it was only later that the need to store state became known.

Adding state storage to an existing design that doesn't already have it is hard. In C, the usual way to do so is to hide it somewhere, as I did with the "noisy" flag here. But that technique can go only so far; here, it became tricky to manage when multiple output files entered the picture. The C++ version was easier, because C++ encourages the use of classes to represent things such as output streams; using a class gives a ready-made place to drop state information when needed.

In effect, C has a bias toward not storing state unless one decides in advance to do so. Thus, C programmers tend to assume that there is an "environment": a collection of places they can go to find the present state of the system. This works fine as long as there is only one environment and one system. But so often, a system grows by taking something that was unique and creating more of them.

0.4 A bigger example

My visitor found the example convincing. After he left, I realized that what I had shown was similar to an experience that some other people I knew had had on a much larger scale.

They were working on an interactive transaction-processing system: the kind of system with a bunch of people sitting at screens that display the electronic equivalents of paper forms. The people fill out the forms, the contents of which are then used to update databases, and so on. The project was nearly complete when their customers asked for a change: They wanted to be able to split the screen and display two unrelated forms at once.

This kind of change can be terrifying. Programs of this kind are typically filled with calls to library functions that assume they know where "the screen" is and how to update it. A change of this sort generally involves finding every piece of code that embodies the notion of "the screen" and replacing it with something that means "the current part of the screen."

Of course, these notions are precisely the kind of hidden state that we saw in the earlier examples. Therefore, it should come as no surprise that this change to the application program was much easier in C++ than experience with C would indicate. All that was necessary was to change the screen-display routines themselves. The relevant state information was already part of a class, which made it trivial to replicate it in multiple objects of that class.

0.5 Conclusion

What made it so easy to change this system was the notion that the state of a computation should be explicitly available, as part of an object, rather than being something that is hidden behind the scenes. Indeed, the very notion that the state of a computation should be made explicit is fundamental to the whole idea of object-oriented programming.*

Such concerns may seem trivial when shown in small examples, but for larger programs they can greatly affect how easy the programs are to understand and change. If we see a snippet of code like this:

```
push(x);
push(y);
add();
z=pop();
```

---

* It is only a little too flip to say that the most fundamental difference between object-oriented programming and functional programming is that, in object-oriented programs, the state that results from a computation usually replaces the prior state, and, in functional programs, it never does.

we can reasonably guess that there is a stack being manipulated somewhere to set z to the sum of x and y, but we have to look elsewhere to find that stack. If, on the other hand, we see

```
s.push(x);
s.push(y);
s.add();
z = s.pop();
```

it is a pretty good bet that the stack is s. It is true that, even in C, we might have seen

```
push(s,x);
push(s,y);
add(s);
z=pop(s);
```

but C exerts enough of a bias against that kind of programming that C programmers often fail to code that way in practice—until they discover that they need more than one stack. The reason is that C++ uses the notion of a class to tie state and action together in a way that C does not. C is biased against this last example because making the example work requires defining the type of s separately from the functions push, add, and pop. C++ offers a single place to describe all those things and to make it clear that they are all connected. By putting connected things together, we can use C++ to express our intentions more clearly.

Part I

Motivation

Abstraction is selective ignorance. Imagine driving a car and having to be aware at every moment of everything going on: in the engine, in the transmission, in the connection between the steering wheel and the tires. Either you'd never make it out of the driveway, or you'd quickly cause an accident.

Similarly, programming rests on choosing what to ignore and when. That is, programming is building abstractions that let us ignore those aspects of the problem that are not important at the moment. C++ is interesting because it lets us describe a particularly wide range of abstractions. C++ makes it easier to think about programs as collections of abstractions and to hide the details of how these abstractions work from users who don't need to care about these details.

C++ is also interesting because it was designed with a particular user community in mind. Some languages are designed to explore particular theoretical principles, others for specific kinds of applications. C++ was designed to let C programmers program in a more abstract style while retaining those aspects of C that are useful or have become "natural" to C programmers. Hence, C++ retains C's emphasis on fast execution, portability, and ease of interfacing with hardware and other software systems.

C++ is intended for a user community that above all is pragmatic. C and C++ programmers routinely deal with messy, real problems; they need tools that let them solve these problems. This pragmatism accounts for a certain degree of informality about both the C++ language and its users. For example, C++ programmers often write incomplete abstractions for limited purposes: They'll design a little class that solves a particular problem without worrying whether that class provides every feature that every user of the class might want. If the class is even barely good enough, they can choose to ignore its incompleteness. Sometimes, an adequate solution now is better than an ideal one later.

There is a difference, however, between pragmatism and laziness. Although it is certainly possible to write C++ programs that are maintenance nightmares, it is also possible to use C++ to partition problems into well-separated pieces, none of which needs to know more about the others than absolutely necessary.

This book keeps returning to these two ideas: pragmatism and abstraction. We begin in this part by looking at how C++ supports these ideas. Later parts will explore the kinds of abstractions C++ lets us write.

1

Why I use C++

This chapter is sort of a personal history: I'll talk about the events that first got me interested in using C++, and some insights I gained while learning it. Thus, I will not say what things I believe are most useful about C++ in general: Instead, I'll talk about how I found C++ useful in my particular situation.

This situation is interesting because it is real. My problem was not one of the "standard object-oriented problems," such as graphics, or interactive user interfaces. Rather, it was the kind of messy problem that people used to solve first in assembly language and then mostly in C. The system had to run efficiently on a number of different machines, to interface with a large body of existing system software, and do so reliably enough to satisfy a demanding user community.

1.1 The problem

I wanted to make it easy for program authors to distribute their work to a growing family of machines. The solution had to be portable and yet use a number of operating-system facilities. C++ did not yet exist, so C was essentially the only choice for these particular machines. My first solution worked well, but proved surprisingly hard to implement, mostly because of the need to avoid arbitrary limits in the program.

The number of machines involved grew until my program needed a major revision to handle the load. But the program was already so complex that I feared that I would not be able to write the new sections in C without making so many mistakes as to compromise reliability.

I decided to try the revisions in C++ instead. The result was successful: My rewrite increased the speed of the old version dramatically, without compromising reliability. Although C++ programs are innately no faster than corresponding C programs, C++ made it intellectually manageable for me to use techniques that would have been too hard for me to implement reliably in C.

What attracted me to C++ had more to do with data abstraction than with object-oriented programming. C++ let me define the characteristics of my data structures, and then to treat these data structures as "black boxes" when it came time to use them. This would have been much harder in C. And no other language would have given me the combination of efficiency and reliability I needed while still allowing me to deal with the systems (and users) that already existed.

1.2 History and context

In 1980, I was a member of the Computing Science Research Center at AT&T Bell Laboratories. Early prototypes of a local-area network were then first becoming available for experiments, and management wanted to encourage people to exploit this new technology. To that end, we were about to acquire five new computers, more than doubling the number of machines available to us. Moreover, it was clear from the trend of hardware prices that we would ultimately have many more machines (indeed, the Center's network has at times comprised as many as 50 machines) and that we would have to deal somehow with the software-maintenance problem that would cause.

That maintenance problem was stickier than you might imagine. On the one hand, critical programs such as compilers were changing constantly. Such programs must be installed carefully; running out of disk space or encountering hardware problems during installation might render an entire machine useless. On the other hand, we did not have anything like a comp-center staff: All the machines were kept going by a cooperative effort among the people who used them. Thus, the only way that a new program could find its way to other machines was for someone to volunteer to take responsibility for getting it there correctly. Of course, program authors were not always eager to do so. Thus, we needed a global solution to this maintenance problem, "yesterday, if possible."

Mike Lesk had tackled the problem a few years before, and had partially solved it with a program called uucp that has since become well known. I say "partially," because Mike deliberately did not address security issues. Moreover, uucp could transfer only a single file at a time, and gave the sender no way of verifying that a transmission had indeed occurred correctly.

1.3 Automatic software distribution

I resolved to carry Mike's banner a few steps further by writing a collection of programs called ASD (Automatic Software Distribution) that, using uucp for transportation, would give program authors a reasonably secure way to propagate their work to what I anticipated would soon be a large fleet of machines. I decided to augment uucp in two ways: by authenticating the sender of an update, and by installing a collection of files in diverse places at the same time.

Neither of these functions was particularly difficult in principle, but both proved messy in practice because of the conflicting desires to be reliable and general. I intended ASD for people who were not in the business of system administration. To get them to use it at all, I would have to give them something that would do what they expected—correctly—and that wouldn't have any niggling restrictions. Thus, for example, I did not want any arbitrary limits on the length of a file name, the size of a file, the number of files that could be handled at one time, and so on. And if a bug in ASD ever distributed an incorrect version of a program, that would be the end of ASD—I would have no second chance.

1.3.1 Reliability versus generality

C has no built-in notion of variable-length arrays: The only alternative to fixing the size of an array during compilation is to allocate memory dynamically. Thus, my desire to avoid arbitrary limits led to a lot of dynamic memory allocation, and consequent complexity. This complexity led me to worry about reliability. For example, here is a typical code fragment from ASD:

```
/* read the file mode in octal */
param = getfield(tf);
mode = cvlong(param, strlen(param), 8);

/* read the user id */
uid = numuid(getfield(tf));

/* read the group id */
gid = numgid(getfield(tf));

/* read the file name (path) */
path = transname(getfield(tf));

/* insist on end of line */
geteol(tf);
```

This fragment reads successive fields from a line of the file identified by tf. To do so, it calls getfield several times, passing the result to various conversion routines.

This may appear straightforward, but appearances deceive: This example conceals an important subtlety. To see it, ask what type getfield might return. Because the value of getfield represents part of an input line, getfield must evidently return a character string. But C has no character strings; the nearest equivalent is a character pointer. That pointer must point somewhere; when and how is that memory reclaimed?

There are several ways to handle this kind of problem in C, all of which have difficulties. One possibility would be to make getfield return a pointer to newly allocated memory each time that it is called, and to make getfield's caller responsible for freeing that memory. Because our fragment calls get-field four times, that would require four calls to free somewhere. I rejected this approach because so many calls would be a nuisance to write, and I would surely forget a few.

Then again, if I could afford to forget one, perhaps I could afford to forget all; another solution would be to abandon all attempts to reclaim memory, and to have getfield allocate memory, at each call, which is never freed. I rejected this approach because it might cause memory exhaustion, where a more careful strategy would avoid running out of memory.

The solution I chose instead was to have getfield return a pointer to memory that would persist only until the next call to getfield. Thus, I would not have to remember to free the result of getfield in general; in exchange for that convenience, I would have to remember to copy the result of getfield (and free the copy) if I wanted to save it somewhere. This exchange was certainly worthwhile for the preceding fragment—and, in fact, for ASD overall—but this strategy definitely made the program harder to write than it would have been if memory were never freed at all. The result of my effort to write a program without arbitrary limits was that most of the work in the program went into book-keeping, rather than into solving the real problem. Because I had to do all that bookkeeping by hand, I constantly worried that a bookkeeping error might make ASD unreliable.

1.3.2 Why C?

At this point, you may be asking yourself "Why did he do this in C?" After all, the bookkeeping I describe could be done much more easily in languages such as Smalltalk, Lisp, or Snobol, all of which have garbage collection and extensible data structures.

It was easy to rule out Smalltalk: It was unavailable for our machines! To a lesser extent, Lisp and Snobol had the same problem: Although they were available on the machines that we had at the time I started to work on ASD, there was no assurance that either language would run on machines that we might acquire later. In fact, C was the only language whose portability was assured in our environment.

But even if some other language were available, I needed an efficient operating-system interface. ASD fiddled a lot with the file system, and that fiddling had to be fast and reliable. People would send hundreds of files at a time, taking up millions of bytes, and they would expect the system to work quickly and correctly the first time.

1.3.3   Dealing with rapid growth

When I began work on ASD, our network was very much a prototype: It was sometimes unavailable, and it was not connected to all machines. Thus, I used uucp for transportation—I had no choice. Over time, however, the network became first reliable and then indispensable. As the network grew, the number of machines using ASD also grew. By the time we reached about 25 machines, uucp proved too slow to handle the load comfortably. It was time to bypass uucp, and start using the network directly.

I had a good idea of what it would take to exploit the network for software distribution: I would have to write a spooler to coordinate distribution activities on a number of machines. This spooler would need a data structure on disk to track which machines had received and installed a package successfully in order to let people find out what had gone wrong if something failed. It would need to be robust enough to run for long periods without human intervention.

Nevertheless, I stalled for quite a while, discouraged by all the clerical details that had beset me while writing the initial version of ASD. I knew the problem I wanted to solve, but couldn't see how to write a C program that would meet all my constraints. To be successful, the new spooler would have to

- Interface with even more operating-system facilities
- Avoid arbitrary limits
- Run substantially more quickly than the old version
- Remain extremely reliable

I could see how to do all these things except the last. Writing a spooler is hard enough, but writing a *reliable* spooler is harder still. A spooler must be able to cope with all kinds of strange failures, and still leave things in a state from which it can recover.

It took years to work the bugs out of uucp, yet I thought that for my new ASD spooler to be a success, it would have to be substantially bugfree immediately.

1.4   Enter C++

At about that time, I decided to see whether I could solve my problems in C++. Although I already had a passing familiarity with C++, I had not done any serious work in it. However, Bjarne Stroustrup's office was not far from mine, and we had talked about the language as it evolved.

There were several aspects of C++ that I thought would help me.

One was the notion of an abstract data type. I knew, for example, that I needed to store the status of a request to send software to each of several machines. I had to be able to store that status in a human-readable file and get it back again, update the status in response to a conversation with a machine, and eventually change the information that constituted the status. All of which needed to be flexible in its memory allocation: Part of the status I wanted to store for a machine was the output of an arbitrary command executed on that machine, and the length of that output was unbounded.

Another help was a package that Jonathan Shopiro had recently written for handling strings and lists. This package let me have truly dynamic character strings without having to worry about bookkeeping details. It also supported the formation of variable-length lists of objects of user-specified type. Thus, once I defined an abstract data type called, say, machine_status, I could use Shopiro's package to define another type that would represent a list of machine_status objects.

To make the design more concrete, here is a code fragment from the C++ ASD spooler. Here, the variable m is of type machine_status:*

```
struct machine_status {
        String p;           // machine name
        List<String> q;     // output, if any
        String s;           // error status; null if successful
};
// ...

m.s = domach(m.p, dfile, m.q);    // try to send a file

if (m.s.length() == 0) {          // did it work?
        sendfile = 1;             // success—remember, we've sent a file
        if (m.q.length() == 0)    // is there any output?
                mli.remove();     // no, we're done with this machine
        else
                mli.replace(m);   // yes, save the output
} else {
        keepfile = 1;             // failure—note it, to try again later
        deadmach += m.p;          // add to the list of dead machines
        mli.replace(m);           // put its status back in the list
}
```

This fragment is executed once for each machine to which we are sending software. The structure m stores the result of an attempt to send a file to another machine in three fields: p is a String that holds the name of the machine; q is a List of Strings that holds the output, if any, from the attempt; and s is a String that either is null if the attempt succeeded or shows the reason for failure.

The domach function is what actually tries to send data to another machine. It returns two results: one explicitly and the other implicitly by modifying its third argument. After we have called domach, m.s tells whether the attempt succeeded, and m.q contains the output, if any.

---

* The more rigorous reader might be surprised that I defined the class with public data members. This was intentional: machine_status is a simple class whose structure is its interface. For simple classes that are their structure, nothing is gained by making the data private.

We therefore check whether `m.s` is empty, by comparing `m.s.length()` to 0. If `m.s` is indeed empty, we set `sendfile` to remember that we sent a file to at least one machine, and then we see whether there is any output. If there is none, we call `mli.remove` to remove the machine currently under consideration from the `List` of machines in the status structure; otherwise, we store the current status in the `List`. The `mli` variable is essentially a pointer into this `List` (`mli` stands for "machine list iterator").

If the attempt failed to talk to the remote machine, we set `keepfile` to remember that we must retain the data file for a subsequent attempt, and then store the current status in the `List`.

There is nothing profound about this program fragment. Every line of it bears an obvious relationship to the problem that it is trying to solve. Unlike in the C fragment, there are no hidden bookkeeping conventions. *And that is exactly the point.* All the bookkeeping can be isolated in the library, debugged once, and then forgotten. The rest of the program can concentrate on solving the problem.

That solution was a success. ASD has sent up to 4000 updates per year to as many as 50 machines. A typical update is a new version of a compiler, or even the operating-system kernel itself. In essence, C++ made it possible for me to write programs that expressed my intentions more accurately than I could in C.

We have already seen one example of a C program fragment that concealed some subtleties; we will now explore what it is about C that makes those subtleties necessary, and how it is possible for the C++ programmer to avoid them.

1.4.1 Hidden conventions in C

Although C has character string literals, it does not really have any true notion of character strings. A string constant is shorthand for an otherwise nameless array of characters (with a null character inserted at the end by the compiler to mark the end of the string), and it is up to the programmer to decide how to deal with those characters. Thus, for instance, although it is legal to say

```
char hello[] = "hello";
```

it is not legal to say

```
char hello[5];
hello = "hello";
```

because C has no built-in way of copying an array. The first of these examples declares a character array with six elements whose initial values are `'h'`, `'e'`, `'l'`, `'l'`, `'o'`, and `'\0'` (a null character). The second example is illegal, because C has no array assignment; the closest approximation is

```
char *hello;
hello = "hello";
```

Here, the variable `hello` is a pointer, not an array: It points to the memory that contains the character constant `"hello"`.

Suppose that we define and initialize two character "strings":

```
char hello[] = "hello";
char world[] = " world";
```

and we want to concatenate them. We'd like the library to provide a `concatenate` function that would enable us to write:

```
char helloworld[];                    // wrong
concatenate(helloworld, hello, world);
```

Unfortunately, this does not work, because we did not say how much memory the `helloworld` array should occupy. We could make it work by saying

```
char helloworld[12];                  // dangerous
concatenate(helloworld, hello, world);
```

but we do not want to have to count characters whenever we wish to concatenate strings. Of course, we could deliberately allocate too much memory, by saying

```
char helloworld[1000];                // wasteful and still dangerous
concatenate(helloworld, hello, world);
```

But how much should we allocate? As long as we have to specify the size of these character arrays as a constant in advance, we are guaranteed to guess wrong at times.

The only way to avoid guessing wrong is to determine string sizes dynamically. Thus, for example, we would like to be able to write

```
char *helloworld;
helloworld = concatenate(hello, world);              // tricky
```

and have the `concatenate` function take responsibility for determining how much memory is needed to contain the concatenation of variables `hello` and `world`, allocate that much memory, form the concatenation, and return a pointer to that memory. Indeed, that is precisely what I did in the initial, C version of ASD: I adopted the convention that all strings or stringlike values would have their sizes determined and memory allocated dynamically. But when is the memory freed?

There is no way for a C string library to know when the programmer is done using a string. Thus, the library must give the programmer the responsibility for deciding when to free string memory. Once we do that, there are many ways to implement dynamic strings in C.

For ASD, I adopted three conventions. The first two are common in C programs; the third is not:

1. A string is represented by a pointer to its initial character.
2. The end of a string is marked by a null character.
3. Functions that generate strings do not share a universal convention about the lifetimes of those strings. For example, some functions return pointers to static buffers that persist until the next call of those functions, whereas others return pointers to memory that their caller is expected to free. It is the responsibility of the user of these strings to take into account those varying lifetimes, use `free` when necessary to free strings that are no longer needed, and not to free strings that will be freed elsewhere automatically.

The lifetime of a string constant such as `"hello"` is effectively unlimited, so that after saying

```
char *hello;
hello = "hello";
```

I must not free the variable `hello`. The preceding `concatenate` function also returns a value that persists indefinitely, but, because the value is in dynamically allocated storage, I should free it when I'm done with it.

Finally, some functions such as `getfield` return a value that persists for a well-defined, but limited, period of time. I shouldn't ever free the value of `getfield`, but if I want to keep the value that it returned around for a long time, I must remember to copy it into less ephemeral storage.

Why deal with three different kinds of storage lifetime? I had no choice about character constants: Their semantics are part of C, and I can't change them. But I could have decided that all other string functions should return a pointer to newly allocated storage. I would then not have to decide whether or not to free such storage: It would always be right to free it when I was done using it.

The main reason that I didn't make all those string functions allocate new memory for each call was that doing so would have made my program significantly larger. For example, I would have had to rewrite the C fragment (Section 1.3.1 (page 13)) to look like this:

```
/*  read the file mode in octal  */
param = getfield(tf);
mode = cvlong(param, strlen (param), 8);
free(param);

/*  read the user id  */
s = getfield(tf);
uid = numuid(s);
free(s);

/*  read the group id  */
s = getfield(tf);
gid = numgid(s);
free(s);
```

```
/*  read the file name (path)  */
s = getfield(tf);
path = transname(s);
free(s);

/*  insist on end of line  */
geteol(tf);
```

It seemed to me that it was worth having a few extra cases to reduce the program size as much as I did.

Using C++ for the revision of ASD allowed me to write programs that were even more compact, and relied on fewer hidden conventions, than I could ever have written in C. For an example, look back at the C++ ASD fragment. The first statement of that fragment assigns a value to m.s:

```
m.s = domach(m.p, dfile, m.q);
```

Of course, m.s is an element of structure m, which in turn may well be part of some larger structure, and so on. If I had to remember the right places to free m.s myself, I would be confident of two things. First, I wouldn't get all the places right the first time; it would probably take many tries before all the bugs were ironed out. Second, I could be confident of introducing new bugs each time that I changed anything significantly.

I found that using C++ freed me from having to worry about all these details. In fact, I cannot think of a single mistake I made while I was writing the C++ ASD spooler that was related in any way to memory allocation.

1.5 Recycled software

The C version of ASD had a number of functions to deal with character strings, but I never considered packaging those functions separately for general use. It was too much trouble to explain the conventions that people would have had to follow to use those functions. Moreover, I know from years of dealing with computer users that most of the people whose programs failed because they hadn't followed the conventions would blame me. C does many things well, but handling flexible character strings isn't one of them.

The C++ ASD spooler used character-string functions, too, and someone else had already written them, so I didn't have to. He was more willing to make the C++ string routines available to others than I would have been to distribute my C string routines, because he didn't have to rely on his users' remembering hidden conventions. Similarly, I used that string library as a basis for routines to implement the specialized pattern matching needed to analyze file names. These routines, in turn, can readily be extracted and used for other work.

I have since had several similar experiences while writing C++ programs. I think of an idea that is fundamental to my problem in some way, define a class that captures that idea, and make sure that that class works in isolation. I then use it to solve my problem in terms of that idea. Surprisingly often, the solution works the first time it compiles.

My C++ programs are so reliable because I can put much more of my ideas directly into C++ class definitions than into anything I could have written in C. Once the class definition is right, I have no choice but to use it in the way I intended when I wrote it. Thus, I think of C++ as helping me keep my ideas straight and holding me to my word.

1.6 Postscript

In the years since I first wrote the column on which this chapter is based, I have been gratified to see that a whole industry of C++ class libraries has formed. There have been widely distributed C libraries, to be sure, but all the C libraries that I know of address specific problem domains. C++, in contrast, has enabled truly general-purpose libraries, where the library authors do not even know about the uses to which their work will be put.

Such is the virtue of abstraction.

2

Why I work on C++

Chapter 1 explained what it was about C++ that interested me, and why I started to use it in my own programming. This chapter complements that one by explaining what it is about C++ that convinced me to spend the past decade developing C++ programming tools, understanding how to use them, writing about and teaching C++, and refining the C++ standard. These chapters cover issues that differ in much the same way that using an automobile to commute to work differs from becoming an automobile designer!

2.1 The success of small projects

It is hard to help noticing how many of the most successful, best known software systems were originally the work of a small number of people. The systems may have grown after they started, but surprisingly many of the real winners started small. The UNIX operating system is a prime example, as is the C programming language. Other examples include the electronic spreadsheet, the Basic and FORTRAN programming languages, MS-DOS, and IBM's VM/370 operating system. VM/370 is particularly interesting because it grew up completely outside IBM's official product line. Although IBM tried for years to discourage customers from using VM/370, that operating system is now solidly in IBM's mainframe mainstream.

Similarly, surprisingly many large projects turn out to be mediocre at best. I'd rather not point fingers in public, but I'm sure you can think of plenty of examples.

What is it about big projects that seems to make it hard for them to succeed? The answer, I think, is that unlike so many other industries, software construction has negative economy of scale. Most competent programmers can dash off a program of a hundred lines in an hour or two, yet the total output from a large project is typically about 10 lines per programmer day.

2.1.1 Overhead

Some of these negative economies come from the amount of time that project members spend communicating with one another. This communication overhead becomes serious as soon as there are too many people on the project to fit at one lunch table at the same time. At that point, some kind of formal mechanism becomes necessary to ensure that each project member knows enough about what the others are doing to make sure that all the pieces fit together. As the project grows, these mechanisms occupy more of everyone's time. There is more to have to understand, too.

This overhead is easy to see, of course. Just look at how members of large software projects spend their time: manipulating trouble report databases; reading, writing, and reviewing requirements documents; going to meetings; dealing with specifications, doing almost anything but programming.

2.1.2 Software factories?

Because this overhead is so visible, many people are looking for ways to reduce it. So far, I haven't seen any approach that appeals to me. It's a hard problem, and we may not be able to solve it. When projects get big enough, it seems that all kinds of things can go wrong in spite of all efforts; the Tacoma Narrows bridge and the space shuttle Challenger come to mind.

Some people treat the overhead of big projects as inevitable. The result of such treatment is a plethora of complicated systems to manage this overhead. All too often, however, the result of such management is merely well-organized overhead. It's still there; it's just been put in neat boxes and charts and thus it seems easy to understand. Some people revel in this overhead. They behave as if it is a Good Thing—almost as if the overhead is really the *cause* of productive software development, rather than something standing in the way. After all, if control and organization are good, more control and organization must be better. I suppose the idea is to bring the same kind of discipline and organization to programming projects as the assembly line is claimed to bring to the factory floor.

I hope that these people aren't right. The software factories I've seen feel to me like unpleasant environments indeed. Each individual functions as a part of a huge automaton, with "the system" controlling everything and the people following its orders. Such rigid control is exactly what has made manufacturing assembly lines the focus of so much tension between labor and management.

Fortunately, I don't think it has to be that way for software. The notion of a software factory overlooks a crucial difference between programming and manufacturing. A factory is a place that fabricates a large number of identical (or nearly identical) objects. It allows economy of scale in such fabrication by taking advantage of division of labor. More recently, its ideal has become the elimination of human effort entirely. Software development, on the other hand, is mostly concerned with producing a relatively small number of artifacts *that are all different from one another.* They may be similar in many ways, but, if they are too similar, then development work becomes a matter of copying things with small variations, and it might as well be done by a program. For that reason, the ideal environment for software development may well look more like a machine shop than a factory—a place in which skilled artisans use the most sophisticated tools they can get their hands on to make their work as efficient as possible.

In fact, programmers (good ones, anyway) continually strive to make their machines do as much of the mechanical part of their work as they can manage. Machines are good at that, after all, and people bore easily.

This view of programmer as artisan is one that becomes progressively harder to maintain as projects become bigger and more anonymous. In consequence, I have been trying to figure out how to treat a large programming problem as a collection of small, independent programming problems. To do that, we need to be able to mechanize the relationships among the small projects that are working on the larger problem. The people involved shouldn't have to check back constantly with one another. In other words, we need interfaces between projects, so that the members of each project rarely need to see beyond the interfaces between them. Those interfaces must be as much a part of the programmer's tool kits as are the more common abstractions of subroutines and data structures.

2.2 Abstraction

Since I started programming more than 25 years ago, I have been fascinated with tools that extend what programmers can do. These tools may be programming languages, or operating systems, or even particular ways of looking at a problem. I know that today I can easily solve problems that I would not have dreamed of trying when I first started programming—and I'm not alone.

The tools that most consistently hold my interest have in common the notion of abstraction. When I'm working on a large problem, such a tool will somehow enable me to break the problem into independent subproblems, and ensure that they remain independent. That is, while I'm working on one piece of the problem, I do not have to worry about any other piece.

For example, if I am writing a program in assembly language, I must constantly worry about the state of the machine. The tools at my disposal are registers, memory, and instructions that operate on those registers and memory. To accomplish anything useful in assembly language, I must express my problem in terms of those particular concepts.

Even assembly languages conceal several useful abstractions. The first is that the program I write is translated before the machine executes it. That is the difference between writing in assembly language and writing directly in machine language. More subtly, the notions of "memory" and "registers" are themselves just abstractions on the part of the machine designer. If that abstraction is stripped away, the execution of the program is expressed in terms of the changes of state of the zillions of gates in the processor. If you're imaginative, you may see a few more levels of abstraction beyond this one.

Higher-level languages offer more sophisticated abstractions. Even the notion of being able to write an expression, instead of a series of separate arithmetic operations, is powerful. This notion was unusual enough when first introduced in the fifties that it formed the basis for the name of FORTRAN: Formula Translation. Abstractions are so useful that successful programmers are constantly inventing them, and incorporating them into their programs. Thus, almost any significant program provides its users with a set of abstractions.

2.2.1   Some abstractions aren't part of a language

Consider the notion of a file. Virtually every operating system makes files available to its users in some form. Every programmer has a notion of what a file is. Under most circumstances, however, files do not have any physical existence! A file is nothing more than a conceptual way of organizing data in long-term storage, supported by a collection of programs and data structures to make that abstraction available.

To do anything useful with files, a programmer has to know what programs to use to access them, and what sequence of requests to make. A typical operating system goes to a good deal of trouble to ensure that a program that makes unreasonable requests receives appropriate diagnostics, rather than crashing the system itself or corrupting the file system! Indeed, one commonly accepted purpose of modern operating systems is to build "firewalls" between files—to make it difficult for a program to modify data unintentionally.

2.2.2   Abstraction and conventions

Operating systems provide a degree of protection that is unusual in programming languages. Programmers who are trying to create abstractions for other programmers to use must often rely on their users to refrain from doing things that the language technically allows. The users must agree to follow not only the rules of the language, but also conventions established by other programmers.

For example, one commonly used abstraction in the C library is the notion of *dynamic memory* implemented by the `malloc` function. You call `malloc` with a number, and it allocates that many characters of memory and gives you its address. When you're done with that memory, you call the `free` function with its address, and the memory is returned to the system for later reuse.

That simple abstraction is useful in a wide range of contexts. It is hard to imagine a C program of any size that does not use `malloc` or `free`. But several conventions lie behind the successful use of that abstraction. To use dynamic memory successfully, the programmer must

- Know how much memory to allocate
- Not use any more memory than was allocated
- Free the memory when it is no longer required
- Not free the memory until it is no longer needed
- Free only memory that has been allocated
- Remember to check each allocation request for success

That's a lot to remember, and it's easy to get wrong. How much of this can be made automatic? In C, not much. If you're writing a program that uses dynamic memory, it's hard to avoid giving your users some responsibility for freeing any dynamic memory that they allocate as part of their requests to your program.

2.2.3 Abstraction and memory management

Some languages solve this problem by using *garbage collection*—a technique for reclaiming memory automatically when the space is no longer needed. Garbage collection makes it much more convenient to write programs with flexible data structures, but often does so at the cost of execution speed and compiler and run-time system complexity. Moreover, garbage collection reclaims only memory: It does not affect other resources. C++ takes another, more unusual route: Its constructors and destructors allow the designer of a data structure that needs dynamic resource allocation to specify exactly how the resources associated with that structure should be freed.

This mechanism is not always as flexible as garbage collection, but, in practice, it comes close in many applications. Moreover, it has the distinct advantage of being far less demanding on its environment than is garbage collection: Memory is freed as soon as it is no longer needed, rather than waiting around until the garbage collector can discover that it is unoccupied.

If that were all C++ had to offer, there would still be good reasons to miss automatic garbage collection. But the notion of constructors and destructors can serve other ends as well. Treated abstractly, many data structures have notions of initialization and termination that extend well beyond mere memory allocation. For example, a data structure that represents a buffered output file must somehow incorporate the idea that the buffer must be flushed before the file is closed. Such a convention can come up in surprisingly subtle places, and the resulting bugs can be annoyingly hard to trace. I once wrote a program in which such a bug* lurked undetected for three years! In C++, a buffered output class definition should have a destructor that flushes the buffer. Such mistakes then become much more difficult to make. Garbage collection would not help here.

Much of C++ is similarly concerned with abstractions and interfaces. The key behind it all is to be able to break a problem into pieces that can be pursued inde-

---

* For an example of this kind of problem, see page 72 of my book *C Traps and Pitfalls* (Addison-Wesley 1989).

pendently. Instead of the pieces' being connected by conventions, they are connected by class definitions and by calls to member and friend functions. Failure
to observe the conventions is met by an immediate diagnostic message from the
compiler, instead of by a program that fails with obscure symptoms.

2.3 Machines should work for people

Why do I care about language and abstraction? Because I think that huge projects are inefficient, uncomfortable to work on, and impossible to manage. I have
neither seen, nor can imagine, a way to cope with a huge project that attacks all
these problems. But if I can help point the way toward breaking up huge projects into bunches of little ones, I will be advancing the cause of the individual
over the anonymous mass, and that of the human over the machine. We must be
the masters of our tools, not the other way around.

3

Living in the real world

I will begin this chapter with two anecdotes that may seem to have nothing to do with C++. Please bear with me.

A successful Boston business executive had recently bought an extremely expensive English luxury car, only to discover during the first cold snap that it wouldn't start. Angry, she explained her problem to the service department. "What?" said the service manager, astonished, "you don't keep it in a heated garage?"

The car was indeed luxurious, with hand-rubbed matched wooden panels in the dash, leather everywhere, and meticulous attention to comfort and style. But winters in Boston are colder than those in England, and the car's designers may not have realized that some of their customers might park their cars outdoors in severe weather.

I first learned APL in 1967.

APL is a remarkable language. It has only two data types—characters and numbers—and arrays are its only data structures. Variables and expressions are dynamically typed. APL programmers never have to worry about memory allocation. The implementation checks all operations, so APL programmers see only APL values and programs.

APL is more than a language—its first implementation included an entire operating system as well. By modern standards, that system was astonishingly efficient: It supported 30 simultaneous time-sharing users on a machine with about as much CPU power and main memory as a typical laptop PC.*

When I was using APL actively, I found my programs to be about one-fifth the size of programs to solve comparable problems in conventional languages such as FORTRAN and PL/I. The programs themselves were not so much simpler as smaller. The built-in APL operations are mostly single characters, rather than

---

* That mainframe had half a megabyte of main memory and ran at about 0.2 MIPS—typical specifications for laptop PCs in 1988, when I originally wrote the column that became this chapter.

identifiers, which encourages APL programmers to pick short names for their variables as well. I think APL's reputation as a write-only language is much exaggerated, and comes about mostly because APL programs are so compact.

In the early 1970's, I was a student at Columbia University. The library there is spread out all over campus: Most of the math books are in the math building, most of the engineering books in the engineering school, and so on. Every day, the library would print a master circulation list, showing every book that was checked out, on reserve, and so on. That list was about 100,000 lines, and was printed on six-part forms so that a copy could go to each of the largest branches of the library. The printers could each handle about 900 lines per minute, so the circulation list took about two hours of printer time per day.

Murphy's Law arranged that the circulation lists would be printed whenever I was waiting for my own jobs to print. Thus, I thought for a time about what it would take to convert the library circulation system to APL. I figured that it would be necessary only to install terminals at every site that now had a copy of the master circulation list; those terminals could interrogate the database directly, and thus could at one stroke do away with the mountains of paper consumed each day. The money saved on paper alone would surely pay for the project before long.

The idea got nowhere, because of questions such as:

- What will we do if the APL system is down when someone wants to check the circulation list?

- Who will fix the terminals when they break?

- Our programmers don't know APL and don't want to learn it. How can we change their minds?

- How will you make APL access our database?

- What about all the COBOL (PL/I, assembly language) programs that we already have?

I don't know whether or not it would have been possible to find satisfactory answers to all these questions. What I do know is that it doesn't matter. Suppose that it had been possible to answer all the objections, and to redo the circulation system in APL. *It would then have been a different system.*

Something like a circulation system does not exist in isolation. There is a whole family of complicated programs, built up over years, to deal with all the aspects of keeping track of a library of millions of books. It is possible to replace one of those programs only if the replacement behaves exactly like the original, especially with regard to its interfaces to the rest of the system.

Thus, it didn't matter how good APL was, or how productive APL programmers were: APL was useless in that context unless an APL program could be substituted invisibly for every COBOL program in the system.

By now, you should begin to see what these stories have in common. It doesn't matter how wonderful a car is if it doesn't start. It doesn't matter how wonderful a programming language is if its programs won't run in your environment.

Cars and programming languages are *tools*. They may have tremendous aesthetic appeal, but ultimately a car is a tool for transportation, and a programming language is a tool for writing programs, which in turn are tools for solving problems. We do not always have the luxury of choosing problems that fit particular tools well. In a place that endures cold winters, we must pick a car that starts in cold weather, supply a heated garage, or do without a car sometimes. We cannot change the weather. If we have to live with a body of existing software, and we can't rewrite all the software to fit our favorite tools, we must choose tools that will coexist with the software.

Now let's think about programming environments.

Most operating systems support what, for want of a better term, I will call a *traditional environment*. You give your program to a compiler, which puts the corresponding machine instructions in a file somewhere. A linker reads that file, combines these machine instructions with other machine instructions from a library, and writes another file. Tell the operating system to execute that file, and it reads the file into memory and jumps to the file's first instruction.

Some operating systems wrap a protection layer around the program first, so that the program can't clobber the system. Some allow several programs to be executed at once. Other environments differ in other details. But this kind of traditional programming environment will coexist with almost all operating systems.

Some languages are normally associated with their own programming environments. APL is one such language; Lisp, Basic, and Smalltalk are others. Some of these languages are harder to separate from their environment than are others; in Smalltalk, it's hard to tell where the language ends and the environment begins.

Basic programs, in contrast, mesh well with conventional notions of files and linkers. Although most Basic implementations are interactive, it is easy to see how to get Basic running in a traditional environment. Basic programs can easily be treated as files, and there can be a clear division between compilation and execution.

Lisp, as another contrast, is pervaded by the notion that programs and data are both instances of internal structures called *S-expressions*. You can write a human-readable representation of a program into a file in exactly the same way that you can write any other S-expression into a file, but the S-expression, not the file, is the program. Thus, Lisp programmers are at a serious disadvantage when they have to deal with data that do not fit the S-expression model neatly. It is hard to write Lisp programs that deal with, say, magnetic tapes of census data, or with strange I/O devices such as local area networks or wind tunnels.

I have met Lisp programmers who react to these disadvantages by arguing that the problems would go away if only the whole world used Lisp and nothing else. And indeed they might! But it doesn't matter: The whole world isn't going to start using Lisp any time soon, and interface problems aren't going to melt away.

The smart programmer will treat Lisp, and any other language, as a tool: Use it when doing so is appropriate and use some other tool when that other tool makes more sense.

Which brings us, finally, to C++.

One of the more common questions that I hear when I give talks on C++ is: Why doesn't C++ have <some particular feature of the questioner's favorite programming environment>? For example, Lisp, Basic, and other languages tend to be implemented interactively: The computer evaluates each expression immediately and prints the result. Why doesn't C++ do that too?

My answer usually boils down to this: "That feature isn't part of a programming language, so whether C++ has it on your system depends on the kind of environment that your system provides." C++ is a programming *language*, not a programming environment in its own right. That can be frustrating when you are trying to run C++ programs under an operating system that provides only a primitive implementation of the traditional environment. But it gives C++ two extremely important attributes: portability and coexistence.

If a machine supports C, there is no fundamental difficulty in getting it to support C++, which means that C++ can run almost anywhere. C++ does not have the kind of intricate operating system dependencies that might be needed to support features such as garbage collection or interactive execution.

Moreover, because C++ can use whatever environment exists on its host system, it lets people write programs that interact with whatever they're already doing. This minimal reliance on an environment also makes it possible for C++ programs to run with almost no supporting environment at all. A garbage collector may have too much overhead in a program that controls, say, a trash compactor.

The ability of C++ to work in whatever environment is already there is what lets people write C++ programs that use large existing bodies of C software without having to rewrite (or even recompile) the C programs. It's also what lets people write entire operating systems in C++.

That's why we're starting to see C++ programs clicking along inside electronic equipment such as cameras.

That's what lets people write C++ programs that can be downloaded into programmable terminals with the simplest of environments.

That's what lets large programming projects that are already using C switch to C++ gradually, without having to rewrite all their code all at once.

That's what lets particle physicists debug their algorithms on their desktop workstations, and then run the same programs on a massively parallel super-computer with an array library that takes advantage of the parallelism.

As C++ becomes more popular, and more people work on supporting C++ development tools, there may someday be a standard C++ environment, just as there is a standard APL environment today. Meanwhile, this ability of C++ pro-grams, to coexist with so many systems that are already there, is what has gotten C++ accepted in so many contexts.

C++ thrives in mixed environments. It lives in the real world.

Part II

Classes and inheritance

Different people mean different things when they talk about object-oriented programming (OOP). Some people think that any application that has a graphical user interface is object oriented. Other people use the term to refer to a particular style of interprocess communication. Still others use it to mean "buy my product."

On the rare occasions when I refer to OOP at all, I mean programming with inheritance and dynamic binding. Although this style of programming is no panacea, it is often useful—particularly in programs that deal with entities that are similar but not identical. Inheritance is a kind of abstraction that allows the programmer to ignore the differences between similar objects at some times, and to exploit these differences at other times.

C++ fills a unique niche in OOP languages. Most such languages provide inheritance and dynamic binding, coupled with dynamic type checking. These languages must therefore look up member functions (methods) while the program is running, to determine which function to call. C++ instead requires the programmer to state which types are "similar" at compile time, and thus can check types during compilation on calls that will later be bound dynamically. This compile-time checking accounts for the fast code that C++ generates for dynamically bound calls. As every C++ programmer should know, run-time polymorphism occurs *only* when a program calls a virtual function through a pointer or reference to a base-class object. This constraint on run-time polymorphism is deliberate.

Less obvious may be the implications of this model. In particular, the fact that object creation and copying are *not* run-time polymorphic profoundly affects class design. Thus, containers—both built-in containers such as arrays or structures, and user defined container classes—can hold only values whose types are known at compile time. This compile time checking introduces a problem for families of classes related by inheritance, when we need to create, copy, or store objects whose precise type is not known until run time.

As usual, the way to solve this problem is to add a level of indirection. The traditional C model would suggest using pointers to achieve the indirection.

Doing so has the unfortunate side effect of requiring users of these classes to get involved in memory management—a tedious and error prone strategy. A more natural approach for C++ is to define a class whose purpose is to provide *and hide* the indirection.

Such classes are often called *handle classes*, and several of the chapters in this part either look at or use this technique. In its simplest form, a handle class lets us attach an object of a single type to an object of any type in a particular inheritance hierarchy. Handles therefore let us ignore the precise type with which we're dealing, while still avoiding the memory-management problems that come with pointers. Chapter 5 presents this kind of basic handle class. A common use for handle classes is to optimize memory management by avoiding unnecessary copies. Chapter 6 presents this technique. The third chapter in this sequence, Chapter 7, looks at a slightly weird implementation technique that combines the time and space efficiencies of the previous two.

The next three chapters explore examples of the handle technique presented in Chapter 6. Chapter 8 uses handles in the context of expression trees, where they hide the inheritance hierarchy altogether. Chapter 9 presents a more complicated example and solves it in conventional style, after which Chapter 10 solves the same problem using inheritance and handles. In all cases, users of these classes write their programs without having to know about the data structure to which the classes they use are attached. By using handles, users can ignore memory management and other such details entirely. In addition, we'll see that handle classes provide a convenient way to reduce memory consumption.

Before launching into solving problems with inheritance, it's important to be comfortable building basic abstractions in C++. We'll begin this part in Chapter 4 by looking at hints for designing effective classes. Then, having seen examples that exploit inheritance, we'll conclude this part in Chapter 11 by examining places where virtual functions might *not* be useful.

4

Checklist for class authors

Every good pilot uses a checklist. This fact sometimes raises naive passengers' eyebrows: Surely someone who knows how to fly the airplane has no need for such a thing! Nevertheless, a pilot who cares about safety will explain that, even though every checklist item is utterly routine, it is still important to have a memory jogger to guard against forgetting anything important during a moment of distraction. Even experienced professional pilots have been known to forget to lower their landing gear until reminded to do so by the warning horn or, worse, by the sound of the propellers destroying themselves on the runway.

A checklist is not a do-list. Its purpose is to help you recall things you might have forgotten, rather than to constrain you. If you blindly follow a checklist without thinking about it, you will probably forget things anyway. With that in mind, here are questions to ask about your classes as you define them. There are no "right" answers to these questions; the point is to get you to think about them, and to make sure that whatever you do is the result of a conscious decision, rather than an accident.

Does your class need a constructor? If the answer is "no," you may be reading this chapter at an inopportune time. Some classes don't need constructors because they are so simple that their structure *is* their interface. We are concerned here, however, primarily with classes that are complicated enough to require a constructor to conceal their inner workings.

Are your data members private? Public data members are often a bad idea because class author has no control over when those members are accessed. Consider, for example, a class that holds a variable-length vector:

```
template<class T> class Vector {
public:
        int length;        // a public data member: a dubious idea
        // ...
};
```

If the class author makes the length of the vector available as a member variable, the author must ensure that the member variable is kept up to date all the time, because there is no way to tell when the user of the class is going to want to access the information. If, on the other hand, the length is made available through a function such as

```
template<class T> class Vector {
public:
        int length() const;                 //  a much better idea
        // ...
};
```

then it is unnecessary for the `Vector` class to calculate the length until the user calls the `length` function. Even if that is not an issue for the present implementation, it may become one later.

Moreover, using a function instead of a variable makes it easy to block write access while still allowing read access. In the first version of the `Vector` class, there is nothing to stop the user from changing the length! It is true in principle that `length` could be made a `const int`, but not if it is ever useful to change the length of a `Vector` object after that object has been created. We could use a reference to allow users read access only:

```
template<class T> class Vector {
public:
        const int& length;          //  each constructor must bind length
                                     //  to true_length

        // ...

private:
        int true_length;
};
```

Indeed that would forestall the latter objection, but it still does not have the flexibility of making `length` a function from the start.

Even if the author of the `Vector` class intended to allow users to change the length of a `Vector`, making the length a public data member is not a good way to do so. Changing the length presumably requires allocating and deallocating memory, as well as copying the `Vector`'s values somewhere else automatically. If the length is a variable that users can set directly, there is no way to detect immediately that a user has changed the length. Thus, the change has to be detected after the fact, probably by checking before *every* operation on a `Vector` whether the most recent operation changed the length. By allowing users to change the length only by calling a member function, we make it possible to know immediately every time that the user changes the length.

There is no single "best" style for writing functions that access or change parts of a class. For example, assume that there are two functions to deal with a vector length. Should they have names such as `set_length` and `get_length`, or should they both be named `length` and distinguished by the number of arguments that they accept? Should the function that modifies the length return `void` or a value? If it returns a value, should that be the previous value of the length or the new value that has just been installed? Or should it return something else entirely, such as an indication of whether it has been successful in dealing with the request? Pick a convention, use it consistently, and document it clearly.

Does your class have a constructor without arguments? If a class has any constructors at all, and you want it to be possible to declare objects of that class without explicitly initializing them, then you must explicitly write a constructor that takes no arguments—for example,

```
class Point {
public:
        Point(int p, int q): x(p), y(q) { }
        // ...

private:
        int x, y;
};
```

Here, we have defined a class with a constructor. Unless this class has a constructor that doesn't require arguments, it will be illegal to say

```
Point p;                // error: no initializer
```

because there will be no way to figure out how to initialize the object p. This may be an intentional part of the design, of course, but don't forget to think about it. Also, remember that if a class demands an explicit initializer, such as the Point class above, it is illegal to try to create an array of objects of that class:

```
Point pa[100];          // error
```

Even if you want to require all instances of your class to be initialized, it is worth thinking about whether to prohibit arrays of objects of that class in exchange for that insistence.

Does every constructor initialize every data member? The purpose of a constructor is to put its object into a well-defined state. The state of an object is reflected by the object's data members. Therefore, it is the responsibility of every constructor to establish well-defined values for all the data members. If any constructor fails to do so, that is a likely sign of trouble ahead.

Of course, this assertion is not always true. Sometimes, classes will have data members that are not given values until their objects have existed for some time. Remember, though, that the purpose of asking these questions is not to demand particular answers, but rather is to encourage you to think about the questions.

Does the class need a destructor? Not all classes with constructors need destructors. For example, a class that represents complex numbers probably does not need a destructor, even if it has constructors. If you think about what a class does, it should be obvious whether or not the class needs a destructor. It usually suffices to ask whether the class allocates any resources that freeing the members of the class will not free automatically. In particular, a class that has new-expressions in its constructors will usually have to have corresponding delete-expressions in its destructor—thus, it will probably need a destructor.

Does the class need a virtual destructor? Some classes need virtual destructors only to say that their destructors are virtual. Of course, a class that is never used as a base class doesn't need a virtual destructor: Virtual functions of any kind are useful only in the presence of inheritance. But suppose that you have written a class called, say, B and someone else derives a class D from it. When does B need a virtual destructor? *When anyone ever executes a* delete *expression on any object of type* B* *that actually points to an object of type* D.

This is true even if neither B nor D has any virtual functions—for example,

```
struct B {
        String s;
};

struct D: B {
        String t;
};

int main()
{
        B* bp = new D;    //  no problem here, but...
        delete bp;        //  this calls the wrong destructor unless
                          //  B has a virtual destructor!
}
```

Here, even though B has no virtual functions, and indeed has no member functions at all, the delete will go awry unless B is given a virtual destructor:

```
struct B {
        String s;
        virtual ~B() { }
};
```

Virtual destructors are often empty.

Does your class need a copy constructor? The answer is often, but not always, "no." The key question is whether there is any difference between copying an object of this class and copying its data members and base classes. You need a copy constructor only if there is a difference.

If your class allocates resources in its constructor, then it probably needs an explicit copy constructor to manage these resources. A class with a destructor (except for an empty virtual destructor) usually has that destructor because it needs to free resources that its constructor allocated, which usually implies that it needs a copy constructor as well. A classic example is a String class:

```
class String {
public:
        String();
        String(const char* s);
        //  other member functions
```

```
private:
        char *data;
};
```

Even without looking at the rest of this class definition, we can guess that it needs a destructor, because its data member points to dynamically allocated memory that must be freed with the corresponding object. It needs an explicit copy constructor for the same reason: Without one, copying a `String` object will be implicitly defined in terms of copying its `data` member. After the copy, the `data` members of both objects will point to the same memory; when the two objects are destroyed, that memory will be freed twice!

If you don't want users to be able to copy objects of a class, make the copy constructor (and probably also the assignment operator) private:

```
class Thing {
public:
        // ...

private:
        Thing(const Thing&);
        Thing& operator=(const Thing&);
};
```

If you don't use these member functions from other members, it is sufficient to declare them as shown. There is no need to define them, because no one calls them: You didn't and the user can't.

Does your class need an assignment operator? If it needs a copy constructor, it probably needs an assignment operator for the same reason. If you don't want users to be able to assign objects of your class, make the assignment operator private.

Assignment for a class X is defined by `X::operator=`. Usually, `operator=` should return an `X&` and end by saying

```
return *this;
```

for consistency with the built-in assignment operators.

Does your assignment operator handle correctly assignment of an object to itself? Self assignment is mishandled so often that more than one C++ book has gotten it wrong. Recall that assignment always replaces an old value in its destination by a new one. If we free the old destination value before copying the source value, and the source and destination are the same object, then we might wind up freeing the source before we copy it. For example, consider a `String` class:

```
class String {
public:
        String& operator=(const String& s);
        // various other members
```

```
private:
        char* data;
};
```

It can be tempting to implement assignment this way:

```
// obvious, but incorrect implementation
String& String::operator=(const String& s)
{
        delete [] data;
        data = new char[strlen(s.data)+1];
        strcpy(data, s.data);
        return *this;
}
```

This approach fails horribly when we assign a String object to itself, because s and *this both refer to the same object. The simplest way to avoid the problem is to guard against it explicitly:

```
// correction 1
String& String::operator=(const String& s)
{
        if (&s != this) {
                delete [] data;
                data = new char[strlen(s.data)+1];
                strcpy(data, s.data);
        }
        return *this;
}
```

Another possibility is to save the old destination value until after you have copied the source value:

```
// correction 2
String& String::operator=(const String& s)
{
        char* newdata = new char[strlen(s.data)+1];
        strcpy(newdata, s.data);
        delete [] data;
        data = newdata;
        return *this;
}
```

Does your class need to define the relational operators? Now that C++ supports templates, general-purpose libraries increasingly include container classes. The classes provide generic definitions of data structures, such as lists, sets, and graphs. These containers rely on operations from the types they contain. A common requirement for containers is the ability to determine whether two values are equivalent. Containers also often rely on being able to determine whether a value is less than or greater than some other value.

Thus, if your class logically can support equality, it may be useful to provide operator== and operator!=. Similarly, if there is some ordering relation on values of your class, you may want to provide the rest of the relational operators. You may need these operators even if you don't expect users to use the relational operations directly. As long as they want to create ordered collections of your type, you'll need to provide the relational operators.

Did you remember to say `delete[]` when deleting an array? The curious [] syntax comes from the effort of C++ to balance C compatibility with efficiency. In particular, C programmers expect to be able to write C functions that use `malloc` to allocate memory, which they will return to C++ functions. They then expect their C++ functions to be able to use `delete` later to free that memory. A C++ implementation that does not wish to preempt an existing C implementation's `malloc` must therefore implement `new` directly in terms of that `malloc`, and must not supply its own. Hence, the C++ library cannot necessarily figure out how large an array is when freeing that array. Even though `malloc` must store that size, it may store the size someplace that the C++ library cannot portably access. As a compromise, C++ therefore requires its users to tell the implementation whether what is being deleted is an array. If it is, the implementation can presumably afford to store the length somewhere else, because the (constant) overhead is likely to be small compared to the amount of memory required for the array.

It is good practice to include the [] when deleting an array of any type, even though some C++ implementations require you to do so only when the objects in the arrays have nontrivial destructors.

Did you remember to say `const` in the argument types of your copy constructor and assignment operator? Some early C++ literature suggested that the copy constructor for class X should be `X::X(X&)`. This suggestion is incorrect: The copy constructor should be `X::X(const X&)`. After all, copying an object does not modify the original! In fact, because it is illegal to bind a `const` to a temporary, using `X::X(X&)` as a copy constructor would not allow the result of any nontrivial expression to be copied.

The same argument applies to assignment: Use `X::operator=(const X&)` and not `X::operator=(X&)`.

When a function has reference parameters, should they be `const` references? The only time that a function should have a reference argument without saying `const` is when it intends to modify the argument. Thus, for example, instead of saying

```
Complex operator+(Complex& x, Complex& y);
```

you should almost certainly say

```
Complex operator+(const Complex& x, const Complex& y);
```

unless you mean to allow adding two `Complex` objects to change their values! Otherwise, expressions such as x+y+z become impossible, because x+y is not an lvalue and therefore may not have a nonconst reference bound to it.

Did you remember to declare your member functions const **appropriately?** When a member function is guaranteed not to modify its object, declare it const so that it can be used for const objects. Therefore, if we use access functions as in our earlier example:

```
template<class T> class Vector {
public:
        int length();                    // get length (wrong)
        int length(int);                 // set length, return previous
        // ...
};
```

the function that fetches the length without changing it should be declared const:

```
template<class T> class Vector {
public:
        int length() const;              // get length (right)
        int length(int);                 // set length, return previous
        // ...
};
```

Otherwise, we will run into trouble in contexts such as this:

```
/* return the larger of n and the length of v */
template<class T>
int padded_length(const Vector<T>& v, int n)
{
        int k = v.length();              // oops!
        return k>n? k: n;
}
```

The line flagged *oops!* won't compile unless the aforementioned const appears in the declaration of length, because v is a reference to const.

This list naturally raises the question of why C++ doesn't somehow handle all these things automatically. The main reason is that it's not possible to do so and still be assured of being right.

Continuing our earlier aviation analogy, making these things automatic would be like designing airplanes to lower their landing gear automatically under the right circumstances. People have tried doing that, with limited success. The trouble is that "the right circumstances" are hard to define in a way that can be reliably handled mechanically. Therefore, in practice, the pilot has to check the "gear down" light before every landing anyway, so the automation doesn't buy much. Of course, leaving the gear extended all the time would solve the problem, but only by introducing unacceptable overhead.

The same argument applies to programming-language design. For example, giving a class a virtual destructor adds overhead. If the class is tiny and has no (other) virtual functions, that overhead can be significant. Causing all classes to have virtual destructors automatically would violate the C++ philosophy of making people pay for only what they use; it would be analogous to leaving the landing gear extended all the time.

The alternative is to have the compiler somehow figure out when a class should have a virtual destructor, and to supply that destructor automatically. Again, the problem lies in defining exactly when to generate such a destructor. If the definition is not perfect, programmers will have to check anyway. Checking will be at least as much work as defining the virtual destructor in the first place.

In other words, C++ is biased toward programmers who think for themselves. Using C++ requires thought, in much the same way as does using any professional tool.

5

Surrogate classes

How can we design a C++ container that can potentially contain objects of diverse but related types? It is difficult to store the objects themselves in the container, because containers generally contain objects of only a single type. Storing pointers to the objects, although it allows inheritance to handle the type diversity, imposes an extra memory-allocation burden.

Here, we'll look at one way of solving this problem by defining objects called *surrogates*, which act mostly like the objects that they represent, but allow a whole hierarchy of types to be collapsed into one. Surrogates are the simplest kind of *handle classes*, as described in the introduction to this part. Subsequent chapters will expand on the essentials presented here.

5.1 The problem

Suppose that we have a class hierarchy that represents different kinds of vehicles:

```
class Vehicle {
public:
        virtual double weight() const = 0;
        virtual void start() = 0;
        // ...
};
class RoadVehicle: public Vehicle { /* ... */ };
class Automobile: public RoadVehicle { /* ... */ };
class Aircraft: public Vehicle { /* ... */ };
class Helicopter: public Aircraft { /* ... */ };
```

and so on. All Vehicles have certain properties in common, which the members of class Vehicle describe. Some Vehicles, however, have properties that others do not share. For example, only an Aircraft can fly, and only a Helicopter can hover.

Suppose next that we wish to keep track of a collection of Vehicles of different kinds. In practice, we would probably use some kind of container class; to keep the presentation simple, however, we'll get by with an array. So, let's try

```
Vehicle parking_lot[1000];
```

This attempt doesn't work. Why not?

The surface reason is that Vehicle is an abstract base class, because its weight and start member functions are *pure virtual functions*. By virtue of saying = 0 in their declarations, those functions are explicitly left undefined. Thus, no objects of class Vehicle can exist—only objects of classes derived from Vehicle can. If no Vehicle objects can exist, we can't have an array of such objects.

There is deeper reason for why our attempt fails, which appears when we ask what would happen if we *could* have objects of class Vehicle. For instance, suppose that we got rid of all the pure virtual functions in class Vehicle. What would happen if we said something like this?

```
Automobile x = /* ... */;
parking_lot[num_vehicles++] = x;
```

The answer is that assigning x to the element of parking_lot would convert x to a Vehicle by discarding all the members not found in the Vehicle class itself. The assignment would then copy this (truncated) object into the parking_lot array.

In effect, we have said that parking_lot is a collection of Vehicles, not a collection of objects of classes derived from Vehicle.

5.2 The classical solution

The usual way to gain flexibility in situations of this kind is to apply a level of indirection. The easiest appropriate form of indirection is to store pointers, rather than the objects themselves:

```
Vehicle* parking_lot[1000];      // an array of pointers
```

Then, we say something like

```
Automobile x = /* ... */;
parking_lot[num_vehicles++] = &x;
```

This approach gets us over our immediate problem, but it introduces two new problems.

First, what we have stored in parking_lot is a pointer to x, which in this example is a local variable. Thus, as soon as that variable x goes away, parking_lot will be left pointing nowhere.

We might solve this new problem by saying that what we will put into
`parking_lot` will be pointers not to the original objects, but rather to copies of
them. We could then adopt the convention that, when we free `parking_lot`,
we will also free the objects to which it points. Thus, we could change our previous example:

```
Automobile x = /* ... */;
parking_lot[num_vehicles++] = new Automobile(x);
```

Although this change avoids storing pointers to local objects, it leaves us instead
with the burden of dynamic memory management. Moreover, this technique
works only as long as we know the static type of the objects that we wish to
install in `parking_lot`. What if we don't? For example, suppose that we want
to make `parking_lot[p]` point to a newly created `Vehicle` that has the same
type and value as the one pointed to by `parking_lot[q]`? We can't say

```
if (p != q) {
        delete parking_lot[p];
        parking_lot[p] = parking_lot[q];
}
```

because then `parking_lot[p]` and `parking_lot[q]` would point to the same
object. Nor can we say

```
if (p != q) {
        delete parking_lot[p];
        parking_lot[p] = new Vehicle(parking_lot[q]);
}
```

because that would get us right back into the previous problem: There are no
objects of type `Vehicle` and, if there were, we wouldn't want one!

5.3 Virtual copy functions

Let's try to find a way of creating copies of objects whose type we do not know at
compile time. We know that the way to do anything with objects of unknown
type in C++ is to use a virtual function. The obvious name for such a function is
`copy`, with `clone` as a plausible alternative.

Because we presumably want to be able to copy any kind of `Vehicle`, we
should augment the `Vehicle` class with an appropriate pure virtual function:

```
class Vehicle {
public:
        virtual double weight() const = 0;
        virtual void start() = 0;
        virtual Vehicle* copy() const = 0;
        // ...
};
```

Next, we define a `copy` member function in every class that is derived from `Vehicle`. The idea is that if `vp` points to an object of some undetermined class derived from `Vehicle`, then `vp->copy()` will yield a pointer to a newly created copy of the object. For example, if class `Truck` is derived (directly or indirectly) from class `Vehicle`, then its `copy` function looks like

```
Vehicle* Truck::copy() const
{
        return new Truck(*this);
};
```

Of course, when we're done with an object, we will want to get rid of it. To be able to do so, we must ensure that class `Vehicle` has a virtual destructor:

```
class Vehicle {
public:
        virtual double weight() const = 0;
        virtual void start() = 0;
        virtual Vehicle* copy() const = 0;
        virtual ~Vehicle() { }
        // ...
};
```

5.4 Defining a surrogate class

We have figured out how to copy objects on demand. Now, let's look at memory allocation. Is there some way that we can avoid having to deal explicitly with memory allocation and still keep the run-time binding properties of our `Vehicle` class?

As is so often true in C++, the key to the solution is to *use classes to represent concepts*. I am often tempted to refer to this notion as the fundamental C++ design rule.

In the context copying objects, applying this design rule means defining something that acts like a `Vehicle` object, but potentially represents an object of any class derived from `Vehicle`. We will call an object of such a class a *surrogate*.

Every `Vehicle` surrogate will stand in for an object of some class derived from `Vehicle`. That object will persist exactly as long as the surrogate is associated with it. Thus, copying the surrogate will copy its corresponding object, and assigning a new value to a surrogate will involve deleting the old object before copying in the new one.* Fortunately, we already have the virtual `copy` function

---

* Dag Brück pointed out that this treatment is subtly different from what we might expect from an assignment, because it changes the type of the object to which the surrogate on the left-hand side is attached.

in the `Vehicle` classes to make these copies. We can therefore start defining our surrogate as follows:

```
class VehicleSurrogate {
public:
        VehicleSurrogate();
        VehicleSurrogate(const Vehicle&);
        ~VehicleSurrogate();
        VehicleSurrogate(const VehicleSurrogate&);
        VehicleSurrogate& operator=(const VehicleSurrogate&);

private:
        Vehicle* vp;
};
```

Our surrogate class has a constructor that takes a `const Vehicle&`, so that we can make a surrogate for an object of any class derived from `Vehicle`. It also has an empty constructor, so that we can create arrays of `VehicleSurrogate` objects.

The empty constructor gives us a problem, however: If `Vehicle` is an abstract base class, what default behavior should we give to `VehicleSurrogate`? What is the type of the object to which it refers? It can't be a `Vehicle`, because there are no `Vehicle` objects.

For want of a better idea, we will coin the notion of an *empty surrogate* that behaves much like a zero pointer. We will be able to create, destroy, and copy such surrogates, but any other operation will be considered an error.

So far, we don't have any other operations, which lack makes it easy to fill in the member-function definitions:

```
VehicleSurrogate::VehicleSurrogate(): vp(0) { }

VehicleSurrogate::VehicleSurrogate(const Vehicle& v):
        vp(v.copy()) { }

VehicleSurrogate::~VehicleSurrogate()
{
        delete vp;
}

VehicleSurrogate::VehicleSurrogate
    (const VehicleSurrogate& v):
        vp(v.vp? v.vp->copy(): 0) { }

VehicleSurrogate&
VehicleSurrogate::operator=(const VehicleSurrogate& v)
{
        if (this != &v) {
                delete vp;
                vp = (v.vp ? v.vp->copy() : 0);
        }
        return *this;
}
```

There are three tricks here worth remembering.

First, note that every call to copy is a virtual call. These calls have no choice but to be virtual, because there are no objects of class Vehicle. Even the call to v.copy in the constructor that takes a const Vehicle& is a virtual call, because v is a reference rather than a plain object.

Second, note the check that v.vp is nonzero in the copy constructor and assignment operator. This check is necessary, because otherwise it would be an error to call v.vp->copy.

Third, notice the check in the assignment operator to make sure that a surrogate is not being assigned to itself.

All we need to complete our surrogate class is to make it support the other operations supported by class Vehicle. In our earlier example, we had weight and start, so let's add those to class VehicleSurrogate:

```
class VehicleSurrogate {
public:
        VehicleSurrogate();
        VehicleSurrogate(const Vehicle&);
        ~VehicleSurrogate();
        VehicleSurrogate(const VehicleSurrogate&);
        VehicleSurrogate& operator=(const VehicleSurrogate&);

        // operations from class Vehicle
        double weight() const;
        void start();
        // ...

private:
        Vehicle* vp;
};
```

Note that these functions are not virtual: The only objects we're using here are of class VehicleSurrogate; none are of anything derived from that class. Of course, the functions themselves call virtual functions in the corresponding Vehicle object. They should also check to make sure that vp is not zero:

```
double VehicleSurrogate::weight() const
{
        if (vp == 0)
                throw "empty VehicleSurrogate.weight()";
        return vp->weight();
}

void VehicleSurrogate::start()
{
        if (vp == 0)
                throw "empty VehicleSurrogate.start()";
        vp->start();
}
```

Once we have done all this work, it is easy to define our parking lot:

```
VehicleSurrogate parking_lot[1000];
Automobile x;
parking_lot[num_vehicles++] = x;
```

This final statement is equivalent to

```
parking_lot[num_vehicles++] = VehicleSurrogate(x);
```

which creates a copy of the object x, binds a VehicleSurrogate object to that copy, and then assigns that object to an element of parking_lot. When the parking_lot array is finally deleted, all those copies will be deleted as well.

5.5 Summary

Mixing inheritance and containers forces us to deal with two issues: controlling memory allocation and putting objects of diverse types into a single container. We can take care of both of these issues with the fundamental C++ technique of using classes to represent concepts. When we do that, we come up with a single class called a surrogate, each object of which represents a single other object that might potentially be of any class in an entire hierarchy. We solve our problems by putting surrogates into our containers to take the place of the objects themselves.

6

Handles: Part 1

Chapter 5 looked at a kind of class, called a surrogate, that let us store objects of diverse, but related, types in a single container. That approach involved creating a surrogate for each object, and storing the surrogate in the container. Creating the surrogate copied the underlying object, as did copying the surrogate.

But what if we want to avoid those copies? This chapter will examine another kind of class, typically called a *handle*, that will allow us to avoid copying objects unnecessarily, while preserving the polymorphic behavior of surrogates.

6.1 The problem

It can be useful to avoid copying objects of a particular class. Perhaps the objects are so large that they are expensive to copy. Each object might represent a resource, such as a file, that cannot readily be copied at all. Some other data structure might "know" the address of the object, and it might be expensive or impossible to insert the address of a copy in the data structure. The objects could be standing in for other objects at the other end of a network connection. Or, as in Chapter 5, we might be in a polymorphic context, where we know the type of a base class of the object, but do not know the type of the object itself or how to copy objects of that type.

On the other hand, C++ functions make it easy to copy things without thinking, because arguments and returned values are normally copied automatically. It is possible to avoid copying arguments by passing them by reference, but we must remember to do this—and anyway, it is less easy for returned values.

It is also possible to avoid copying objects by using pointers. Indeed, pointers (or references) are essential to C++ polymorphism. However, we must still remember consistently to write functions that accept pointers instead of objects. Moreover, it can be harder to use pointers to objects than to use the objects directly.

Uninitialized pointers are dangerous, but there is no simple way to avoid them. On some implementations, merely copying such a pointer might cause a crash:

```
void f()
{
        int* p;        // uninitialized
        int* q = p;    // undefined behavior
}
```

In such implementations, the memory-management hardware typically checks that every pointer being copied actually points to a memory location that the program has allocated. Thus, merely copying p might cause a hardware trap.

Moreover, whenever there are several pointers to the same object, we must think about when to delete the object. If we delete the object too early, that means there is still a pointer somewhere else that points to it. Using that pointer will thereafter cause undefined behavior. If we delete the object too late, we will be occupying memory that we might have been able to use for some other purpose. Indeed, if we wait too long, we might lose the last pointer to the object and be unable to free the object at all.

What we need is a way to obtain some of the advantages of pointers, particularly the ability to avoid copying objects and to use objects polymorphically, while avoiding some of the disadvantages, such as the lack of safety. The solution in C++ is to define an appropriate class. Because objects of such classes are usually *attached* to objects of the classes they control, these classes are often called *handle classes*. Because handles behave somewhat like pointers, people sometimes also call them *smart pointers*. However, handles can behave differently enough from pointers that thinking of them as just a kind of pointer is probably too restrictive.

In this chapter, we'll develop a straightforward, but complete, handle class. Along the way, we'll point out several places where things might be done differently from the particular way we chose. At one point, we will show where a small change in the implementation of the handle class produces a large change in behavior.

6.2 A simple class

To make our discussion concrete, we need to be able to attach our handles to objects, so we need a class definition for those objects. To be interesting, our object class should have some data. Classes with two or more data members are more interesting than classes with only a single data member—otherwise, we could just use a single object. Integers are probably the easiest type for these data members to have, so we will imagine a class that contains two integers.

What might be the purpose of such a class? These days, the most likely use is to store the coordinates of a point on a bitmap display. We will therefore call the class Point.* We can imagine many operations that our class might support; here is an arbitrary selection:

```
class Point {
public:
        Point(): xval(0), yval(0) { }
        Point(int x, int y): xval(x), yval(y) { }
        int x() const { return xval; }
        int y() const { return yval; }
        Point& x(int xv) { xval = xv; return *this; }
        Point& y(int yv) { yval = yv; return *this; }

private:
        int xval, yval;
};
```

There is a constructor with no arguments, to make it possible to create a Point without explicitly supplying coordinates. That is essential, for example, to make it possible to create arrays of Points. We could have used a single constructor with default arguments, instead of the two constructors:

```
        Point(int x = 0, int y = 0): xval(x), yval(y) { }
```

Then, however, it would have been possible to construct a Point with a single argument (the other being zero by default); doing so is almost surely a mistake.

The compiler-generated assignment operator and copy constructor will, by default, behave the way we want, so we don't need to define them explicitly. This situation often holds for classes that have no pointers as members.

Of course, we need a way to access the elements of our Point objects. We probably also need a way to change those elements—and there are about as many different ways to change class elements as there are class authors. The technique in our present example overloads the x and y member functions so that, for example, if p is a point, then

```
        int x = p.x();
```

copies the x coordinate of p into x, and

```
        p.x(42);
```

sets the x coordinate of p to 42. The mutative operations return a reference to their object, so p.x(42).y(24) will set the x coordinate of p to 42 and the y coordinate to 24. Readers who prefer a different approach are invited to follow their own taste.

---

* We note in passing that, had the data members of our class been real numbers instead of integers, we probably would have wanted to call our class Complex. Integers as data members are therefore a less complex choice.

6.3 Attaching a handle

What should it mean to initialize a handle from a `Point` object?

```
Point p;
Handle h(p);    // what should this mean?
```

Superficially, we might expect that this code should attach a handle h directly to the object p, but a little reflection should lead us to the conclusion that that will not work. The problem is that the object p is directly under the user's control. What happens to the handle when the user deletes p? Evidently, deleting p must invalidate the handle, but how does the handle know that p was deleted? Similarly, should deleting the handle delete p as well? If it does, and if p is a local variable, then p will be deleted twice: once when the handle goes away and once when p itself goes out of scope. If saying

```
Handle h(p);
```

attaches a handle directly to the object p, then our handle had better have nothing to do with the allocation or deallocation of p. When that is acceptable, we can just as well use pointers or references, and not build a separate class at all.

This reasoning suggests that a handle should "own" the object to which it is attached, in turn suggesting that the handle should create and destroy that object. Then, we have two possibilities: We might create our own `Point` object and give it to the handle to copy, or we might give the handle the arguments that we would have used to create a `Point`. We will allow both alternatives, so we will want to give the handle class the same constructors as the `Point` class. In other words, we would like

```
Handle h0(123, 456);
```

to create a `Handle` that is attached to a newly allocated `Point` with coordinates 123 and 456, and

```
Handle h(p);
```

to make a copy of p and to attach the handle to the copy. After that, the handle will control what happens to the copy, and the owner of p has no restrictions that were not there already. In effect, a handle is a kind of container that contains only a single object.

6.4 Getting at the object

Suppose that we have a `Handle` attached to a `Point`. What operations should we use to access the `Point`? If a handle is to act like a pointer, we might think it sufficient to use `operator->` to forward all the relevant `Handle` operations to the corresponding `Point` operations:

```
class Handle {
public:
        Point* operator->();
        // ...
};
```

Indeed, this simple approach almost works—but it yields a handle that is too much like a pointer. Using `operator->` forwards *all* the `Point` operations, and there's no easy way to turn them off or to override them selectively.

For example, if we want handles to have complete control over allocating and deallocating our objects, it would be nice to prevent users from obtaining the addresses of those objects directly. Doing otherwise reveals enough of the allocation strategy to make it difficult to change that strategy in the future. But if our handle has an `operator->`, we can call that `operator->` directly by saying:

```
Point* adr = h.operator->();
```

thereby obtaining the address of the underlying `Point`.

To hide that address, then, we must avoid `operator->`, and must choose explicitly which `Point` operations we want our handles to make available.

6.5 Simple implementation

We now already know enough to begin implementing our handle class. If we want to avoid `operator->()`, we will have to give our handle its own x and y operations, each of which will presumably return an `int` (if called without an argument) or a `Handle&` (if called with an argument). We will give our class a default constructor, for the same reason that we gave `Point` a default constructor: to allow arrays and other containers to contain `Handles`. Having decided on the x and y operations, we can define much of our class:

```
class Handle {
public:
        Handle();
        Handle(int, int);
        Handle(const Point&);
        Handle(const Handle&);
        Handle& operator=(const Handle&);
        ~Handle();

        int x() const;
        Handle& x(int);
        int y() const;
        Handle& y(int);

private:
        // ...
};
```

All that is left is to fill in the private data and the definitions of the member functions—and it is here that the semantic variations become possible.

6.6 Use-counted handles

One reason for using handles is to avoid copying objects. Thus, we will want to allow a single object to have many handles attached to it; otherwise, it is hard to see how to pass a handle as a function argument, thereby copying the handle, without copying the object as well. We must keep track of how many handles are attached to each individual object, so that we will know when to delete the object. The usual way to do that is with a use count.

The use count cannot, of course, be part of the handle. That would require each handle to know where all the others are that are attached the same object, to make it possible to update the other handles' use counts. Nor can the use count be part of the object, because in that case, we would have to rewrite the object's class. Thus, we must define a new class that contains a use count and a `Point`. We will call it `UPoint`. This class will be used only for implementation, so we will make all its members private, and will nominate our handle class as a friend. When we create one of these `UPoint` objects, the use count will always be `1`, because we will immediately be storing the object's address in a `Handle` object. On the other hand, we will want to create an object of this class in all the ways that we can create a `Point`, so we will duplicate the `Point` constructors:

```
class UPoint {
        // all members are private
        friend class Handle;
        Point p;
        int u;

        UPoint(): u(1) { }
        UPoint(int x, int y): p(x, y), u(1) { }
        UPoint(const Point& p0): p(p0), u(1) { }
};
```

Aside from these operations, we will deal with `UPoint` objects by referring to their components directly.

Now we can return to our handle class to fill in the rest of the details:

```
class Handle {
public:
        // as before
        Handle();
        Handle(int, int);
        Handle(const Point&);
        Handle(const Handle&);
        Handle& operator=(const Handle&);
        ~Handle();
```

```
            int x() const;
            Handle& x(int);
            int y() const;
            Handle& y(int);
    private:
            // added
            UPoint* up;
    };
```

Most of the constructors are easy—each one allocates a `UPoint` with the appropriate arguments:

```
Handle::Handle(): up(new UPoint) { }

Handle::Handle(int x, int y): up(new UPoint(x, y)) { }

Handle::Handle(const Point& p): up(new UPoint(p)) { }
```

The destructor is also easy—it decrements the use count and deletes the `UPoint` if the use count reaches zero:

```
Handle::~Handle()
{
        if (--up->u == 0)
                delete up;
}
```

Even the copy constructor is straightforward, as long as we remember that the use count is there to avoid copying `Point`s:

```
Handle::Handle(const Handle& h): up(h.up) { ++up->u; }
```

All it does is increment the use count of the object that it is "copying," so that the original and the copy now point to the same `UPoint` object.

The assignment operator is only slightly less simple. Because we are overwriting the left-hand side, we will have to decrement the use count of the (old) `Upoint` referred to by the left-hand side. Doing so will reflect that, after the assignment, the left-hand side will be pointing to a different `Upoint`. However, when we decrement the use count, we must be sure to do so in a way that will behave properly even when the left-hand and right-hand sides refer to the same `Upoint` object.

The easiest way to obtain that assurance is to increment the use count of the right-hand side first, and only then to decrement the left-hand-side use count:

```
Handle& Handle::operator=(const Handle& h)
{
        ++h.up->u;
        if (--up->u == 0)
                delete up;
        return *this;
}
```

The access functions are straightforward as well:

```
int Handle::x() const { return up->p.x(); }
int Handle::y() const { return up->p.y(); }
```

When we come to the modification functions, however, things suddenly become interesting. The reason is that we must now decide whether we want our handles to have value semantics or pointer semantics.

6.7 Copy on write

From an implementation viewpoint, we have arranged for our handles to make it unnecessary to copy Point objects. The key question is whether or not we wish the user-visible behavior of our handle class to be the same. For example,

```
Handle h(3, 4);
Handle h2 = h;          // copy the Handle
h2.x(5);                // change the Point
int n = h.y();          // 3 or 5?
```

If we want handles to act like values, we will want n to be 3 in this example, because copying h into h2 and then changing the value of h2 should not affect the value of h. On the other hand, we might want handles to behave like pointers or references, in which case we might say that h and h2 are bound to the same object, and changing one should change the other. We can have it either way, but we must choose.

Suppose that we want pointer semantics. Then, it is never necessary to copy a UPoint object, and the modification functions are almost trivial:

```
Handle& Handle::x(int x0)
{
        up->p.x(x0);
        return *this;
}

Handle& Handle::y(int y0)
{
        up->p.y(y0);
        return *this;
}
```

However, if we want value semantics, we have to ensure that the particular UPoint that we are modifying is not in use by any other Handle. The way to do that is to look at the use count. If it is 1, then our Handle is the only one using the UPoint; if it is anything else, then we can make it 1 by copying the UPoint:

```
Handle& Handle::x(int x0)
{
        if (up->u != 1) {
                --up->u;
                up = new UPoint(up->p);
        }
        up->p.x(x0);
}
```

Similarly for `Handle::y`. Having rewritten `Handle::x`, we can see that the code

```
if (up->u != 1) {
        --up->u;
        up = new UPoint(up->p);
}
```

will have to be replicated in every member that changes the `UPoint`, which observation suggests that we should create a private member function that ensures that our `Handle` has a use count of `1`. We will leave that as an (easy) exercise.

This technique is commonly called *copy on write*. It has the advantage of avoiding copies except when they are truly necessary, and it carries only a small overhead. Such techniques often turn up in library classes that involve handles.

6.8 Discussion

Programmers expect to see pointer semantics or value semantics, depending on context and on how they were brought up. For example, C programmers often simulate character strings in a way that suggests pointer semantics. Both C and FORTRAN programmers tend to expect arrays to have pointer semantics. Handles attached to things that are intended to be used for object-oriented programming usually should have pointer semantics. On the other hand, most languages that support variable-length strings—either as built-in types or through libraries— offer value semantics.

We were able to get almost all the way through implementing our handle class without caring whether we used pointer or value semantics. Indeed, the only time that it mattered was when we were trying to modify the object. More generally, *the difference between objects and values shows up only when we try to change the objects*. In other words, values and immutable objects are indistinguishable. Having said that, I must hedge slightly: It may be possible to tell whether an object was copied by comparing the addresses of the original and the copy. But that is an artificial distinction, in the sense that, if the address is the *only* thing that can ever be made to differ between two objects that started out as copies of each other, then that difference is not terribly useful.

Because immutable objects act like values, copy on write is an optimization that is needed for only mutable objects. Saying it that way makes it almost obvious: If you never write, you don't need copy on write! This assertion is true even for assignment, because we implemented assignment as a rebinding, rather than as a copy. That is, if h and k are handles, we implemented h = k by detaching h from whatever Point it was formerly attached to and reattaching it to the Point to which k is attached. This operation is done purely on handles: It does not change the value of any Point. It relies on the fact that assignment changes the value of every component of the Point, so that assigning a handle is equivalent to throwing out the old Point and reattaching the handle to a new one.

We could have implemented the other mutative operations (such as the x and y member functions) similarly. For example,

```
p.x(42);
```

is equivalent to

```
p = Point(42, p.y());
```

except that the latter does no mutative operations. However, it avoids them by copying all the components of p except for the one that it is assigning. If p had many components, this strategy could be expensive. Our actual implementation copies *all* the components of the Point, and then changes one of them. It saves time, however, by doing so only when the object being modified has two or more handles attached to it.

We have seen two variations on the handle theme, both with use counts. One implements value semantics through copy on write; the other implements pointer semantics. Other variations are possible.

In Chapter 5, for example, we saw a kind of handle, called a surrogate, that always copied its object. A program that uses a surrogate is likely to be slower than one that uses a use-counted implementation, but the surrogate strategy avoids the space overhead of the use count. Moreover, the run-time cost may not be much if such handles are copied infrequently.

Another variation, which we have not seen, is a handle for which copying is a destructive operation—that is, making a "copy" of a handle detaches the original handle from its object. So, for example, if h is a handle of this kind that is attached to some object, then

```
h1 = h;
```

would attach h1 to the object and detach h from it.

This approach can ensure that no object ever has more than one handle attached to it, which guarantee makes use counting unnecessary. On examination, this technique of ensuring that each object has at most one handle attached to it, turns out to combine the space efficiency of surrogates with the time efficiency of use-counted handles (and then some). However, using such handles can be dangerous, because we can easily detach a handle from its object without realizing that we have done so.

Finally, it is possible to separate the use count from its object by putting extra information into the handle. That is the subject of Chapter 7.

7

Handles: Part 2

Chapter 6 talked about a technique for adding handles and use counts to a class to be able to "copy" objects of that class efficiently by just manipulating the use counts. That technique had a significant disadvantage: To attach a handle to an object of class T, we had to define a new class with a member of type T. This requirement would make it hard, for example, to attach such a handle to an object of a (statically) unknown class derived from T.

There is another way to define handle classes that removes that disadvantage. Although Bjarne Stroustrup mentions this technique in *The C++ Programming Language* (Addison-Wesley 1991), it does not seem to be widely used. Briefly, the idea is to separate the use count from the data, putting the use count into its own object, so that, instead of two objects, as in

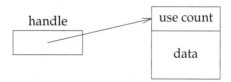

there are three:

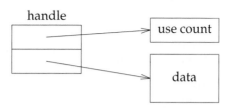

At first glance, it is hard to see why replacing two data structures by three should help. It turns out, however, that the extra modularity more than makes up for the extra complexity. The gain comes from making it unnecessary to attach anything directly to the class object itself. The rest of this chapter will explore the details.

7.1 Review

Suppose that we have a class that represents the coordinates of a point on a bitmap display. Such a class might look like this:

```
class Point {
public:
        Point(): xval(0), yval(0) { }
        Point(int x, int y): xval(x), yval(y) { }
        int x() const { return xval; }
        int y() const { return yval; }
        Point& x(int xv) { xval = xv; return *this; }
        Point& y(int yv) { yval = yv; return *this; }

private:
        int xval, yval;
};
```

The technique described in Chapter 6 involved creating a new class to contain a
Point and a use count:

```
class UPoint {
        //  all members are private
        friend class Handle;
        Point p;
        int u;

        UPoint(): u(1) { }
        UPoint(int x, int y): p(x, y), u(1) { }
        UPoint(const Point& p0): p(p0), u(1) { }
};
```

Then we defined a handle class that contains a pointer to a Upoint object, along
with the relevant construction, destruction, and access functions:

```
class Handle {
public:
        Handle();
        Handle(int, int);
        Handle(const Point&);
        Handle(const Handle&);
        Handle& operator=(const Handle&);
        ~Handle();
        int x() const;
        Handle& x(int);
        int y() const;
        Handle& y(int);

private:
        UPoint* up;
};
```

7.2 Separating the use count

The technique from Chapter 6 requires that we construct a new class that depends on the `Point` class. That is fine for this particular class, but makes it hard to attach a handle not just to a `Point`, but also to an object of any class derived from `Point`. The trouble is that we might not have known all the relevant types at the time that we were defining our handle class.

If we treat the use count separately from the `Point`, that changes the implementation of our handle class:

```
class Handle {
public:
        // as before

private:
        Point* p;
        int* u;          // pointer to use count
};
```

Here, the public declarations of our `Handle` class are unchanged from the previous version; the user sees no difference. However, class `UPoint` is gone; instead of a pointer to `UPoint`, we have a pointer to `Point` and a pointer to an `int` that represents the use count. We will come back later and define an auxiliary class to make it easier to deal with use counts.

The use of `Point*` instead of `UPoint*` is important, because it is what lets us potentially attach a `Handle` not just to a `Point`, but also to an object of a class derived from `Point`.

Having changed the data-structure part of our implementation, let's see whether we can implement the rest of it. The ordinary constructors are straightforward enough. They allocate memory for the use count and the data, and set the use count to `1`:

```
Handle::Handle():
        u(new int(1)), p(new Point) { }

Handle::Handle(int x, int y):
        u(new int(1)), p(new Point(x, y)) { }

Handle::Handle(const Point& p0):
        u(new int(1)), p(new Point(p0)) { }
```

The copy constructor and assignment are also simple. By incrementing and decrementing the use counts in the right order, we do the right thing when assigning a handle to itself:

```
Handle::Handle(const Handle& h):
        u(h.u), p(h.p) { ++*u; }
```

```
Handle& operator=(const handle& h)
{
        ++*h.u;
        if (--*u == 0) {
                delete u;
                delete p;
        }
        u = h.u;
        p = h.p;
        return *this;
}
```

The destructor is not hard either:

```
Handle::~Handle()
{
        if (--*u == 0) {
                delete u;
                delete p;
        }
}
```

All this is slightly more complicated than the corresponding implementation with the use count attached directly to the `Point`. In particular, our uses of `new` and `delete` seem to come in pairs: one dealing with the use count, and the other dealing with the data. How we deal with the data will presumably differ from one handle to another. Is there some way that we can abstract out our work with the use counts?

7.3 Abstraction of use counts

We would like to make our use-counted handles easier to implement. It is probably unwise to try for too general an abstraction, lest we wind up reimplementing the handle class itself. In particular, we will assume that our use-count class knows nothing about the nature of the object to which our handle is attached. Given that assumption, what can we say about our use counts?

First, if our goal is to reimplement what we have so far, a use-count object should contain a pointer to an `int`. Moreover, at the very least, it needs a constructor, destructor, assignment operator, and copy constructor:

```
class UseCount {
public:
        UseCount();
        UseCount(const UseCount&);
        UseCount& operator=(const UseCount&);
        ~UseCount();
        // other stuff to be determined
```

```
private:
        int* p;
};
```

What about implementation? We have already seen that use counts always start out at `1`. This gives us the default constructor:

```
UseCount::UseCount(): p(new int(1)) { }
```

Similarly, we can see that constructing one `UseCount` from another makes them both point to the same counter and increments the counter:

```
UseCount::UseCount(const UseCount& u): p(u.p) { ++*p; }
```

Destroying a `UseCount` decrements the counter and deletes the counter when it reaches zero:

```
UseCount::~UseCount() { if (--*p == 0) delete p; }
```

At this point, we can start rewriting our `Handle` class:

```
class Handle {
public:
        // as before

private:
        Point* p;
        UseCount u;
};
```

The constructors now become simpler because they can rely on the behavior of the default `UseCount` constructor:

```
Handle::Handle(): p(new Point) { }
Handle::Handle(int x, int y): p(new Point(x, y)) { }
Handle::Handle(const Point& p0): p(new Point(p0)) { }
Handle::Handle(const Handle& h): u(h.u), p(h.p) { }
```

The copy constructor is a nice surprise: It now just copies the components of the `Handle`, which means that, if we wanted to, we could omit the copy constructor entirely.

What about the destructor? It has a problem: It needs to know whether the use count is about to become `0` so that it knows whether to delete the handle's data. As it stands, class `UseCount` does not supply that information. Let's add a member called `only`, which says whether this particular `UseCount` object is the only one pointing at its counter:

```
class UseCount {
        // as before

public:
        bool only();
};

bool UseCount::only() { return *p == 1; }
```

Now we can write the new `Handle` destructor:

```
Handle::~Handle()
{
        if (u.only())
                delete p;
}
```

What about the `Handle` assignment operator? That requires several operations that class `UseCount` does not support directly: We must increment one
counter, decrement another, and possibly delete a counter. Moreover, we must
later decide whether or not to delete the data being assigned. Because many of
these operations involve fiddling with use counts, we should probably add
another operation to class `UseCount`. Because of the implementation-specific
nature of this operation, it resists attempts to find a good name for it; `reattach`
seems as good as any. While we're at it, we will make assignment private for
`UseCount` objects. That way, we won't have to think about what assigning a
`UseCount` might mean:

```
class UseCount {
        // as before

public:
        bool reattach(const UseCount&);

private:
        UseCount& operator=(const UseCount&);
};
```

Here is the definition of `reattach`:

```
bool UseCount::reattach(const UseCount& u)
{
        ++*u.p;
        if (--p == 0) {
                delete p;
                p = u.p;
                return true;
        }
        p = u.p;
        return false;
}
```

Now we can write `handle` assignment:

```
Handle& Handle::operator=(const Handle& h)
{
        if (u.reattach(h.u))
                delete p;
        p = h.p;
        return *this;
}
```

7.4 Access functions and copy on write

What remains is reading and writing individual elements of `Point` objects. As in Chapter 6, we will implement value semantics through copy on write, so that before we change a component of a `Point`, we will ensure that its handle is the only one that is using that particular `Point` object. The `UseCount::only` member lets us find out whether a particular handle is the only one using that handle's object, but it doesn't give us a way to force that handle to be the only one. We will need another `UseCount` member to help us. Like `reattach`, it will manipulate the use counts appropriately, and will return a result that says whether we need to copy the object itself:

```
class UseCount {
        // as before

public:
        bool makeonly();
};
```

The definition of `makeonly` is straightforward:

```
bool UseCount::makeonly() {
        if (*p == 1)
                return false;
        --*p;
        p = new int(1);
        return true;
}
```

Now we can write the access functions. We show only the ones for x; the ones for y are similar:

```
int Handle::x() const {
        return p->x();
}

Handle& Handle::x(int x0) {
        if (u.makeonly())
                p = new Point(*p);
        p->x(x0);
        return *this;
}
```

7.5 Discussion

This example shows what at first may appear to be a weird division of effort. In several cases, class `Handle` asks class `UseCount` to do something, and then does almost the same thing again. For example, the `Handle::x` access function uses `makeonly` to ensure that the use count is 1 and then, if the counter was copied (and therefore if `makeonly` returned `true`), copies the underlying `Point` object. At first glance, it appears that these two tasks could be merged, and indeed that approach probably would make this example slightly faster.

The particular strategy that we followed, however, has an important advantage: class `UseCount` incorporates no knowledge at all about the classes with which it will be used. Thus, we can use this class as part of the implementation of handles to be attached to a variety of different data structures.

Class `UseCount` simplifies a particular implementation subproblem: It is not intended for "end users." The specification of class `UseCount` is far from obvious. Its interface grew out of a desire to simplify the implementation of use-counted handles. The overall effect, however, is a reasonably clean separation of concerns in the solution to a messy problem. Moreover, the resulting `Handle` class is as easy to use as are those constructed along more traditional lines—and more flexible as well.

8

An object-oriented program

Object-oriented programming is often said to comprise three parts: data abstraction, inheritance, and dynamic binding. Here is a small but complete C++ program that demonstrates all three.

These techniques are most useful in large programs and particularly so in large, changing programs. There is not enough space here to explain a large program, though, so what you will see is a toy program instead. This program illustrates each of these ideas despite its small size, and will repay careful study.

8.1 The problem

The program deals with trees that represent arithmetic expressions. For example, the expression (-5) * (3+4) corresponds to

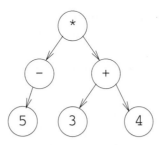

An expression tree contains nodes that represent constants, unary operators, and binary operators. Such a tree might be used in a compiler or calculator program.

We want to be able to create such a tree by calling appropriate functions, and then to print a fully parenthesized representation of the tree. For example, we would like

```
#include <iostream.h>

int main()
{
        Expr t = Expr("*", Expr("-", 5), Expr("+", 3, 4));
        cout << t << endl;
        t = Expr("*", t, t);
        cout << t << endl;
}
```

to print

```
((-5)*(3+4))
(((-5)*(3+4))*((-5)*(3+4)))
```

as output. Moreover, we do not want to have to worry about how these expressions are represented, or about when or how to allocate and free their memory.

This toy program does things that are typical of many larger programs—such as compilers, editors, and CAD/CAM systems—that deal with complicated input. Much of the effort in such programs is in manipulating trees, graphs, and similar data structures. Authors of such programs perennially face problems of memory allocation, flexibility, and efficiency. Object-oriented techniques allow the solutions of these problems to be localized, so that each subsequent change does not require parallel changes all over the program.

8.2 An object-oriented solution

The diagram in Section 8.1 (page 75) contains two distinct kinds of objects: *nodes* (represented by circles) and *edges* (represented by arrows). Let's see how far we can get by looking first at just the nodes.

Each node contains a value—an operand or an operator—and each has zero, one, or two children. We might be tempted to represent a node as a class with a union to represent the value and a List to represent the children. But this representation would require a type field to say what kind of node we have. Whenever you need a type field, you should stop to think whether defining a set of classes related by inheritance might solve the problem more effectively.

We will follow our own advice here. The classes will have some things in common: Each will store a value and some number of children. They will also have some things that differ from each other, such as what kind of value they store, and how many children they have. Inheritance lets us capture the similarities between the types of nodes. Dynamic binding lets nodes "know" what type they are, making it unnecessary to incorporate this knowledge in every operation on these objects.

If we look more closely at the tree, we see that there are three kinds of nodes. One represents an integer expression. It holds an integer value and has no children. The others represent unary and binary expressions, and hold an operand and one or two children, respectively. We want to be able to print any node, but how we do so depends on the kind of node we're printing. This is where dynamic binding comes in: We can define a `virtual` function to say how to print each type of node. Dynamic binding will take care of calling the right function at run time, based on the actual type of node that we're printing.

What kind of inheritance relates these nodes? Each type of node seems to stand independently from the others. That is, a node with no children is not "a kind of" node with one child, nor vice versa. Apparently, we'll need another class that captures what it means to be a node, but that is not a concrete node itself. Each of our actual types will derive from this common base class.

We'll call this common base class an `Expr_node`. Not surprisingly, this class is simple:

```
class Expr_node {
        friend ostream& operator<<
                           (ostream&, const Expr_node&);

protected:
        virtual void print(ostream&) const = 0;
        virtual ~Expr_node() { }
};
```

Because we know that we'll create objects of types derived from `Expr_node`, we've provided a virtual destructor. It will ensure that deleting an object pointed to by an `Expr_node*` will invoke the right derived class destructor.

We know that we want dynamic binding to apply to the `print` operation, but our sample program used the `<<` output operator to print an expression tree. Dynamic binding applies only to member functions, so we've declared a virtual `print` function that the output operator will call to do the actual work. Because we want users to use the output operator, not the `print` function, we've made `print` private and declared `operator<<` as a `friend`.

The declaration of `print` says that `print` is a pure virtual function, which makes `Expr_node` an abstract base class. This captures our intent that no objects of type `Expr_node` ever exist—only objects of classes derived from `Expr_node`. The `Expr_node` class exists simply to capture a common interface.

Finally, we define the output operator to call the appropriate `print` function:

```
ostream&
operator<<(ostream&, const Expr_node& e)
{
        e.print(o);
        return o;
}
```

Now we can use inheritance to declare our concrete types. The first thing to note about these types is that objects of those types will have to be constructed in response to our users' requests to create expression trees. Although we have not yet thought much about how the user is going to construct these trees, it should take only a little foresight to realize that class Expr will play a key role. We will therefore declare class Expr as a friend of each of our concrete types.

The simplest of these concrete types is a node that contains an integer value and has no children:

```
class Int_node: public Expr_node {
        friend class Expr;

        int n;

        Int_node(int k): n(k) { }
        void print(ostream& o) const { o << n; }
};
```

But what about the other types? In each case, we need to store an operator (which is easy), but how can we store the children? We won't know until run time what kinds of nodes the children will be, so we can't store the children by value; we'll have to store pointers. Assuming that we have a general-purpose String class to represent the operator gives us unary and binary node classes that look like

```
class Unary_node: public Expr_node {
        friend class Expr;

        String op;
        Expr_node* opnd;

        Unary_node(const String& a, Expr_node* b):
                op(a), opnd(b) { }
        void print(ostream& o) const
                { o << "(" << op << *opnd << ")"; }
};

class Binary_node: public Expr_node {
        friend class Expr;

        String op;
        Expr_node* left;
        Expr_node* right;

        Binary_node(const String& a,
                    Expr_node* b, Expr_node* c):
                op(a), left(b), right(c) { }
        void print(ostream& o) const
                { o << "(" << *left << op << *right << ")"; }
};
```

This design will work, but there's a problem. The user has to deal with pointers instead of values; and will therefore have to allocate and remember to deallocate objects. For example, we wanted to create an expression tree as

```
Expr t = Expr("*", Expr("-", 5), Expr("+", 3, 4));
```

But this won't work—the constructors that build binary and unary expressions expect pointers, not objects. Instead, we could allocate the nodes dynamically:

```
Binary_node *t = new Binary_node("*",
                      new Unary_node("-", new Int_node(5)),
                      new Binary_node("+",
                          new Int_node(3), new Int_node(4)));
```

Of course, we must then remember to delete the nodes. But how would we delete them? We no longer have pointers to the objects that we created in the inner `new` calls. We might try letting the `Binary_node` and `Unary_node` destructors delete their operands, but that won't work either. If the destructors deleted their operands, we might delete objects more than once, because more than one `Expr_node` could point to the same underlying expression.

8.3 Handle classes

Things are getting messy. Not only have we pushed off memory management onto the user, but there's no convenient way for the user to manage memory. We need to think again.

First, let's look back at the problem. If we look at the tree in Section 8.1 (page 75), we can see that we've captured the circles in the `Expr_node` family of classes, but we haven't modeled the arrows. We're getting into trouble because we're representing the arrows as simple pointers. We've compounded our troubles by forcing the users of our classes to deal with these pointers by themselves. These difficulties are similar to the ones that we solved in Chapters 5 and 6 by introducing a handle class to manage the pointers. In the present case, such a class appears to model our abstraction more accurately anyway.

Understanding these troubles convinces us that class `Expr` should be a kind of handle class that represents an edge—or equivalently, the tree rooted at an edge. Because users care about only (sub)trees, not individual nodes in the tree, we can also use `Expr` to hide the `Expr_node` inheritance hierarchy altogether. Each `Expr` will contain a pointer to an `Expr_node`. Because users will create `Exprs` and not `Expr_nodes`, we'll need `Expr` constructors that represent all three kinds of `Expr_nodes`. Each `Expr` constructor will create an object of an appropriate class derived from `Expr_node`, and will store the address of that object in the `Expr` object that is under construction. The user of class `Expr` will not see the `Expr_node` objects directly.

So now we have

```
class Expr {
        friend ostream& operator<<(ostream&, const Expr&);

        Expr_node* p;
```

```
public:
        Expr(int);                              // create an Int_node
        Expr(const String&, Expr);              // create a Unary_node
        Expr(const String&, Expr, Expr); // create a Binary_node
        Expr(const Expr&);
        Expr& operator=(const Expr&);
        ~Expr() { delete p; }
};
```

The constructors create an appropriate Expr_node and store its address in p:

```
Expr::Expr(int n)
{
        p = new Int_node(n);
}

Expr::Expr(const String& op, Expr t)
{
        p = new Unary_node(op, t);
}

Expr::Expr(const String& op, Expr left, Expr right)
{
        p = new Binary_node(op, left, right);
}
```

The destructor takes care of freeing the node allocated in the constructor. No further memory management is needed, as we shall see.

Because the Expr constructors allocate Expr_nodes, we'll need to implement the copy constructor and assignment operator to manage these underlying Expr_nodes. Because the destructor destroys p, we'll need to create a new copy whenever we copy or assign an Expr. As we saw in Section 5.3 (page 49), we can add a virtual copy function to the Expr_node hierarchy, and use that function to implement copy and assign in class Expr.

Before rushing into this implementation, we should first think about whether we need to make all these copies. As it stands, the operations on Exprs never change the underlying Expr_node. It's likely to be more efficient to avoid copying the underlying Expr_node if possible.

The usual way to avoid copying is to make each Expr_node contain a use count, which records how many Exprs point at that particular Expr_node. Classes Expr and Expr_node will cooperate to manage the use count, and will arrange to delete an Expr_node when, and only when, its use count goes to 0.

For this to work, we'll need to add a use count to class Expr_node, and to initialize it to 1 when a new object of type (derived from) Expr_node is created. Class Expr will help manage the use count, so we'll nominate it as a friend:

```
class Expr_node {
        friend ostream& operator<<(ostream&, const Expr&);
        friend class Expr;

        int use;
```

```
protected:
        Expr_node(): use(1) { }
        virtual void print(ostream&) const = 0;
        virtual ~Expr_node() { }
};
```

Class `Expr` increments the use count whenever it "copies" an `Expr_node`, and arranges to delete the underlying `Expr_node` when there are no more users:

```
class Expr {
        // as before

public:
        Expr(const Expr& t) { p = t.p; ++p->use; }
        ~Expr() { if (--p->use == 0) delete p; }
        Expr& operator=(const Expr& t);
};
```

The copy constructor increments the use count and points p at the same `Expr_node` pointed to by the object that it is copying. The destructor decrements the use count and destroys the underlying `Expr_node` if this use of the object is the final one. The assignment operator has to increment and decrement the use counts of the right-hand and left-hand sides, respectively. By working on the use count of the right-hand side first, we can guard against self assignment:

```
Expr&
Expr::operator=(const Expr& rhs)
{
        rhs.p->use++;
        if (--p->use == 0)
                delete p;
        p = rhs.p;
        return *this;
}
```

We must still define the output operator, which now operates on `Expr`s instead of on `Expr_node`s. The implementation reflects the extra indirection:

```
ostream&
operator<<(ostream& o, const Expr& t)
{
        t.p->print(o);
        return o;
}
```

Finally, we'll need to change each of the classes derived from `Expr_node` to make their operations private, to nominate class `Expr` as a `friend`, and to store `Expr`s, not pointers to `Expr_node`s. For example,

```
class Binary_node: public Expr_node {

        friend class Expr;
```

```
String op;
Expr left;
Expr right;

Binary_node(const String& a, Expr b, Expr c):
        op(a), left(b), right(c) { }

void print(ostream& o) const {
        o << "(" << left << op << right << ")";
}
};
```

With this, our original main program works, and users can freely declare objects and temporaries of type Expr. Moreover, they can build up arbitrarily complicated expressions, and print them, without having to think about memory management.

8.4 Extension 1: New operations

As it stands, our system is weak—it allows us only to build and print expressions. One obvious extension that our users will request is operations to evaluate the expression once it is built up. So, for example, we'd like to alter our original program slightly:

```
int main()
{
        Expr t = Expr("*", Expr("-", 5), Expr("+", 3, 4));
        cout << t << " = " << t.eval() << endl;
        t = Expr("*", t, t);
        cout << t << " = " << t.eval() << endl;
}
```

Running this program should yield

```
((-5)*(3+4)) = -35
(((-5)*(3+4))*((-5)*(3+4))) = 1225
```

Simply stating the problem gives us insight into its solution: Evaluating an Expr can work the same way as printing one. Users will invoke eval on some Expr; eval can delegate the real work to the nodes that make up the Expr.

So our Expr class now looks like

```
class Expr {
        friend class Expr_node;
        friend ostream& operator<<(ostream&, const Expr&);

        Expr_node* p;
```

```
      public:
            Expr(int);
            Expr(const String&, Expr);
            Expr(const String&, Expr, Expr);
            Expr(const Expr& t) { p = t.p; ++p->use; }
            ~Expr() { if (--p->use == 0) delete p; }
            Expr& operator=(const Expr& t);
            int eval() const { return p->eval(); }     // added
      };
```

where all `eval` has to do is pass the request to evaluate the expression to the `Expr_node` to which it points.

Class `Expr_node` in turn, will get another pure virtual function:

```
class Expr_node {
protected:

            virtual int eval() const = 0;
            // as before
      };
```

We'll also have to add a function to do the evaluation to each class derived from `Expr_node`. `Int_nodes` are simplest. Evaluating an `Int_node` just requires returning its value:

```
class Int_node: public Expr_node {
            friend class Expr;

            int n;

            Int_node(int k): n(k) { }
            void print(ostream& o) const { o << n; }
            int eval() const { return n; }                // added
      };
```

In principle, `Unary_nodes` are simple too: We evaluate the operand and then do the operation.

At this point, however, we realize that we've built up `Expr_nodes` without regard to the operators stored in them. To evaluate the expression, we need to restrict the applicable operators to those we know how to evaluate. What we'll do is simply to check that some sensible arithmetic operator has been stored. If not, we'll throw an exception. For `Unary_nodes`, we'll allow use of unary minus:

```
class Unary_node: public Expr_node {
            friend class Expr;

            String op;
            Expr opnd;
```

```
                Unary_node(const String& a, Expr b):
                        op(a), opnd(b) { }
                void print(ostream& o) const
                        { o << "(" << op << opnd << ")"; }
                int eval() const;                               // added
        };

        int
        Unary_node::eval() const
        {
                if (op == "-")
                        return -opnd.eval();
                throw "error, bad op " + op + " in UnaryNode";
        }
```

Here the call to

```
        opnd.eval();
```

calls the `eval` member of class `Expr`, which in turns invokes the virtual `eval` operation for the `Expr_node` to which it points. This ensures that the right `eval` operation is performed, depending on the kind of `Expr_node` that is the operand of this `Unary_node`.

By now, it should also be clear that evaluating a `Binary_node` will be easy (if tedious). Here's the `eval` function for `Binary_node`s:

```
        int
        Binary_node::eval() const
        {
                int op1 = left.eval();
                int op2 = right.eval();

                if (op == "-")  return op1 - op2;
                if (op == "+")  return op1 + op2;
                if (op == "*")  return op1 * op2;
                if (op == "/" && op2 != 0)  return op1 / op2;

                throw "error, bad op " + op + " in BinaryNode";
        }
```

Now, we can evaluate arithmetic expressions properly.

Think for a bit about what we had to do and, perhaps as important, what we didn't have to do. Adding the new operation touched no code that would affect existing operations. Because our class abstractions accurately modeled arithmetic expressions, extending the program to evaluate those expressions required about as little new code as could be imagined. As with printing an expression, the dynamic-binding facilities make evaluating expressions a simple process of saying how to evaluate each kind of node, and then letting the run-time system figure out which `eval` function to invoke, as appropriate.

8.5 Extension 2: New node types

We've seen how data abstraction and dynamic binding made it easy to add new operations to the system. Now let's look at how they also make it possible to add new kinds of nodes without changing all the code that uses nodes.

Suppose we want to add a `Ternary_node` to represent ternary operators such as `?:` (the *if-then-else* operator). First, we declare `Ternary_node` and define its operations:

```
class Ternary_node: public Expr_node {
        friend class Expr;

        String op;
        Expr left;
        Expr middle;
        Expr right;

        Ternary_node(const String& a, Expr b, Expr c, Expr d):
                op(a), left(b), middle(c), right(d) { }
        void print(ostream& o) const;
        int eval() const;
};

void
Ternary_node::print(ostream& o) const
{
        o << "(" << left << " ? " <<
            middle << " : " << right << ")";
}

int
Ternary_node::eval() const
{
        if (left.eval())
                return middle.eval();
        else
                return right.eval();
}
```

These declarations are similar to the declaration of class `Binary_node` and, in fact, started as a copy of it. Next, we define an `Expr` constructor for a `Ternary_node`:

```
Expr::Expr
    (const String& op, Expr left, Expr middle, Expr right)
{
        p = new Ternary_node(op, left, middle, right);
}
```

We insert a declaration for this constructor into the class definition for `Expr`:

```
class Expr {
        friend class Expr_node;
        friend ostream& operator<<(ostream&, const Expr&);
```

```
              Expr_node* p;
public:
              Expr(int);
              Expr(const String&, Expr);
              Expr(const String&, Expr, Expr);
              Expr(const String&, Expr, Expr, Expr);        // added
              Expr(const Expr& t) { p = t.p; ++p->use; }
              ~Expr() { if (--p->use == 0) delete p; }
              Expr& operator=(const Expr& t);
              int eval() const { return p->eval(); }
     };
```

We are done!

One person who had worked on a C compiler saw this example and said: "We despaired at adding the ? : operator to our compiler, because it would have taken weeks or months—and you just did it in 18 lines of code!" Although the compiler was much bigger than this example, that comment is right on the mark. Making this change entailed only adding new classes and functions: not a single line of existing executable code changed, and only one declaration was added to an existing class definition. And, as is so common with C++ and its strong type checking, this revised program ran correctly the first time it compiled.

8.6 Reflections

We've seen how to use object-oriented programming to simplify the design and evolution of an application. The essence of the solution was to model the objects in the underlying system that we wanted to simulate. Once we recognized that expression trees comprise nodes and edges, we could design data abstractions that modeled these trees. Inheritance let us capture the similarities among the types of nodes. Dynamic binding let us define the operations on each type of node, leaving it to the compiler to arrange to call the right function at run time. Thus, data abstraction plus dynamic binding let us think about only the behavior and implementation of each type, without having to be concerned about interactions with other objects.

We've already seen that our object-oriented design made it easy to add new operations and new types to the application. In practice, we'd want to add many more, including

- Having added Ternary_nodes, we're going to need relational operations. This addition is easy: We just need to modify the Binary_node::eval function to support relational operators.
- We'll also want to add assignment expressions. This is a bit trickier. Assignment requires that we add a variable type to our expression trees. We can avoid a full-fledged symbol table by adding a new class to represent a cell

that would contain a name and its value. Then, we'll need to define two new expression types: one to represent a variable and one to assign a value to a variable.

- Expression trees are useful, but statements would be even more powerful. We can design a parallel statement hierarchy with operations to print and execute statements.

The point is that this application can grow gracefully. We can start with a simple specification, design a solution, use that design, and see that the model works. As our needs change, we can more easily add operations and new types, growing the application and testing each change as we make it. The changes that we need to make are isolated. Each change requires work proportional to the description of the change.

Think what it would take to represent expression trees without dynamic binding.

9

Analysis of
a classroom exercise: Part 1

In August 1992, the two of us taught a weeklong C++ course at Stanford University under the auspices of the Western Institute in Computer Science. To succeed, such a course needs good classroom exercises. The only way to learn to write programs in a new language is to write them.

The first edition of Stroustrup's *The C++ Programming Language* (Addison-Wesley 1991) inspired a particularly interesting exercise. Like most classroom exercises, this one is a simplification of what happens in real applications—in this case, applications based on bitmap graphics. The simplifications are to use characters instead of bits, and to write into ordinary files instead of displaying on graphical hardware. It then becomes unnecessary to deal with the complexities of the typical graphics system. Moreover, there is no need to tie the solution to any one system: All computers that can run C++ programs can display characters. In effect, we are treating characters as great big pixels.

This chapter will describe the problem, and will present a fairly traditional solution. Chapter 10 will revisit the problem from an object-oriented viewpoint.

9.1 The problem

The object of the game is to write a collection of classes and functions to manipulate *character pictures*. A character picture is a rectangular array of characters that can be printed.

The first thing we need, of course, is a way of creating pictures. To create a picture, we must have a way of getting characters into the picture. One straightforward way of doing so is by putting the characters right into a program, as parts of string literals. We can then define a way of creating a picture from (a data structure that is initialized from) a collection of string literals that appear as part of a C++ program.

Thus, for example, we can imagine writing a program such as

```
#include <iostream.h>
#include "Picture.h"

char *init[] = { "Paris", "in the", "Spring" };

int main()
{
        Picture p(init, 3);
        cout << p << endl;
}
```

and having it print

```
Paris
in the
Spring
```

The idea, of course, is that the Picture object called p contains information copied from the array init, and we can use an appropriately overloaded oper-ator<< to print it.

By itself, this example isn't very interesting. The fun part of the assignment is to design operations that do interesting things with pictures. We suggested three: framing, and horizontal and vertical concatenation.

For example, if p is our picture, framing p and printing the result should yield

```
+------+
|Paris |
|in the|
|Spring|
+------+
```

The choice of the particular characters to use for the frame is arbitrary; the place-ment of the frame is not. Because a picture is a rectangular array, the frame should adjoin the picture on all sides. Note in particular that that implies putting a space after the s in Paris, even though ideally we would not want to send that space to the output file when printing the unframed picture.

We have now generated two pictures—one framed and one unframed. Con-catenating them horizontally with the first one on the left should yield

```
Paris +------+
in the|Paris |
Spring|in the|
      |Spring|
      +------+
```

This result involves an arbitrary decision: How do we concatenate two pictures of two different sizes? The course exercise specified lining them up along their top edges, as shown.

The final picture operation is vertical concatenation. Again, we must make an arbitrary decision about how to combine pictures of different sizes; the exercise

said that the pictures should be lined up along their left edges. Thus, if we concatenate the most recent two pictures vertically, in order of creation, we get

```
+-------+
|Paris  |
|in the |
|Spring |
+-------+
Paris +-------+
in the|Paris  |
Spring|in the |
      |Spring |
      +-------+
```

Moreover, framing this picture would yield

```
+----------------+
|+-------+        |
||Paris  |        |
||in the |        |
||Spring |        |
|+-------+        |
|Paris +-------+  |
|in the|Paris  | |
|Spring|in the | |
|      |Spring | |
|      +-------+ |
+----------------+
```

And, of course, we'd like to be able to continue to create new pictures by framing
and concatenating them without limit.

9.2 Designing the interface

When we are solving problems of this kind, it is often useful to try to stand in the
user's place, and to ask: "What operations would I like to have, and how might I
express them?" The problem specification has already answered part of that
question for us, in the sense that we know that we need to be able to create and
print pictures, and to combine them in three ways, but it says nothing about
what forms those operations might take. Finding a solution often starts with
deciding on such details.

One good way to decide what forms operations should take is to try using the
operations. It can be easier to infer how to define operations from usage examples than it is to invent the operations from scratch. In the case of our picture
exercise, we can learn some things about the operations we want by looking
again at our earlier program example:

```
#include <iostream.h>
#include "Picture.h"

char *init[] = { "Paris", "in the", "Spring" };

int main()
{
        Picture p(init, 3);
        cout << p << endl;
}
```

This example already fixes four decisions about the solution, none of which was specified in the course assignment except by example. First, the example uses a class called `Picture` to represent a picture—or at least a picture that is composed directly of strings. Second, the definition of class `Picture` is evidently contained in a file called `Picture.h`. Third, we build up a `Picture` from strings by constructing it with two arguments: a pointer to the initial element of an array of character pointers, and the number of pointers in the array. Finally, we use `operator<<` to print a picture.

These decisions allow us to start writing `Picture.h` right away:

```
#include <iostream.h>

class Picture {
public:
        Picture(const char* const*, int);
};

ostream& operator<<(ostream&, const Picture&);
```

We may wish to change this code later, but it is a reasonably accurate rendition of the decisions that we have made so far.

The next choice is to decide how to represent the other operations on pictures: framing and the two varieties of concatenation. Suppose, for example, that p is a `Picture`; how might we ask to frame it?

One possibility is `p.frame()`; another is `frame(p)`. Is one better than the other? To an extent, it depends on whether we wish framing a picture to modify the original picture or to yield a new one. If framing a picture modifies it, `p.frame()` is probably easier to understand. On the other hand, if we will be writing complicated expressions that construct pictures, `frame(p)` may be easier to understand than `p.frame()`, especially when p is an expression that itself includes parentheses.

Our earlier examples involved combining pictures into others, suggesting that the nonmember form makes more sense. Moreover, the two forms of concatenation seem (to me, anyway) like binary operators, perhaps by analogy with string concatenation. Therefore, for the purpose of this discussion, we will pick the `frame(p)` syntax. It may be a useful exercise to try doing it the other way.

We now need to choose a way to express horizontal and vertical concatenation. If p and q are `Pictures`, we might imagine writing `hcat(p,q)` and vcat(p,q), or we might look for something more compact. Again, ease of constructing complicated pictures suggests the compact route, so we should seek a pair of likely operators.

Two pairs suggest themselves: +/* and &/|. The relationship between & and | feels (to me) more like the relationship between horizontal and vertical than does the relationship between + and *, so those are the ones we'll use. Because p|q looks a little like "p next to q," we'll use | for horizontal concatenation and & for vertical concatenation.

Some people are bound to dislike this choice. Is it really easier to understand p|q than hcat(p,q)? Fortunately, people who dislike overloaded operators are free to write

```
Picture hcat(const Picture& p, const Picture& q)
{
        return p | q;
}
```

and so on.

Swallowing that syntactic sugar, we have a Picture.h that looks like this:

```
#include <iostream.h>

class Picture {

public:
        Picture(const char* const*, int);
};

ostream& operator<<(ostream&, const Picture&);

Picture frame(const Picture&);

Picture operator&(const Picture&, const Picture&);

Picture operator|(const Picture&, const Picture&);
```

9.3 A few loose ends

Before we think about implementation, we should include a few other details that will surely be necessary. A Picture will inevitably include a pointer to some kind of auxiliary memory that will contain the characters themselves. That means that the class will need a copy constructor, a destructor, and an assignment operator. It should probably also have an empty constructor, to make it possible to define an array of Pictures. Adding these members gives us the following Picture.h:

```
#include <iostream.h>

class Picture {
public:
        Picture();
        Picture(const char* const*, int);
        Picture(const Picture&);
        ~Picture();

        Picture& operator=(const Picture&);
};

ostream& operator<<(ostream&, const Picture&);

Picture frame(const Picture&);
Picture operator&(const Picture&, const Picture&);
Picture operator|(const Picture&, const Picture&);
```

9.4 Testing the interface

At this point, we can use `Picture.h` to compile the `main` program presented in
Section 9.1 (page 89). Of course, we can't link it, because we'll get complaints
about undefined members:

```
Picture::Picture(const char* const*, int)
operator<<(ostream&, const Picture&)
Picture::~Picture()
```

We can also compile (but not run) a program to build and print the other pictures in Section 9.1 (page 89)

```
#include <stream.h>
#include "Picture.h"

char *init[] = { "Paris", "in the", "Spring" };

int main()
{
        Picture p(init, 3);
        cout << p << endl;

        Picture q = frame(p);
        cout << q << endl;

        Picture r = p | q;
        cout << r << endl;

        Picture s = q & r;
        cout << s << endl << frame(s) << endl;
}
```

More compactly, we could also write

```
Picture p(init, 3);
Picture q = frame(p);
cout << frame(q & (p | q)) << endl;
```

which would print the final fully nested picture.

The syntax that we've chosen appears to be usable as a first try; the next step is to implement the classes and functions that we've declared.

9.5 Strategy

We are now ready to begin our implementation. Let's think a bit about how to organize it. The central question is how we will represent a `Picture`. Each `Picture` object represents a two-dimensional array of characters, so the most direct way of implementing class `Picture` would be to store the contents as such an array. There's only one catch: C++ doesn't directly implement two-dimensional arrays. The nearest we can come is a one-dimensional array of one-dimensional arrays. Arrays of arrays work fine if the size is known during compilation, but are a bit more difficult to implement when the size is known only during execution.

Of course, the most general way to deal with two-dimensional arrays is to define an appropriate class. Our purpose in this chapter, however, is to show a straightforward solution, rather than a general one. We will, therefore, solve only as much of this subproblem as we need in order to get the main job done.

If all we have is one-dimensional arrays, that's what we'll have to use. If a picture has height h and width w, an array of h*w characters will serve nicely. Using the same convention that built-in arrays use, we will assume that all the characters of each row are contiguous. We can immediately conclude that character n of row 0 is at position n in the array. Now, what about rows after the initial one? Each row is w characters long, so moving from character n in row 0 to character n in row k will be equivalent to moving k*w characters further into the array. The character position that corresponds to character n of row k is therefore k*w+n. To keep the presentation simpler, we'll define member functions to use this formula:

```
class Picture {

private:
        int height, width;
        char* data;

        char& position(int row, int col) {
                return data[row * width + col];
        }
```

```
char position(int row, int col) const {
       return data[row * width + col];
}
// ...
};
```

The two `position` member functions differ in that one works on a const `Pic-`
`ture` and returns a copy of the requested character, while the other grants both
read and write access to a given character of a `Picture` lvalue.

9.6 Tactics

Having decided on a representation, we can start defining member functions of
class `Picture`. When we run into difficulty, we will take a step back, to see
whether we have to revisit any design decisions that we've made so far.

The first member is the default constructor—the one invoked by

```
Picture p;
```

Such a picture will be empty, of course: Its `height` and `width` will both be zero.
What about the `data`? Because there's nothing there, the `data` member can
point anywhere at all, as long as we don't try to delete it! However, if we want
to avoid trouble in the long run, it's simplest to make the pointer zero as well.
That gives us the following constructor:

```
Picture::Picture(): height(0), width(0), data(0) { }
```

Now we have to look at the first constructor that does any real work:

```
Picture(const char* const*, int);
```

The arguments to this constructor effectively describe a ragged array: one whose
rows are not necessarily all the same size. The constructor has to copy these
rows into a rectangular array. To do that, it must first allocate memory for that
array; the amount to allocate is the product of the number of rows and the length
of the longest row.

Thus, the constructor must first determine the length of the longest row.
Only then can it allocate memory for the array and copy in the characters. Before
writing the rest of the member functions, we note that other functions are likely
to need to do these operations too. So let's start by defining a `static` member
function to find the larger of two integers:

```
int Picture::max(int m, int n)
{
       return m > n ? m: n;
}
```

We'll need another member to allocate memory, and to put the address of that memory in the `data` member:

```
void Picture::init(int h, int w)
{
        height = h;
        width = w;
        data = new char[height * width];
}
```

Now we can write the constructor itself:

```
Picture::Picture(const char* const* array, int n)
{
        int w = 0;
        int i;

        for (i = 0; i < n; i++)
                w = Picture::max(w, strlen(array[i]));

        init(n, w);
```

At this point, `height`, `width`, and `data` have appropriate values; it remains only to copy the characters in from the source. We will do that one row at a time, using `position` to copy characters from the source into the next row of `data`. Because the input strings may be of differing lengths, we have to remember to fill the rest of each row with blanks.

```
        for (i = 0; i < n; i++) {
                const char* src = array[i];
                int len = strlen(src);
                int j = 0;

                while (j < len) {
                        position(i, j) = src[j];
                        ++j;
                }

                while (j < width) {
                        position(i,j) = ' ';
                        ++j;
                }
        }
}
```

Next come the copy constructor and the assignment operator. These two members do similar things. It seems therefore to make sense to define a private function that will do the common part of the work. Indeed, with a little forethought, we may be able to make this function useful for the other operations as well.

The fundamental operation is to copy the contents of some other `Picture` into the picture on which we're working at the moment. For the copy constructor and assignment operator, the sizes of the two pictures will be the same.

Even in the concatenation case, we can confidently assume that the destination is at least as large as the source, because no operation ever throws away picture characters.

Because the destination can be larger than the source, it will be useful to be able to supply the starting point in the destination into which to copy the source. Row and column number, as measured in the destination, provide a good way to do this. We therefore have use for a `private` function such as

```
class Picture {
private:
        void copyblock(int, int, const Picture&);
        // ...
};
```

With the help of this function, the `Picture` copy constructor becomes almost trivial:

```
Picture::Picture(const Picture& p):
        height(p.height), width(p.width),
        data(new char[p.height * p.width])
{
        copyblock(0, 0, p);
}
```

The destructor is even simpler:

```
Picture::~Picture() { delete [] data; }
```

Now, what about that assignment operator? Essentially, all we have to do is to throw out (and remember to delete) the data for the current object, and to copy in the data from the source. As usual, the one trick is to ensure that the source and destination are not the same:

```
Picture& Picture::operator=(const Picture& p)
{
        if (this != &p) {
                delete[] data;
                init(p.height, p.width);
                copyblock(0, 0, p);
        }
        return *this;
}
```

The `copyblock` function has proved its worth: We have used it twice already. The function itself is straightforward, particularly given our `position` function. The trick is to remember to offset the position in the output array by the starting row and `col`:

```
void Picture::copyblock(int row, int col, const Picture& p)
{
        for (int i = 0; i < p.height; ++i) {
                for (int j = 0; j < p.width; ++j)
                        position(i + row, j + col) =
                                        p.position(i, j);
        }
}
```

The output operation is equally simple:

```
ostream& operator<<(ostream& o, const Picture& p)
{
        for (int i = 0; i < p.height; ++i) {
                for (int j = 0; j < p.width; ++j)
                        o << p.position(i, j);
                o << endl;
        }

        return o;
}
```

At this point, we are far enough along to be able to try a simple program:

```
#include "Picture.h"

char *init[] = { "Paris", "in the", "Spring" };

int main()
{
        Picture p(init, 3);
        cout << p << endl;
        Picture q = p;
        cout << q << endl;
}
```

It works; as long as we don't call the frame or concatenation functions, we don't need to define them. Getting a piece of a program working before finishing the rest of it can reassure us that the overall design is on track.

9.7 Combining pictures

Let's look now at the frame function. It builds up a picture from another picture, and adds some additional information. It has to do three things: allocate memory for the result, store appropriate characters for the frame, and copy in the source. Because it is a friend, it will be able to use knowledge of how pictures are implemented.

We will assume that frames are always one character wide. That means that a framed picture will be two characters longer in each dimension than the original. The first part of the frame function therefore looks like this:

```
Picture frame(const Picture& p)
{
        Picture r;

        r.init(p.height + 2, p.width + 2);
```

Building the frame itself turns out to be a bit of a pain, because the frame has so many components. First, we put | characters along both sides of the picture:

```
        for (int i = 1; i < r.height - 1; ++i) {
                r.position(i, 0) = '|';
                r.position(i, r.width - 1) = '|';
        }
```

Next we put – characters along the top and bottom of the picture:

```
        for (int j = 1; j < r.width - 1; ++j) {
                r.position(0, j) = '-';
                r.position(r.height - 1, j) = '-';
        }
```

Finally, we put + characters in the four corners:

```
        r.position(0, 0) = '+';
        r.position(0, r.width - 1) = '+';
        r.position(r.height - 1, 0) = '+';
        r.position(r.height - 1, r.width - 1) = '+';
```

Once that's done, we've built the frame; all that remains is to copy the source picture into the appropriate spot, with its corner at (1,1):

```
        r.copyblock(1, 1, p);
        return r;
}
```

Concatenation is easier. Again there are three steps: calculate how much memory we need, fill the unused parts of the newly allocated memory with blanks, and then copy in the operands.

For vertical concatenation, the height of the result will be the sum of the operand heights, and the width will be the greater of the widths. The first step therefore looks like this:

```
Picture operator&(const Picture& p, const Picture& q)
{
        Picture r;

        r.init(p.height + q.height,
                Picture::max(p.width, q.width));
```

We can use copyblock to copy the operands into the output Picture, but first we must initialize the unused portion of data with blanks. It looks like we'll need another utility function to clear the unused portions of the array. For now, let's assume we have a function clear that takes four int arguments. These arguments, taken in pairs, will denote opposite corners of a rectangle in the output array to clear:

```
r.clear(0, p.width, p.height, r.width);
r.clear(p.height, q.width, r.height, r.width);
```

These two calls to `clear` will clear the rectangle to the right of each of the two pictures that we are concatenating vertically. One or both of those rectangles will be empty, because at least one of the two argument pictures will fill the horizontal extent of the result picture.

Finally, we use `copyblock` twice to put the operand pictures in their places:

```
r.copyblock(0, 0, p);
r.copyblock(p.height, 0, q);

return r;
}
```

Horizontal concatenation is much the same, except that coordinates are swapped in various places. We invite you to compare it with vertical concatenation. Again, one or both of the two calls to `clear` will clear an empty rectangle:

```
Picture operator|(const Picture& p, const Picture& q)
{
        Picture r;

        r.init(Picture::max(p.height, q.height),
               p.width + q.width);

        r.clear(p.height, 0, r.height, p.width);
        r.clear(q.height, p.width, r.height, r.width);

        r.copyblock(0, 0, p);
        r.copyblock(0, p.width, q);

        return r;
}
```

Finally, we need to define `clear`:

```
void Picture::clear(int r1, int c1, int r2, int c2)
{
        for (int r = r1; r < r2; ++r)
                for (int c = c1; c < c2; ++c)
                        position(r, c) = ' ';
}
```

For completeness, here is the class declaration again, with all the added pieces in place:

```
class Picture {
friend ostream& operator<<(ostream&, const Picture&);
friend Picture frame(const Picture&);
friend Picture operator&(const Picture&, const Picture&);
friend Picture operator|(const Picture&, const Picture&);
```

```
public:
        Picture();
        Picture(const char* const*, int);
        Picture(const Picture&);
        ~Picture();

        Picture& operator=(const Picture&);
private:
        int height, width;
        char* data;
        void copyblock(int, int, const Picture&);
        char& position(int, int);
        char position(int, int) const;
        void clear(int, int, int, int);
        void init(int, int);
        static int max(int, int);
};
```

9.8 Conclusion

This solution to the picture problem is neither very long nor very difficult. It has the advantages of being straightforward and easy to understand. It also has several disadvantages.

First, copying a picture always copies its characters. Moreover, incorporating a picture into a bigger one copies the characters of the inner picture, as well. Second, this solution potentially devotes a lot of memory to blanks. All it takes is for a picture to have one line much longer than the rest. Finally, the solution throws away all structural information about the picture. Suppose, for example, that we wanted to write a function that would remove the frame from a framed picture. As the program stands, we have no way to distinguish a framed picture from one that just happens to have characters along its edges that look like a frame.

These disadvantages all stem from one source: We have implemented the Picture class to store the *representation* of a picture, not its structure. We cannot solve such problems merely by patching: If we want to store structure, we must completely redesign the program.

That redesign is the subject of Chapter 10.

10

Analysis of
a classroom exercise: Part 2

In Chapter 9, we looked at a problem that formed the basis for an interesting homework assignment during a C++ course. We also saw a straightforward solution to that problem that did just what the problem said and no more. This solution had shortcomings: It potentially wasted a lot of space and was fundamentally inflexible.

The problem before us now is how to represent pictures in a way that does not have these disadvantages. Here, we'll solve that problem by preserving information that, although not part of the problem specification, will give us the ability to modify our solution in useful ways.

As we'll see, our new design will be similar to the one that we developed for expression trees in Chapter 8. By reflecting, in a class hierarchy, the structure of the pictures that we're manipulating, we can preserve that structure for later use. We'll also provide a handle class to hide the implementation detail that we're using inheritance, and to protect the user from having to deal with memory management.

10.1 Strategy

The trouble with the strategy in Chapter 9 was that it destroyed the structure of a picture as soon as that picture was created. Suppose that we adopt the opposite strategy, by keeping structural information around as long as possible? How might we do that? What would it do for us?

The first, almost immediate conclusion is that we would have to store several different kinds of pictures. After all, the most obvious aspect of a picture's structure is the way that that picture was formed: It was generated directly from an array of character strings, it is a framed picture, or it is the result of a horizontal or vertical concatenation.

The next conclusion, which is somewhat less obvious, is that it is unnecessary ever to copy the contents of pictures. If, for example, we obtain a picture y by framing some other picture x, that fact does not change x. That means that the representation of y can somehow refer to the representation of x without having to copy it.

Pointers come to mind here, obviously, as does using inheritance to distinguish among the various kinds of pictures. But, in C++, using pointers requires thinking about memory allocation. Because we already decided what interface we should let our users see, we can't pass the memory-allocation problem along to the users. We need a way to hide the implementation details.

These are the same issues that we faced in Chapter 8. What we need is a handle class, which we'll call `Picture`, to hide an inheritance hierarchy that captures the structure of the pictures that we're building. Once we have a handle class, it will be easy to implement a use-counted memory-allocation strategy to avoid copying the underlying characters that make up a picture.

To make this strategy a little more concrete, we can begin with the `Picture` class that users see. Class `Picture` will contain a pointer to an object of some other class; that object will say what kind of picture it really is. Using inheritance to distinguish among kinds of pictures will yield a structure in which Class `Picture` contains a (private) pointer to a class that we shall call `P_Node`, an abstract base class with derived classes:

- `String_Pic`, for a picture obtained directly from strings
- `Frame_Pic`, which represents a picture obtained by framing another picture
- `Hcat_Pic`, for a picture that is the horizontal concatenation of two pictures
- `Vcat_Pic`, for the vertical concatenation of two other pictures

The `Picture` and `P_Node` classes will cooperate to solve the memory-allocation problem.

10.1.1 Tactics

Let us begin by writing down what we have so far. Class `Picture` has an interface that has already been chosen for us:

```
class Picture {
public:
        Picture();
        Picture(const char* const*, int);
        Picture(const Picture&);
        ~Picture();

        Picture& operator=(const Picture&);
};
```

We also know a bit about the other classes we'll need:

```
class P_Node { };
```

```
class String_Pic: public P_Node { };

class Frame_Pic: public P_Node { };

class VCat_Pic: public P_Node { };

class HCat_Pic: public P_Node { };
```

So now all we have to do is fill in the details.

We can start by declaring the P_Node pointer that we know is in every Picture object, and adding friend declarations for the operations that will need to
know about the structure of Pictures:

```
class P_Node;

class Picture {
        friend ostream& operator<<(ostream&, const Picture&);
        friend Picture frame(const Picture&);
        friend Picture operator&
                (const Picture&, const Picture&);
        friend Picture operator|
                (const Picture&, const Picture&);

public:
        Picture(const char* const*, int);
        Picture(const Picture&);
        ~Picture();
        Picture& operator=(const Picture&);

private:
        P_Node* p;
};
```

The declaration

```
class P_Node;
```

tells the compiler that P_Node names a class; it is necessary because we are
declaring a pointer to P_Node before we've declared the class itself.

10.1.2 Memory allocation

Every Picture will point to a P_Node, but several Pictures might point to
the *same* P_Node. For example, after

```
Picture p1 = /* some picture */;
Picture p2 = p1;
```

there is no reason to require the entire contents of p1 to be copied. Instead, we'll
give every P_Node object a use count, which will keep track of how many
Pictures point at that particular P_Node. Of course, if we are going to rely on
these use counts, we must make sure no one else fiddles with them. We can do
that by making the use count private, and by making class Picture a friend
of class P_Node. Let's write that down:

```
class P_Node {
        friend class Picture;

protected:
        int use;
};
```

Surprisingly, we now have enough information to write the copy constructor, destructor, and assignment operator for class `Picture`. We know that every `Picture` points at a `P_Node`, so the copy constructor will make the new `Picture` point at the same `P_Node` as the old one, and will increment the use count:

```
Picture::Picture(const Picture& orig): p(orig.p)
{
        orig.p->use++;
}
```

Similarly, the `Picture` destructor will decrement the use count and delete the `P_Node` if this `P_Node` is the only one pointed to by the `Picture` being destroyed:

```
Picture::~Picture()
{
        if (--p->use == 0)
                delete p;
}
```

Finally, the assignment operator always replaces an old value by a new one. It therefore increments the use count of the new value and decrements the use count of the old one, taking care to do so in an order that will ensure correct results even if we are assigning a `Picture` to itself:

```
Picture& Picture::operator=(const Picture& orig)
{
        orig.p->use++;
        if (--p->use == 0)
                delete p;
        p = orig.p;
        return *this;
}
```

As usual, the problem with self assignment is that `orig` and `*this` refer to the same object.

Now, let's look at the constructor and destructor for class `P_Node`. We expect that there will be no independent `P_Node` objects, but rather only objects of classes derived from `P_Node`. That immediately argues that we will need a virtual destructor. Consider, for example, the statement

```
delete p;
```

in the `Picture` destructor. Although p is a `P_Node*`, it will actually point at an object of a derived class. This case is precisely the one in which a virtual destructor is essential. We therefore augment our `P_Node` class

```
class P_Node {
        friend class Picture;

protected:
        virtual ~P_Node();

private:
        int use;
};
```

and define the destructor:

```
P_Node::~P_Node() { }
```

Now, what about constructors? Again, we expect `P_Node` objects to exist only as parts of larger objects. Even so, every `P_Node` has a use count, for which we must find an initial value.

Although we don't yet know everything that we're going to do with `P_Nodes`, we can make a pretty good guess that, when we create an object of class (derived from) `P_Node`, we will store the address of that object in some `Picture`. Because the `P_Node` is newly created, it will have only the one `Picture` pointing to it, so we should start off the use count at 1. Our `P_Node` class

```
class P_Node {
        friend class Picture;

protected:
        P_Node();
        virtual ~P_Node();

private:
        int use;
};
```

has gained a constructor, which we must define:

```
P_Node::P_Node(): use(1) { }
```

10.1.3 Building the structure

It is time to consider how to construct `Picture` objects that will represent the various kinds of pictures. We'll begin with the constructor

```
Picture::Picture(const char* const*, int);
```

We have already decided that the constructor will work by creating a `String_Pic` object and storing its address in the `Picture`. We haven't defined class `String_Pic` yet, though, so let's assume that it will have an appropriate constructor. That allows us to write our `Picture` constructor easily:

```
Picture::Picture(const char* const* str, int n):
        p(new String_Pic(str, n)) { }
```

Of course, this definition just postpones the problem: What do we need in class
String_Pic? We need to store the number of strings and a pointer to a copy of
the characters we were given. We don't want to store pointers directly to the
user's characters, because the user might change or destroy those characters
later. All the members of String_Pic can be private: We will nominate class
Picture as a friend, and the only other possible access will be through virtual
functions. That gives us

```
class String_Pic: public P_Node {
        friend class Picture;

        String_Pic(const char* const*, int);
        ~String_Pic();

        char** data;
        int size;
};
```

Implementing the constructor and destructor is not hard:

```
String_Pic::String_Pic(const char* const* p, int n):
        data(new char* [n]), size(n)
{
        for (int i = 0; i < n; i++) {
                data[i] = new char[strlen(p[i])+1];
                strcpy(data[i], p[i]);
        }
}

String_Pic::~String_Pic()
{
        for (int i = 0; i < size; i++)
                delete[] data[i];
        delete[] data;
}
```

Note that the nontrivial destructor for class String_Pic makes the virtual
destructor essential in class P_Node.

Making a framed picture also is easy. We note first that a Frame_Pic needs,
somewhat surprisingly, to contain a Picture:

```
class Frame_Pic: public P_Node {
        friend Picture frame(const Picture&);

        Frame_Pic(const Picture&);
        Picture p;
};
```

That is the most straightforward way to represent the structure we want. A
framed picture, after all, is just a Picture with extra information. The

Frame_Pic represents the extra information, leaving the Picture to represent
what is inside the frame.

It is therefore trivial to construct a Frame_Pic:

```
Frame_Pic::Frame_Pic(const Picture& pic): p(pic) { }
```

All that remains is to write the function frame, which users will use in place of a
constructor. Here, we run into a little trouble:

```
Picture frame(const Picture& pic)
{
        Frame_Pic* p = new Frame_Pic(pic.p);
        // now what?
};
```

We have created a pointer p, which points to a newly created Frame_Pic object.
How do we get this pointer into a Picture so that we can return it to our user?

One way is to go back, and to give class Picture a private constructor,
whose purpose will be exactly that:

```
class Picture {
        // as before

private:
        Picture(P_Node*);                   // added
        P_Node* p;
};
```

Of course, we must define that constructor:

```
Picture::Picture(P_Node* p_node): p(p_node) { }
```

Now, we can complete the definition of frame:

```
Picture frame(const Picture& pic)
{
        return new Frame_Pic(pic.p);
};
```

Here, we are using our newly defined Picture constructor as an implicit conversion operator.

A similar strategy works for the concatenation operators. We derive two
more classes from P_Node:

```
class VCat_Pic: public P_Node {
        friend Picture operator&
                    (const Picture&, const Picture&);

        VCat_Pic(const Picture&, const Picture&);
        Picture top, bottom;
};

class HCat_Pic: public P_Node {
        friend Picture operator|
                    (const Picture&, const Picture&);
```

```
              HCat_Pic(const Picture&, const Picture&);
              Picture left, right;
    };
```

We then define the appropriate constructors and `operator&` and `operator|` functions to use them:

```
    VCat_Pic::VCat_Pic(const Picture& t, const Picture& b):
            top(t), bottom(b) { }

    Picture operator&(const Picture& t, const Picture& b)
    {
            return new VCat_Pic(t.p, b.p);
    };

    HCat_Pic::HCat_Pic(const Picture& l, const Picture& r):
            left(l), right(r) { }

    Picture operator|(const Picture& l, const Picture& r)
    {
            return new HCat_Pic(l.p, r.p);
    };
```

10.1.4 Displaying the picture

We now have a hierarchy of classes that lets us construct pictures in a way that preserves their structure. Unfortunately, it is lacking one important aspect: It doesn't give us any way to display a `Picture`!

Before plunging into implementation, let's think about it. We will presumably print a `Picture` with an algorithm that reflects the `Picture`'s structure. The obvious way to print a `String_Pic` is to print each of its strings, followed by a newline. Suppose, though, that we were to do it that way. Then, the only display operation would be to print the entire picture. In that case, how would we implement the function that displays a `Frame_Pic`? The difficulty is that we need to print part of the frame on every line of the picture, which means that our display operation is not powerful enough.

If we need to get control at the beginning and end of every line, that suggests that, instead of displaying the entire picture, what we want is to display a given line of the picture, *without the newline that ordinarily ends a line*. Then, the framing operation becomes easy. First, we print the top line of the frame. Then, for each line in the picture, we print the left side of the frame, the picture line, and the right side of the frame. Finally, we print the bottom line of the frame.

Looking at this procedure carefully, we see that we will also need to determine the height and width of a picture. For example, when we are displaying a framed picture, we will need to know the width of the (unframed) picture to know how wide to make the top and bottom rows of the frame. We will also need to know the height to know how many rows to print.

Is that all? Not quite. Suppose that we are displaying a `String_Pic`. Then, we want the display of each line to end as soon as the corresponding string ends; there's no need to fill up the page with spaces. However, if we are displaying a `Frame_Pic` that contains (only) a `String_Pic`, it is essential to pad each line of the `String_Pic` to the width of the longest string, lest the frame have a ragged right margin.

Therefore, the display operation needs two arguments: the number of the row to display, and the minimum width required. The row will be padded with blanks as necessary to make up the minimum. While we're at it, we'll add another argument: the file on which we want to display the output.

The classes derived from `P_Node` will use the `height`, `width`, and `display` functions that we have added. However, we made those functions private to keep ordinary users from using them. The decision to do so keeps the functions from leaking out into the interface of class `Picture`, but in exchange, it forces us to nominate, as friends of class `Picture`, the classes derived from `P_Node`. Our `Picture` class now looks like this:

```
class Picture {
        // as before
        friend class String_pic;
        friend class Frame_Pic;
        friend class HCat_pic;
        friend class VCat_pic;

private:
        Picture(P_Node*);
        int height() const;                                    // added
        int width() const;                                     // added
        void display(ostream&, int, int) const;  // added
        P_Node* p;
};
```

The `height`, `width`, and `display` functions forward their arguments to corresponding functions that we must still add to class `P_Node`:

```
int Picture::height() const
{
        return p->height();
}

int Picture::width() const
{
        return p->width();
}

void Picture::display(ostream& o, int x, int y) const
{
        p->display(o, x, y);
}
```

Now what about that `operator<<`? It uses `display` to pick out one line at a time from the picture, with no padding:

```
ostream& operator<<(ostream& os, const Picture& picture)
{
        int ht = picture.height();
        for (int i = 0; i < ht; i++) {
                picture.display(os, i, 0);
                os << endl;
        }
        return os;
}
```

In class `P_Node`, we need not define the `height`, `width`, and `display` functions. After all, there are no objects of class `P_Node`, so the functions will never be called. We will therefore make them pure virtual. Class `P_Node` now looks like this:

```
class P_Node {
        friend class Picture;

protected:
        P_Node();
        virtual ~P_Node();
        virtual int height() const = 0;          // added
        virtual int width() const = 0;           // added
        virtual void display
                (ostream&, int, int) const = 0;  // added

private:
        int use;
};
```

All that remains is to define `height`, `width`, and `display` in each of the four derived classes. There are, of course, a zillion ways to define them; what follows is slanted toward compactness, rather than toward execution efficiency.

For completeness, we first give the full declarations of the four derived classes:

```
class String_Pic: public P_Node {
        friend class Picture;

        String_Pic(const char* const*, int);
        ~String_Pic();
        int height() const;                      // added
        int width() const;                       // added
        void display(ostream&, int, int) const;  // added

        char** data;
        int size;
};

class Frame_Pic: public P_Node {
        friend Picture frame(const Picture&);
```

```
            Frame_Pic(const Picture&);
            int height() const;                          // added
            int width() const;                           // added
            void display(ostream&, int, int) const;      // added

            Picture p;
    };

class VCat_Pic: public P_Node {
        friend Picture operator&
                (const Picture&, const Picture&);

        VCat_Pic(const Picture&, const Picture&);
        int height() const;                          // added
        int width() const;                           // added
        void display(ostream&, int, int) const;      // added

        Picture top, bottom;
    };

class HCat_Pic: public P_Node {
        friend Picture operator|
                (const Picture&, const Picture&);

        HCat_Pic(const Picture&, const Picture&);
        int height() const;                          // added
        int width() const;                           // added
        void display(ostream&, int, int) const;      // added

        Picture left, right;
    };
```

The height of a `String_Pic` is simply the number of strings, which we have already stored; the width is the size of the longest string. So let's start by defining a utility function to find the larger of two integers:

```
int P_node::max(int x, int y)
{
        return x > y ? x: y;
}
```

With that done, we can define the `height`, `width`, and `display` members of class `String_Pic`:

```
int String_Pic::height() const
{
        return size;
}

int String_Pic::width() const
{
        int n = 0;
```

```
        for (int i = 0; i < size; i++) {
                n = max(n, strlen(data[i]));
        }
        return n;
    }
```

To define `String_Pic::display`, we will find it useful first to define an auxiliary function called `pad`. This function takes a file and two arguments x and y; if
x<y, it prints y−x blanks on the file:

```
static void pad(ostream& os, int x, int y)
{
        for (int i = x; i < y; i++)
                os << " ";
}
```

For `String_Pic::display` itself, we will print the given line, padded out to
the minimum width as necessary. While we're at it, we must decide what to do
if the line is out of range. We will pretend that lines out of range are empty, so
that we can take advantage of that behavior later if we wish:

```
void
String_Pic::display(ostream& os, int row, int width) const
{
        int start = 0;
        if (row >= 0 && row < height()) {
                os << data[row];
                start = strlen(data[row]);
        }
        pad(os, start, width);
}
```

Finding the height and width of a framed picture is trivial: We add 2 to both the
height and the width of the picture inside the frame.

```
int Frame_Pic::height() const
{
        return p.height() + 2;
}

int Frame_Pic::width() const
{
        return p.width() + 2;
}
```

Printing a framed picture is tedious, but not difficult. There are three cases: the
row requested is outside the picture altogether, it's the top or bottom row of the
frame, or it's one of the rows of the interior picture.

```
void Frame_Pic::display(ostream& os, int row, int wd) const
{
        if (row < 0 || row >= height()) {
```

```
                    // out of range
                    pad(os, 0, wd);
        } else {
                    if (row == 0 || row == height() - 1) {
                            // top or bottom border
                            os << "+";
                            int i = p.width();
                            while (--i >= 0)
                                    os << "-";
                            os << "+";
                    } else {
                            // interior row
                            os << "|";
                            p.display(os, row - 1, p.width());
                            os << "|";
                    }
                    pad(os, width(), wd);
        }
}
```

Finally, we have to print concatenated pictures. The heights and widths are easy. For example, the height of a vertically concatenated picture is the sum of the heights of that picture's components, and the width is the larger of the component widths. Similar reasoning applies to horizontally concatenated pictures:

```
int VCat_Pic::height() const
{
        return top.height() + bottom.height();
}

int VCat_Pic::width() const
{
        return max(top.width(), bottom.width());
}

int HCat_Pic::height() const
{
        return max(left.height(), right.height());
}

int HCat_Pic::width() const
{
        return left.width() + right.width();
}
```

Displaying concatenated pictures is a little harder; the neat duality between horizontal and vertical no longer applies. Vertical concatenation is the easy one, dividing into three cases. We've been asked to display a row, which is out of range, part of the top picture, or part of the bottom picture. In each case, we pass along the width that we've been given:

```
void VCat_Pic::display(ostream& os, int row, int wd) const
{
        if (row > 0 && row < top.height())
                top.display(os, row, wd);
        else if (row < top.height() + bottom.height())
                bottom.display(os, row - top.height(), wd);
        else
                pad(os, 0, wd);
}
```

Note that, when we are displaying the bottom picture, the row number must be offset by the size of the top picture.

Next, we must handle horizontal concatenation. This operation may seem hard at first, but is surprisingly easy: We print the corresponding row of the left picture, then that of the right picture. Finally we pad as necessary to the given width:

```
void HCat_Pic::display(ostream& os, int row, int wd) const
{
        left.display(os, row, left.width());
        right.display(os, row, right.width());
        pad(os, width(), wd);
}
```

That is all we need in order to solve the original problem.

10.2 Exploiting the structure

One of our objectives in designing a new solution was greater flexibility. To illustrate this flexibility, we shall add a new operation to the system: reframing an existing picture.

Reframing a picture should allow the user to specify a new value for the corners, and for the top or bottom borders of the frame, and should change the current frame characters to the new ones for all the component pictures within a Picture. For example: If pic is this picture from Section 9.1 (page 89)

```
+--------------+
|+------+      |
||Paris |      |
||in the|      |
||Spring|      |
|+------+      |
|Paris +------+|
|in the|Paris ||
|Spring|in the||
|      |Spring||
|      +------+|
+--------------+
```

then `reframe(pic, '*', '*', '*')` should generate

```
****************
********       *
**Paris *      *
**in the*      *
**Spring*      *
********       *
*Paris ********
*in the*Paris **
*Spring*in the**
*       *Spring**
*       ********
****************
```

Before exploring how to do this in the current design, you might consider how and, indeed, whether it's even possible to do it using the initial design developed in Chapter 9. In that design, there is no way to determine whether a given character is part of a `Picture` or part of the frame around a component `Picture`. Therefore, it's hard to see how we could even find the frame in order to reframe it! In the present solution, though, the structure of a `Picture` is captured explicitly in the types of the `P_Node`s. This structure should give us the handle we need to provide a `reframe` operation.

First, we note that reframing a `Picture`, like our other operations, is a non-member function. This implies that we'll need to add a friend declaration to class `Picture` and, as we did in the other operations, we'll forward the work to the underlying `P_Node`. With this, we can write the new `Picture` class:

```
class Picture {
        friend ostream& operator<<(ostream&, const Picture&);
        friend Picture frame(const Picture&);
        friend Picture reframe                          // added
                (const Picture&, char, char, char);
        // ...
};
```

We can also write the `reframe` function:

```
Picture reframe (const Picture& pic, char c, char s, char t)
{
        return pic.p->reframe(c,s,t);
}
```

We'll need to add another pure virtual function to the `P_Node` class, and to make the global `reframe` function a friend:

```
class P_Node {
        friend Picture reframe(char, char, char);
        virtual Picture reframe(char, char, char) = 0;
        // ...
};
```

Each of the classes derived from `P_Node` will also need to define a `reframe` operation. For brevity, we'll omit showing the new class declarations with the `reframe` operation.

Now, let's look at how we'll implement `reframe` for each type. Starting with the easiest, we can observe that reframing a `String_Pic` is trivial—there is no frame to change. We'll treat this as a no-op, and will generate another pointer to the `String_Pic` as the resulting `Picture`:

```
Picture String_Pic::reframe(char, char, char)
{
        use++;
        return this;    // uses the private Picture constructor
}
```

Note that we increment the use count to indicate that there is another user of the underlying `String_Pic`, and use the conversion operator from `P_node*` to generate a new `Picture` from `this`.

To `reframe` a `HCat_Pic` or a `VCat_Pic` is a simple matter of building a new `Picture` by reframing the component `Picture`s:

```
Picture VCat_Pic::reframe(char c, char s, char t)
{
        return new VCat_Pic(
                ::reframe(top,c,s,t),
                ::reframe(bottom,c,s,t)
        );
}

Picture HCat_Pic::reframe(char c, char s, char t)
{
        return new HCat_Pic(
                ::reframe(left,c,s,t),
                ::reframe(right,c,s,t)
        );
}
```

Note the use of the scope operator `::` to invoke the global `reframe` function explicitly when we are reframing the component `Picture`s. Without it, references to `reframe` would call the wrong function—they would be recursive calls to the member functions themselves. The program would therefore not compile, because the global `reframe` function takes one more argument than do the member `reframe` functions.

Next, let's look at `Frame_Pic`s. Before thinking about the `reframe` operation itself, let's think about what changing the frame characters implies. In our current scheme, the `Frame_Pic::display` function *knows* what values to use for the frame. Clearly, this will have to change. Instead, we'll need to store in the `Frame_Pic` object itself the characters used to create the frame, and to rewrite the `display` function to use these values. This implies that we'll need to add data members to `Frame_Pic`, and to provide a way to get these frame values into a `Frame_Pic` object. Now, we can write a new `Frame_Pic` class:

```
class Frame_Pic: public P_Node {
        friend Picture frame(const Picture&);

        Frame_Pic(const Picture&,
                char = '+', char = '|', char = '-');
        int height() const;
        int width() const;
        void display(ostream&, int, int) const;
        Picture reframe(char, char, char);

        Picture p;
        char corner;
        char sideborder;
        char topborder;
};
```

Here, we've updated the `Frame_Pic` constructor to capture the characters that will make up the frame. For compatibility with existing code, we gave default values to these new arguments that match the characters, we used to generate in the `display` operation:

```
Frame_Pic::Frame_Pic
        (const Picture& pic, char c, char s, char t):
        p(pic), corner(c), sideborder(s), topborder(t) { }
```

Given this new constructor, we can now finally write the `reframe` function. First, note that, to `reframe` a `Frame_Pic`, we need to `reframe` its component `Picture` with the new values, and then generate a new `Frame_Pic` initialized with that new `Picture` and the new frame values:

```
Picture Frame_Pic::reframe(char c, char s, char t)
{
        return new Frame_Pic(::reframe(p,c,s,t), c, s, t);
}
```

Finally, we will need to rewrite the `display` function to use the stored values of the frame characters. We leave that as an exercise for the reader.

10.3 Conclusion

When solving a problem, it is important to keep in mind not only what the immediate problem is, but also how the problem might change in the future. For this particular problem, the key realization was that pictures have structure, and that we might need someday to take that structure into account. That, in turn, led us to look for a way to store the structure, instead of merely storing the contents, of a picture.

The next insight was that we could use inheritance to model the structure. This should not be surprising; inheritance is most useful in precisely the kinds of circumstances that we can express by saying things like "Any picture can be framed to yield another picture."

Once we decided to use inheritance, it became apparent that we did not need to copy the contents of a picture. This realization led to use counts as a memory-management technique; we discovered that we could limit memory-allocation concerns to only two classes in our family.

Finally, we learned that we did not need to reconstitute the characters of the picture, even when we were displaying it. Instead, we could go over the picture one line at a time, building up the characters on the fly and writing them out immediately.

This solution is significantly larger than the one presented in Chapter 9, but for complicated pictures it will use much less memory. More important, it is much more flexible. We were able to implement a `reframe` operation that would have been impossible given the initial implementation.

Does that make this program better or worse? As usual, it depends. For a classroom exercise, the value lies in doing it both ways, and in understanding both. Flexibility is usually worth something in real-world programs, too, because it saves us from having to rewrite them in the face of changing require-ments. How much we can afford to pay for flexibility is, of course, one of those engineering tradeoffs that we can make only when the surrounding context is understood. One must understand the problem and its context before choosing a solution.

11

When not to use
virtual functions

Chapter 9 solved a fairly hard problem without using virtual functions; Chapter 10 used virtual functions to solve the same problem. If we had made all the functions virtual in Chapter 9, we would not have affected the behavior of the examples there, because there is no inheritance. On the other hand, virtual functions are crucial to the behavior of the Chapter 10 examples.

One can argue along such lines to claim that virtual functions are somehow more fundamental than nonvirtual ones, and that all member functions should therefore be virtual by default. Indeed, some people have suggested that there is no reason ever not to use a virtual function, and that all member functions should therefore be virtual automatically. The reasoning behind this argument appears attractive at first; it is worth examining carefully to understand where the problems lie.

11.1 The case for

We note first that, if we look only at program behavior, and if there is no inheritance, then it makes no difference whether or not a function is virtual. Therefore, goes the argument, programmers who *don't* use inheritance can make all their functions virtual without thinking about it. Only when inheritance enters the picture is there anything to consider.

In programs that use inheritance, the argument continues, making all functions virtual allows for much more flexibility. As a somewhat simplified example, consider an IntArray class that represents an array of integers:*

---

* In this example and those that follow, we will simplify the presentation by using an array of values of one specific type. In practice, of course, it would be much more useful to generalize the examples by using templates. That alternative would not affect any of the reasoning.

```
class IntArray {
public:
        // ...
        unsigned size() const;
        int& operator[](unsigned n);
};
```

We might write a function that sets all the elements of the array to zero:

```
void zero(IntArray& x)
{
        for (int i = 0; i < x.size(); i++)
                x[n] = 0;
}
```

The argument is that, in cases such as this one, IntArray::operator[] and IntArray::size() should be virtual. For example, someone might want to derive a class from IntArray called, say, IntFileArray, which would store its integers in a file, rather than directly in memory. If the member functions IntArray::operator[] and IntArray::size are virtual, the zero function will work correctly on IntFileArray objects; if they aren't, the zero function will probably fail.

11.2 The case against

Despite its appeal, this argument has several problems:
- Virtual functions are not terribly expensive, yet neither are they free; it is important to think about what they cost before using them.
- There are cases where nonvirtual functions behave "correctly," and virtual functions do not.
- Not every class is designed for inheritance.

11.2.1 Efficiency

A good compiler will impose no overhead on a program that calls a virtual function that is a member of an explicitly supplied object; for example

```
T x;
x.f();
```

Here, we have defined an object x of class T, and have called its member function f. Whether f is virtual should not matter; the compiler can determine that x is an object of class T, and not of some class derived from T, so it can generate a direct call to T::f. However, if all calls to member functions were through explicitly specified objects, it would never matter whether or not the member functions were virtual.

Where it does matter is if the call is through a pointer or reference:

```
void call_f(T* tp)
{
        tp->f();
}
```

Here, `tp` points to an object of class `T` or of some class derived from `T`, so, if `T::f` is virtual, the call must go through the virtual-function mechanism. Does the virtual lookup cost enough to matter?

It depends. It is hard to know how much a particular program costs without measuring the cost on a variety of machines, but it is possible to get a rough approximation by counting memory references.* For example, let's look back at the `IntArray::operator[]` member function. A typical way to implement an array class is to have its constructor allocate an appropriate amount of memory somewhere, in which case `operator[]` might look like this:

```
int& IntArray::operator[](unsigned n)
{
        if (n >= arraysize)
                throw "subscript out of range";
        return data[n];
}
```

Aside from function-call overhead, this function requires three memory references, to fetch the values of `n`, `arraysize`, and `data`. How does this overhead compare with the cost of calling a virtual function? For that matter, how does the overhead compare with the cost of calling a nonvirtual member function?

Because we are assuming that overhead matters, we will presumably have coded this function inline. Thus, a good implementation will introduce no overhead at all when applying `operator[]` directly to an object. The cost of applying it through a pointer or reference is probably about three memory references: one for the pointer itself, one to initialize the `this` pointer for the member function, and one for the call–return sequence. Thus, we can expect this little member function to take about twice as long when we call it through a pointer or reference as it does to call it directly for an object. Calling a virtual function typically takes three memory references: one to fetch from the object the address of the table that describes its type, another to fetch the address of the virtual function, and the third to fetch the object's offset in the larger object that may enclose it. In such an implementation, making a function virtual will triple, rather than double the execution time.

---

* This technique may well become more accurate as microprocessors become faster and memory references increasingly dominate computation time. Or it may become less accurate as processors incorporate huge caches to compensate for the delay in fetching information from outside the chip. The time estimates that follow are necessarily crude; if you want greater accuracy, run your own tests on your own implementation.

Is this overhead a problem? It depends on the application. Clearly, the bigger a member function is, the less of a problem making it virtual is. Indeed, the same argument might well be applied to the bounds check: Removing it would remove one of the three memory references in the function itself, so we might reasonably say that the bounds check made the function 50% slower. Moreover, a good optimizing compiler may render all our estimates moot. If you care about how long things take, you should measure them. Nevertheless, this rough analysis suggests that virtual-function overhead may be significant.

Sometimes, a little thought will let us keep the flexibility of virtual functions without incurring any significant overhead at all. Consider, for example, a class that represents an input buffer. By analogy with the C library function getc, we might want our class to have a member function named get that returns an int. The return value will contain either a character or EOF. Moreover, we want people to be able to derive classes from ours that implement completely different buffering strategies.

The obvious approach is to write

```
class InputBuffer {
public:
        // ...
        virtual int get();
        // ...
};
```

so that whoever inherits from this class will be able to override get as necessary.

However, this approach is potentially expensive. Consider the following function that counts the lines in a buffer:

```
int countlines(InputBuffer& b)
{
        int n = 0;
        int c;

        while ((c = b.get()) != EOF) {
                if (c == '\n')
                        n++;
        }

        return n;
}
```

This function is flexible, in the sense that it will work for classes derived from InputBuffer. However, every call to get is a virtual function call, and therefore costs about six memory references (three for the function, three more because it's virtual). Thus, the function-call overhead is likely to dominate the loop execution time.

We can do substantially better in designing the InputBuffer class if we realize that buffering applications are likely to make multiple characters available to us at a time. Suppose, for example, that we do this:

```
class InputBuffer {
public:
        // ...
        int get() {
                if (next >= limit)
                        return refill();
                return *next++;
        }
protected:
        virtual int refill();

private:
        char* next;
        char* limit;
};
```

We also assume here that we will have some number of characters waiting in the buffer. The data member `next` points to the first such character; the member `limit` points to the first memory location beyond the final character. The test `next >= limit` therefore determines whether the available characters are exhausted. If they are, we call the `refill` function, which tries to obtain more characters. If it succeeds, it resets `next` and `limit` appropriately, and returns the first such character; if it fails, it returns `EOF`.

We assume that, in the most common case, there *are* characters remaining; in this case we simply return `*next++`. That yields the next available character and also steps to the next one.

The point is that `get` is now inline and not virtual. If there is a character available, it takes about four memory references to execute: two for the comparison, one to fetch the character, and one more to store the updated value of `next`. If we must call `refill`, of course, it will probably cost considerably more, but if `refill` gets a large enough chunk from its input, that doesn't matter much.

In this example, we have therefore reduced the typical cost of `get` from six memory references plus the body of the virtual `get` to slightly more than four memory references overall. If we assume that the virtual version of `get` does as much work as the nonvirtual one (and it is hard to see how to do much less), our shift in strategy has reduced `get` from 10 memory references to four, more than doubling the speed.

11.2.2 What behavior do you want?

Derived classes often strictly extend the behavior of their base classes. That is, it is often possible for a derived class object to take the place of a base class object without changing the behavior of the program. However, there are cases where that is not so; in such cases, virtual functions may cause undesired behavior.

We can build an example of that on top of our `IntArray` class. First, we will flesh out its declaration slightly:

```
class IntArray {
public:
        IntArray(unsigned);
        int& operator[](unsigned);
        unsigned size() const;
        // ...
};
```

We assume that we will construct an `IntArray` by giving it a size, and that we have a subscript operation.

Suppose now that we derive from this class an `IntBlock` class that behaves like an `IntArray`, except that its initial element's index need not be zero:

```
class IntBlock: public IntArray {
public:
        IntBlock(int l, int h): low(l), high(h),
            IntArray(l > h? 0: h - l + 1) { }
        int& operator[](int n) {
            return IntArray::operator[](n - low);
        }

private:
        int low, high;
};
```

This class definition is fairly straightforward: To construct an `IntBlock` with a lower bound of l and an upper bound of h, we construct the underlying array with h-l+1 elements, except that we force a negative number of elements to zero. The subscript operation is simple too: We use the appropriate index as an argument to the base-class subscript operator.

Now, consider a function that adds all the elements of an `IntArray`:

```
int sum(IntArray& x)
{
        int result = 0;
        for (int i = 0; i < x.size(); i++)
                result += x[i];
        return result;
}
```

What happens if we give this function an `IntBlock`, instead of an `IntArray`?

The answer is that it will add the elements of the `IntBlock` correctly *only* if `operator[]` is not virtual! The point is that `sum` treats its argument as an `IntArray` to the extent that it really expects `IntArray` behavior from its argument. In particular, it expects the initial element to have an index of 0 and it expects the `size` function to return the number of elements. Because `IntBlock` is not a strict extension of `IntArray`, this behavior appears only if `operator[]` is not virtual.

11.2.3 Not all classes are general

The third reason that it makes sense not to use virtual functions is that some classes are designed for specific, limited purposes.

We usually think of a class as having an *interface*, which consists of its public members, and an *implementation*, which comprises everything else. An interface, however, is a way of communicating with users, and classes can have two different kinds of users: the people who use objects of that class, and the people who derive other classes from it.

Every class will have users of the first kind, even if the only user is the author, but some classes may be deliberately intended not to have any users of the second kind. In other words, we might sometimes write a class with the explicit intention of *not* thinking about how other people might want to change its behavior through inheritance.

At this point, I can imagine people accusing me of advocating deliberately bad design. I can't help thinking, though, of a project I once heard of that required its developers to document every subroutine that they wrote, and to make the subroutines available to the rest of the project. The rationale was that, if a subroutine was useful to one developer, it would probably be useful to others as well. Why shouldn't the whole project benefit?

Of course, it's not hard to predict what happened: Developers soon started avoiding subroutines when they didn't absolutely need them. Instead the developers used their text editors to copy chunks of code, and to make whatever local changes they wanted. The result was a system that was harder to maintain, understand, and change.

Similarly, we sometimes write classes for limited purposes. For example, I remember one tiny class I wrote, as part of the ASD system described in Chapter 1, which calculated a checksum of data handed to it. It had a constructor, a member function to give it data, another to extract the checksum—and that was about it. Had I taken the time to consider how other people might generalize that class, it would have taken time away from the rest of the system. It's not clear that my providing this class would have made anyone else's life easier anyway; no one has ever asked me about that class.

11.3 Destructors are special

If you do intend to support inheritance from your class, even if you don't use other virtual functions, you may still need a virtual destructor.

Recall that the difference between a virtual and a nonvirtual function shows up in only one specific set of circumstances: when using a base class pointer or reference to point or refer to a derived class object. An illustrative case follows:

```
class Base {
public:
        void f();
        virtual void g();
};
class Derived: public Base {
public:
        void f();
        virtual void g();
};
```

We can now create objects of `Base` and `Derived` classes, and can obtain pointers to them:

```
Base b;
Derived d;

Base* bp = &b;
Base* bq = &d;
Derived* dp = &d;
```

Here, bp points at a `Base` object, and bq and dp point at `Derived` objects. What happens when we use these pointers to call the member functions f and g?

```
bp->f();   /* Base::f */        bp->g();   /* Base::g */
bq->f();   /* Base::f */        bq->g();   /* Derived::g */
dp->g();   /* Derived::g */     dp->f();   /* Derived::f */
```

You can see that the only time that the nonvirtual function f and the virtual function g behave differently from each other is when the static type of the pointer differs from the type of the actual object to which it points. It follows then that virtual destructors are needed when both of the following are true:

- Something happens that requires a destructor.
- It happens in a context where a pointer or reference has a static type referring to a base class and is actually pointing or referring to an object of a derived class.

Destructors are required only to destroy objects. The only way to destroy an object through a pointer is to use a `delete` expression.* Therefore, the only time that virtual destructors matter is when using a pointer to a base class to `delete` an object of a derived class. Thus, for example:

```
Base* bp;
Derived* dp;

bp = new Derived;
dp = new Derived;

delete bp;        // Base must have a virtual destructor
delete dp;        // virtual destructors are irrelevant here
```

---

* This assertion is not quite true: We can call a destructor explicitly. You shouldn't be doing that, however, unless you understand C++ memory management well enough not to need this chapter.

Here we are using `bp`, a base-class pointer, to delete a derived-class object. Thus, `Base` must have a virtual destructor for this example to work correctly.

Some implementations might get this example right anyway—but don't count on it. Notice that it may be necessary to use a virtual destructor even if your class doesn't have any virtual functions at all.

If you need a virtual destructor, it suffices to define an empty one:

```
class Base {
public:
        // ...
        virtual ~Base() { }
};
```

Moreover, if a class has a base class with a virtual destructor, the class itself automatically acquires a virtual destructor as well, so a single virtual destructor is sufficient to pervade an entire class hierarchy.

11.4 Summary

Virtual functions are a fundamental part of C++ and are essential to object-oriented programs. However, even though something may be useful, that does not excuse us from thinking about when it is right to use it.

We have seen three reasons why virtual functions are not always appropriate: They carry a cost that is sometimes significant, they do not always offer appropriate behavior, and we may sometimes want to write classes without thinking about how people might inherit from them.

On the other hand, we've also seen one case where a virtual function may be necessary. Virtual destructors are needed whenever you want to allow `delete` of a pointer to base that is actually pointing to a derived object.

More generally, it is essential for us to think about what we are doing when we write programs. Acting by rule and reflex is not enough.

Part III

Templates

We can look at templates in several ways. In a sense, templates are just a constrained form of syntactic macros. Since the days of macro assemblers, many languages have provided some kind of macro facility. So why are templates so important?

The answer, as is so often true in C++, is pragmatic. Yes, templates can be a bit messy. But, unlike ordinary macros, C++ templates are safe enough that we can program with them confidently without fear that some undetected error will turn our program into an undiagnosable mess. Moreover, they take enough burden off the programmer's shoulders to make them pleasant to use. Because templates are close to macros, though, the code that is generated can run as fast as it would by writing each instantiation by hand.

A more interesting way to look at templates is to see them as compile-time functions that take types as parameters and generate code. In a sense, templates make it possible to abstract away the type details involved in writing a program. The second half of this part, Chapters 16 through 21, explores this way of thinking about templates. The notion of generic (type-independent) programming pervades the Standard Template Library (STL), and those chapters introduce the ideas embodied in that library.

The first half of this part looks at a traditional use for templates: container classes. In Chapters 12 through 14, we'll explore the kind of containers that most libraries provide. Chapter 15 takes a different, lightweight approach to containers and presents an implementation of a list class heavily influenced by good old-fashioned Lisp.

Perhaps the wide range of abstractions presented in this part is the best evidence for the importance of templates.

12

Designing a container class

A container is a data structure that holds a collection of values. C has two kinds of containers built in: arrays and structures. C++ might have provided additional containers, but didn't. Instead, it offers ways for users to write their own. This means that the C++ language does not lock in any single approach to container design—although the standard library will encourage a particular approach.

Designing a successful container is not automatic: If there were only one right way to do it, why not build that right way into the language? This chapter will begin by examining questions about container design. We'll conclude by answering those questions in the context of a simple container, which behaves much like a (built-in) array but allows the size of the container to be established at the time that it is created. Chapters 13 and 14 will build on this simple class, and will look at ways that we can improve on built-in arrays.

12.1 What does it contain?

The first decision to make about a container is what to put into it. That might seem obvious: A container contains objects, right? But exactly what does it mean to contain an object?

To make this question more concrete, let's assume that c1 and c2 are containers, and that obj is an object. Assume further that our containers, whatever they are, have a member function insert to put an object into them. Also assume that obj has a member function mutate that will change its value somehow. Then we can say

```
c1.insert(obj);
```

after which obj is "in" container c1. If we now say

```
obj.mutate();
```

does that change the value of the object in c1 as well, or did we really insert only a *copy* of obj?

Similarly, if instead we had inserted `obj` into two containers:

```
c1.insert(obj);
c2.insert(obj);
```

would changing the object in one of the containers change the other?

Object deallocation raises a related question. For example,

```
void f()
{
        Container c;
        {
                Object obj;
                c.insert(obj);
        }
        //  is c still valid here?
}
```

Here we have created a container, inserted an object into it, and then deleted the object. If the object itself is in the container, rather than a copy of the object, then how does the container know that the object has gone away? One possibility is to say "it doesn't," and to require users of our container to ensure that their objects stay around at least as long as the container does. But if that's the behavior we want, why don't we clarify things by putting *pointers* to the objects, rather than the objects themselves, into the container?

This line of reasoning suggests that containers generally should contain copies of the objects placed in them, rather than the original objects themselves. A user who wants to preserve object identity—that is, a user who really wants the same object to be in multiple containers—can put pointers to the objects into the container. One advantage of this strategy is that users don't have to learn a new set of semantics; they presumably already know how to handle pointers. Indeed, copying values into a container, rather than remembering specific objects, is exactly the way built-in arrays work, so users don't have to learn new semantics to deal with that either.

12.2 What does copying the container mean?

The usual way to express a container is as a template, with the parameter being the type of the objects in the container. Thus, for an arbitrary type T, we can imagine containers like `List<T>` or `Set<T>`. For the moment, let's use `Container<T>` to refer to a container that contains objects of type T, when we don't really care what kind of container it is. If putting an object into a container copies the object, should copying a container also copy the objects in it? For example, after executing

```
Container<T> c1;
```

we need to decide what happens when we write

```
Container<T> c2(c1);
```

or

```
Container<T> c2;
c2 = c1;
```

More specifically, we need to decide whether changing an object in c2 will affect c1, or vice versa. For example, given

```
c1 = c2;
// add a new value to c2
c2.insert(some_new_obj);

// change some existing value in c2
c2.update(some_existing_obj, some_new_value);
```

what, if any, is the effect on c1?

If copying c2 into c1 caused c1 and c2 to refer to the same underlying object, then later changes to c2 will be reflected in c1. On the other hand, if we defined copying to mean putting the *value* of c2 into c1 then these changes to c2 will not be reflected in c1.

As usual, it may be useful to look at what C and C++ do about related built-in types. For our purposes, we'll want to see what copying means for the built-in aggregates: structures and arrays. Unusually, this time, looking at how C does things isn't much help.

If we look at how structures are copied or assigned, then we know that the answer is that the values are copied, so that

```
struct C {
        int i;
        double d;
} c1, c2;
/* ... */
c1 = c2;
```

means that the values stored in c2.i and c2.d are copied into the correspond-ing members of c1. If we now assign to c2.i:

```
c2.i = /* some new value */ ;
```

then c1.i remains unmodified.

For C arrays, the case is more complicated. At one level, it seems that the question has no meaning, because assignment of arrays isn't allowed, and we can't initialize one array from another:

```
int x[N];
int y[N] = x;        /* illegal */

int y[N];
y = x;                   /* illegal */
```

However, it appears to be possible to "copy" an array in one circumstance—namely, when calling a function:

```
void f(int[N]);
int x[N];

void g()
{
        f(x);
}
```

Here, we might expect that call-by-value semantics would cause a copy of x to be passed to f. In fact, what happens is that f is effectively recast to operate on an int*, and the call to f is transformed to pass to f the address of the initial element of x. It is as though we had instead written

```
void f(int*);
int x[N];

void g()
{
        f(&x[0]);
}
```

If f modifies an element of its argument, then the changes that f makes will be reflected in x.

Thus, built-in aggregates in both C and C++ implement two different approaches to what copying means:

- Structures implement value semantics: After a copy, both variables have independent copies of the value.
- Arrays implement reference semantics: After a copy, both variables refer to the same underlying object.

If looking at C doesn't answer the question, perhaps efficiency arguments can. Clearly, it is more efficient if copying a container simply causes the two containers to refer to the same underlying object than it is if copying a container copies the elements in the container. After all, most copies will happen in function invocation anyway, and a common mistake will be to write

```
void f(Container<T>)
```

when

```
void f(const Container<T>&)
```

would have been better. If copying a container means copying each of the elements of the container, then this mistake is potentially expensive. Why penalize the careless or novice user when we could help out by defining copy to have reference semantics?

But if we want to protect the unwary from inadvertently copying a large object, why not prohibit implicit copies of that object by making its copy constructor private? If the user really wants to pass a potentially modifiable reference to the container to a function, there are already two ways to do that:

```
void f(Container<T>&);
void f(Container<T>*);
```

Moreover, use counting and copy-on-write techniques can make it inexpensive to form what behaves like a copy of a container.

This last argument seems to indicate that we should define copying a container as copying the values stored in the container. Note that doing so usually involves allocating space to hold the values to be copied, and then copying the old values into the new space.

There is one exception to this general rule, which is if the type of the container itself implies something about whether copying should create a new value or result in a new reference to the same object. For example, a container intended to mimic a file might logically define copying as resulting in another reference to the same underlying file in the file system.

These arguments are not absolute—a certain amount of personal bias creeps in. Still, in future examples, we will adopt the strategy that copying a container copies its contents unless there is an overwhelming reason to do otherwise.

12.3 How do you get at container elements?

We have already argued that putting an object into a container should copy that object. What about taking an object out again? In other words, when we take objects out of a Container<T>, should we get something of type T or of type T&? There are arguments on both sides.

Objects are often fetched many times from containers, even when they are stored only once, so it may be more important to avoid the overhead of copying objects out of a container than to avoid the overhead of copying objects into the container. This is particularly true when the objects are themselves aggregates of some kind: One often fetches an object from a container to inspect only a small part of it. Moreover—and this argument can be decisive—if fetching an object yields a reference, that makes it much easier to modify the object while that object is still in the container. Indeed, if it is important to be able to modify objects in a container, then either the container must somehow provide object references or it must give its user some other way to change the objects that it contains.

On the other hand, the efficiency argument is not necessarily overwhelming. If the most common use of objects obtained from containers is to copy them somewhere else immediately, then a reasonably clever compiler can change two copies into one, and most of the efficiency problem evaporates. Moreover, allowing the user to obtain references to objects in a container opens the possibility that the user might take the address of one of these arguments and save it for later use—or misuse.

For example, consider an arraylike container c with the property that, for an integral value i, c[i] is a reference to one of the objects in the container. Assume that trying to refer to a nonexistent element of our container causes the container to grow automatically to accommodate the element, and that this growth potentially copies all the existing elements of the container so as to keep them in contiguous memory. Then, the innocuous statement

```
c[i] = c[j];
```

can fail horribly if the compiler evaluates c[j] to a reference, saves the resulting address, and then evaluates c[i]. If evaluating c[i] relocates element j in the container, the reference that the compiler saved may no longer refer to anything!

This example shows that containers that yield references must be careful about relocating the objects they contain. Indeed, it may be wise never to relocate such objects at all if it is possible to avoid doing so. In any event, it is crucial for the class author to document what the class does.

12.4 How do you distinguish reading from writing?

Given these difficulties with operator[], it may be worthwhile to use operator[] only for fetching, and to define some other way of storing elements. For example, it might make sense to fetch the element with index i from a container c by saying c[i], but to change the value of that element to, say, x by saying c.update(i,x). This dichotomy may look a little strange for simple classes, but it becomes more natural when there is more than one way of modifying a container.

For example, in *A Discipline of Programming* (Prentice-Hall, 1976), Edsger Dijkstra proposes an arraylike data structure in which elements can be appended or removed at either end. He also suggests operations for finding the number of elements, for renumbering the elements, for exchanging two elements, and so on. Interestingly, he also uses a syntax for updating an element that is different from the one that he uses for fetching an element. In a C++ container, each of Dijkstra's operations—with the possible exception of fetching an element—would best be implemented as a separate, member function that is not an operator.

One possibly surprising consequence of a separate update function is that containers of containers designed in this way are likely to be useless. Consider

```
template <class T> class Container {
        // ...
public:
        T operator[](Index) const;          // copy the element
        void update(Index, const T&);       // update in place
        // ...
};
```

where `Index` is an appropriate type to identify an element in this `Container`. Here, we have no way to utter the address of any element in the `Container`, so that we cannot get at any element directly. Instead, we use `update` to change the value stored at some `Index`, and we can read values through `operator[]`.

But what about this case:

```
Container< Container<int> > c;
Index i, j;
int k = c[i][j];             // fetch element j from Container[i]
// how do we update c[i][j]???
```

The problem is that the `update` function takes only one `Index`, so that although it can get us to the `i`th `Container`, it can't get us to element `j` of that `Container`. Thus, we might attempt to solve the problem by overloading `update`:

```
void update(Index, const T&);
void update(Index, Index, const T&);
```

But we haven't solved the problem, only postponed it. We can handle two-dimensional `Container`s, but not `Container`s of higher dimensions.

Another possibility is to use `operator[]` to fetch the `i`th `Container`, and then to use `update` on that element:

```
c[i].update(j, new_value);
```

Unfortunately, this doesn't work either: `c[i]` returns a `T`, not a `T&`. So, when we call `update` on `c[i]`, we're updating a temporary *copy* of the `i`th `Container`. Once we've done the change, that copy will be discarded.

It appears, then, that the best compromise is to allow `c[i]` to yield a reference, and to warn users to use such references only immediately after creating them.

12.5 How do you handle container growth?

Every container needs some way of putting elements into it. It is often useful to distinguish between adding a new element to a container and changing the value of an element already there. What, for example, should happen if we try to store an element that does not already exist? What about fetching such an element?

There is no single best answer to these questions. For example, if a container has setlike behavior, there is little difficulty in storing a brand-new element. On the other hand, if the container behaves more like an array, the new element probably has an associated index, which means that there may be intervening elements to deal with as well. Suppose, for example, that c is an (initially) empty, arraylike container of integers, and we say

```
c[0] = 1;
c[100000] = 3;
```

We have given values to c[0] and c[100000], but what about c[1] through c[99999]? If we allow new elements to be created discontiguously in such a container, we have to decide what value to give to the intervening elements, when our user has never explicitly done so.

Moreover, if we truly want our container to act like an array by using c[i] both for fetching and storing values, then a previously nonexistent c[i] must be set to some value, even if that value is going to be overwritten immediately. The reason is that the user might say

```
int* ip = &c[i];
```

and later might either assign a value to *ip or try to fetch the value that is presumably already there. At the time that we evaluate c[i], we don't know which alternative the user intends.

If we do not have separate operations for fetching and storing, we must evidently do the same thing when a user tries to fetch a nonexistent element as we do when trying to store it. But exactly what should happen depends on the application. One sensible approach is to provide a way to create new container elements explicitly and then to throw an exception whenever someone tries to access an element without creating it first. Another approach is simply to yield some canonical value, such as the value returned by the empty constructor. In other words, accessing a nonexistent element of a container with objects of class T in it might yield the value of T(). Choosing which of these approaches to take is one of those decisions where knowing about the intended application helps.

When designing a container that can grow gradually, it is important to think about how to allocate memory for the container's elements so as to avoid unacceptable overhead in common cases. For example, imagine an arraylike container with an operation to append a single element to the end of the array. A naive way to implement that operation is to copy the entire contents of the container into new memory just big enough to hold the old contents plus the new element. The problem with that, of course, is that the run time needed to build up a container is quadratic in the size of the container. A less naive allocation strategy is to increase the container's size in chunks, so that new memory must be allocated only once in a while. This can work well, but it does require care to choose an appropriate strategy for calculating new chunk sizes.

It is also important to think about when to give back memory to the system. A container that grows one element at a time is potentially inefficient, as is one that shrinks one element at a time. On the other hand, in some applications, it may be important not to hold onto memory any longer than necessary. Again, this is a case where the application dictates the implementation strategy.

12.6 What operations does the container provide?

As we do for any class, we have to decide what operations to support. As usual, it is important to understand how the container is intended to be used. For example, is it ever useful to allow a container of containers? If so, then it is important to implement for the containers themselves every operation that the container requires for objects stored therein. In other words, if the container copies objects into itself, it is important to allow entire containers to be copied. A similar argument applies to assignment and to the default constructor. If this seems too picky, remember that we can view every multidimensional array as a container of containers. Remember also that, unless a container has a default constructor, it is impossible to create a built-in array of containers.

Finally, there is the question of how to step "sequentially" through all the elements of a container. The quotation marks on "sequentially" are there because before it is even possible to ask this question, one must first impose a sequence on the elements!

There is a whole spectrum of techniques for dealing with this problem. The solutions are often called *iterators*, and there is enough to say about them that we will defer these issues to Chapter 14.

12.7 What do you assume about the container element type?

In Section 12.1 (page 133), we concluded that container elements ought to be copies, rather than the original objects. This decision implies that
- We can copy elements of type T.
- Copying elements does the right thing.

A little thinking should convince us that the more generally useful a container is intended to be, the fewer assumptions it should make about the types that it will store. Another way of looking at this is that the more operations T is assumed to provide, the fewer types there will be that provide all these operations.

Once we've decided to rely on a particular operation, we use the most common name for the operation. For example, if we assume that we can copy elements, we should also assume that the function that does the copy is spelled

`T::T(const T&)`, not `copy` or `clone` or something else. Not only is this the most likely "name" for the copy operation in user classes, but also it allows us to create containers of the built-in types directly. If we assumed that `copy` copied elements into the container, then we would have to provide a `copy` function for each of the built-in types that we wanted to store in the container. This argues that we'll use overloaded operators, rather than ordinary functions, whenever an operator captures the semantics we need. Also, whatever requirements there are on type `T`, it is important that they be documented along with the container, so that users can see whether the container can be used with some particular type.

At a minimum, containers seem to require operations to copy, assign and destroy objects of type `T`. After all, these operations are so fundamental that the system will provide them for any type that doesn't otherwise say what they mean. Relying on the existence of a default constructor is probably safe also. The built-in containers—both structures and arrays—usually rely on the default constructor. We are therefore not imposing any constraints beyond those already imposed for the built-in aggregates. But not all types provide a default constructor. Some types will be ineligible for use by a container that relies on the default constructor—just not many.

What other operations are sensible to assume? Many kinds of containers must rely on being able to distinguish whether two elements are equal. For example, a `Set` should include the ability to interrogate for set membership. Users should be able to ask, for any given value x of type `T`, whether x is in the `Set`. One way to answer this question is to ask whether the equality operator `operator==(const T&, const T&)` exists. Although we can get by with just the equality operator, performance is likely to be so poor that most such containers also impose other requirements as well. A common technique is to store set elements in some order, and to require a sensible definition for an inequality relation, such as `operator<(const T&, const T&)`.

At first glance, it may seem useful to include input and output operations for a container. It's tempting to provide

```
template <class T>
ostream& operator<<(ostream&, const Container<T>&);
```

But what if your users don't want to do I/O, or have their own I/O library? Some applications—especially those for embedded systems—may not even have an I/O library available and don't ever intend to do any I/O.

Even if users of the container want to be able to do I/O, the preceding declaration ties the container to a specific library. A more general solution might be to provide a mechanism to iterate through the container, and then to let the user write specific I/O routines using this mechanism. Chapter 30 discusses another approach. In that chapter, we explore a method to define an abstract interface, which results in a library-independent way to do I/O.

On the other hand, tying a container to the standard `iostream` library is not necessarily the wrong decision. The point is that such decisions should be conscious, not accidental.

Beyond these few operations, additional requirements on type `T` will reduce the generality of the container—even though those requirements on `T` may extend the usefulness of the container in some specific instances. As usual, there is no simple right answer. Instead, the ways in which the container is intended to be used should dictate what operations to assume about `T`.

12.8 Containers and inheritance

Arrays and inheritance don't mix. The problem is that C arrays assume that their elements are all the same size. C arrays know the type of the elements stored in them and use the size of objects of that type to get from one element to another within the array. Because types related by inheritance can have different sizes, arrays of the base-class type are not useful when used to store objects of some type derived from the base. Not surprisingly, we'll see that similar issues arise for other containers of objects related by inheritance.

Suppose that we have a base class `B` and a derived class `D`. What happens when we try to put a `D` object into a `Container<B>`? Logically, this should have the same effect as copying a `D` object into a `B`: The object gets cut down into a `B`—for example,

```
class Vehicle { /* ... */ };
class Airplane: public Vehicle { /* ... */ };
```

If we have a `Container<Vehicle>`, and we try to put an `Airplane` into it, we will get a copy of the `Vehicle` part of our `Airplane` and nothing else. As before, if we want to remember the entire `Airplane`, we can use a `Container<Vehicle*>` and store a pointer to the `Airplane`. Alternatively, to simplify memory management, it may be desirable to write an intermediate class such as a `VehicleSurrogate` as defined in Section 5.4 (page 50).

One might think that it would be nice for `Container<Airplane>` to be derived from `Container<Vehicle>`. Doing so, however, would open a hole in the type system:

```
Vehicle v;
Container<Airplane> ca;
```

We most definitely do not want to be able to put `v` into `ca`; `ca` is only for `Airplanes`. In particular, we should be able to go through all the elements of `ca` and do things to them that can be done to only `Airplanes`, such as making them fly. That's why we made `ca` a `Container<Airplane>`, and not a `Container<Vehicle>`.

But if `Container<Airplane>` were derived from `Container<Vehicle>`, we could do the following:

```
Container<Vehicle>& vp = ca;
vp.insert(v);              // oops!
```

We could then insert a (plain) `Vehicle` into a `Container<Airplane>` without further ado. Causing all the `Vehicles` in the container to fly would then produce quite a spectacle.

Indeed, if inheritance were to apply to containers at all, it would be necessary for `Container<Vehicle>` to be derived from `Container<Airplane>`, rather than the other way around. `Container<Vehicle>` also would have to be derived from every `Container<V>` for which `V` is derived from `Vehicle`.

This daunting prospect should be a convincing argument that containers of different types should not inherit from each other; `Container<Vehicle>` and `Container<Airplane>` should be completely different classes.

12.9 Designing an arraylike class

We've seen a number of questions we need to ask when designing a container class. In the remainder of this chapter, we'll explore these design issues in the context of creating an arraylike container class called `Array`. Given that we want to build something like a built-in array, a good place to start is to outline the properties of built-in arrays.

C arrays have a small set of operations. We can create them:

```
T x[N];
```

defines `x` as an array with `N` elements, each of type `T`. The only requirement on `T` is that it have a default constructor. As we'll see shortly, it's also useful for `T` to support assignment but that's not strictly required. Notice that arrays themselves meet these requirements for `T`. Hence, we can have arrays of arrays. Once an array is created, its size is fixed. We can neither grow nor shrink a built-in array.

To access elements, for both store and fetch, we use `[]` syntax.

```
T i = x[0];
```

assigns element 0 from the array into `i`. What this means depends on the definition of `T::operator=`.

Because the size of the array is fixed, subscripting off the end of the array

```
x[N + 100]
```

is undefined.

We can convert an array into a pointer:

```
T* p = x;
```

initializes p to point to the first element of x.

Built-in arrays can be neither assigned nor copied.*

And that's it.

This is a deceptively simple description. Before we design our Array class, it is important that we understand the relationship between arrays and pointers. To do so, let's consider how programmers use arrays. For example, suppose that we want to do something to each element of x. If we use a function f to represent that something, there are two typical ways to solve that problem in C. One is to use a subscript:

```
int i;
for (i = 0; i < N; i++)
        f(x[i]);
```

The other is to use a pointer:

```
T *p;
for (p = x; p < x + N; p++)
        f(*p);
```

The second form is often abbreviated along these lines:

```
T* p = &x;
while (p < x + N)
        f(*p++);
```

If we were to ask a typical C programmer (assuming such a person exists) the difference between pointers and subscripts, a likely answer would be that subscripts are easier to understand but pointers are more efficient. I suspect that few C programmers would mention two deeper differences between the examples:

1. In the subscript example, the value of the subscript is meaningful in itself, independently of its use as a subscript.
2. In the pointer example, it is not necessary to know the identity of the container to access the container's elements: The pointer itself contains all the necessary information.

Distinctions of this kind can be far more important than issues of efficiency, because they affect design. A program that has access to a pointer to an array element implicitly has access to the whole array, whereas a program that can access only a subscript needs to know separately which array to use. On the other hand, the notion of "the corresponding elements of several arrays" is much easier to implement using subscripts than it is using pointers. Moreover, deallocating an array invalidates all pointers to its elements without notice to the own-

---

* You can pass a built-in array to a function, but that array is not copied. Instead, the array is converted to a pointer to the first element of the array and that pointer is passed to the function. Built-in arrays also support { } initialization syntax, but, as there is no hope of emulating that in a container class, we won't try.

ers of those pointers, whereas the value of a subscript remains potentially meaningful by itself.

So what does that tell us about our container-design issues?

- Because the cells in the `Array` are allocated when the `Array` is created, the question of whether to store objects or copies in the `Array` is moot. There is no way to store the user's object in the `Array`. Instead, the `Array` "owns" the objects in it, and starts them off with the default value for type `T`. The value stored in an element can be modified subsequently; whether that is a copy of the user's object's value or a pointer or reference to that object depends on the definition of `T::operator=`.
- What to do about copy and assignment is easy: they're not allowed.
- We'll use `operator[]` to access to elements, both for storing and fetching values.
- Like copying, what to do about growing arrays is easy: they're of fixed size. Furthermore, subscripting past this fixed size is undefined; we can do what we like when that happens.
- We can think of arrays as having a "default constructor" in the sense that we can create arrays of arrays.
- There is a conversion from an array to a pointer to its initial element.

We now know enough to write our class definition:

```
template<class T> class Array {
public:
        Array(): data(0), sz(0) { }
        Array(unsigned size):
                sz(size), data(new T[size]) { }
        ~Array() { delete [] data; }

        const T& operator[](unsigned n) const
        {
                if (n >= sz || data == 0)
                        throw "Array subscript out of range";
                return data[n];
        }
        T& operator[](unsigned n)
        {
                if (n >= sz || data == 0)
                        throw "Array subscript out of range";
                return data[n];
        }

        operator const T*() const
        {
                return data;
        }
        operator T*()
        {
                return data;
        }
```

```
private:
        T* data;
        unsigned sz;
        Array(const Array& a);
        Array& operator=(const Array&);
};
```

This class definition should come as no surprise. The constructor allocates enough memory to hold the array, and the destructor deletes that memory. We have declared a copy constructor and assignment operator, but have made them private, so that users of `Array` will not be able to copy or assign them. We also assume that the element class T has a default constructor, so that new `T[size]` is meaningful. This is consistent with the restriction on T for built-in arrays.

Because subscripting off the end of a built-in array is an undefined operation, we'll check and throw an exception in the interest of robustness. Note that, in the subscript operators, we need only check for n >= sz; we can safely ignore n < 0, because n is `unsigned`.

We include a default constructor for `Array` to allow usage such as

```
Array< Array<int> > ai(10);
```

Thus, as we cannot do with built-in arrays, we can create an `Array` of size 0. This seems harmless enough, and we make sure the trouble is limited by checking all dereferences of `data`.

Finally, we provide conversion operators to T* and const T*.

We can use objects of this class similarly to built-in arrays:

```
Array<int> x(N);
int i;
for(i = 0; i < N; i++)
        x[i] = i;
```

will allocate an `Array<int>` of size N and will assign the values 0 through N-1 to its elements. The only real difference between this example and the earlier one is that we must say

```
Array<int> x(N);
```

instead of

```
int x[N];
```

In exchange for this minor inconvenience, we can defer fixing the size of the array until execution time.

Because we provided a conversion to T*, we can also manipulate `Array`s in terms of pointers. Given the preceding definition of x, executing

```
int* p = x;
int* q = x + N;
while (p != q)
        cout << *p++ << " ";
```

will print the elements of x.

However, our class has at least two significant pitfalls. One of them is also present with built-in arrays: It is possible to keep around the address of an element even after the Array that contains it has vanished, as in

```
void f()
{
        int* p;
        {
                Array<int> x(20);
                p = &x[10];
        }
        cout << *p;        // disaster!
}
```

Because Array<T>::operator[] returns a T&, there is nothing to stop the user from taking the address of the object that it returns. In the preceding example, the Array object x goes out of scope while p still points at one of its elements.

The other pitfall is more subtle: By allowing users access to the address of its elements, the Array class implicitly makes promises about its implementation. In other words, it tells its users enough about its inner workings to violate the notion of encapsulation. It is one thing to assume that x[5] represents the element that follows x[4]; that is implicit in the abstract definition of an array. It is quite another to assume that those elements are stored in contiguous memory.

These pitfalls become much more important if we try to extend our class, even in natural ways. Suppose, for instance, that we decide to allow the size of an Array to change after it has been constructed. We might do so by adding a member function called, say, resize(unsigned), which we would call with the new size of the Array.

How would such a function work? It would have to allocate memory for the new elements, copy their values from the old ones, and then delete the old memory. A clever implementation might sometimes be able to take advantage of overlap, but that is not assured.

That means that resizing an Array potentially invalidates every pointer to any of its elements. Thus, for example, after

```
Array<int> x(20);
int* p = &x[10];
x.resize(30);
```

there is no guarantee that p now points anywhere sensible.

Of course, we might argue that this is just an extension of the pitfall shared by built-in arrays. However, it is an extension in a direction that may not be obvious: The Array still exists, it hasn't lost any information, its subscripts are still valid, and yet the pointers to its elements are no longer valid! In effect, by maintaining the relationship between Arrays and pointers, we have forced ourselves to be aware of implementation details that would have been irrelevant otherwise.

So far, then, we have learned the following:

- Using pointers for built-in arrays can be more convenient than using subscripts, because using a subscript requires knowing which array to use as well.
- But allowing pointers into arraylike *classes* adds a pitfall: Changing the implementation or augmenting the operations of such classes may suddenly invalidate pointers to its elements.

Is there some way that we can gain the convenience of pointers without the pitfalls? It turns out that there is, but only by sacrificing other useful properties. This tradeoff will be the topic of Chapter 13.

13

Accessing container elements

In Chapter 12, we designed and implemented a class called `Array<T>`, which behaves like a built-in array, but allows the size of the `Array` to be established when the `Array` is created. We intended class `Array` to preserve as much array-like behavior as possible: In particular, it preserves the close relationship between an `Array<T>` and a pointer to T.

We discovered that maintaining this relationship between `Arrays` and pointers has its costs. As when using built-in arrays, it is easy for a user to retain a pointer into the `Array` even after the `Array` itself has vanished. In addition, the relationship between `Arrays` and pointers forces us to reveal the inner workings of the class. Because a user can obtain a pointer into the `Array`, changing the underlying memory that an `Array` occupies will almost certainly lead to user errors. This makes obvious extensions, such as providing a `resize` operation, problematical.

In this chapter, we'll see how close we can come to retaining the expressiveness of pointers, while avoiding these drawbacks.

13.1 Imitating a pointer

The fundamental rule of C++ design is: *Use classes to represent concepts.* A pointer incorporates the identity of an array, along with a place in it. If we wish to imitate arrays, we should therefore begin by defining a class that will identify an `Array` and a place in it. Such a class might contain a subscript and a pointer to the corresponding `Array`. Because an object of that class behaves like a pointer, we will call the class `Pointer`:

```
template<class T> class Pointer {
private:
        Array<T>* ap;
        unsigned sub;
        // ...
};
```

This way of designing a class is somewhat unusual. Usually, one begins by asking what operations or characteristics are useful: Only then does one think about implementation. In this case, we start by knowing what information objects of our class will contain, and then think about what operations people might want to perform on that information. Thus, we know that a `Pointer` will encapsulate a (pointer to an) `Array` and a place within that `Array`; now we have to decide what operations to allow on `Pointer` objects.

A good place to start is to look at constructors, destructors, copying, and assignment. There appears to be only one sensible meaning to ascribe to the last two: After copying a `Pointer`, the original and the copy should point to the same place. Because we are trying to make our class behave like built-in pointers, there seems to be no reason to cause anything special to happen when a `Pointer` is destroyed. Thus, the default definitions of the destructor, copy constructor, and assignment operator do the right things, and no explicit effort is needed to override them.

What about constructors? We'll want to be able to construct a `Pointer` from an `Array` and a subscript. Should constructors require both arguments? If not, should we be allowed to omit just the subscript, or both arguments?

It is tempting to require both arguments, thereby banishing unbound `Pointers` entirely. That, however, would prohibit arrays (and `Arrays`) of `Pointers`. Instead, we'll say that constructing a `Pointer` without an associated `Array` will yield a `Pointer` that doesn't point anywhere, and that leaving out the subscript will give a default of zero. That gives us the following definition so far:

```
template<class T> class Pointer {
public:
        Pointer(Array<T>& a, unsigned n = 0):
              ap(&a), sub(n) { }
        Pointer(): ap(0), sub(0) { }
        // ...

private:
        Array<T>* ap;
        unsigned sub;
};
```

We used a default value for n to make it possible to define two constructors instead of three, but we did not give a default value for a because there is no value that we could use as the default: A reference must always be bound to some object.

We now know how to create, destroy, and copy `Pointer` objects. We must next decide how to access the `Array` element to which a `Pointer` points, and it is here that things become interesting.

13.2 Getting at the data

At first glance, one might think that the obvious way to access an `Array` element
is simply to define `operator*() const` along the following lines:

```
template<class T> class Pointer {
public:
        T& operator*() const {
                if (ap == 0)
                        throw "* of unbound Pointer";
                return (*ap)[sub];
        }
        // ...
};
```

But this gets us back into the same problems that we wished to avoid by defining
the `Pointer` class in the first place! The trouble is that this definition of `opera-`
`tor*` yields a reference to an element of the data structure that underlies the corresponding `Array`, which means that the implementation details are again visible to the user.

   Of course, if we change the definition of `operator*()` a bit, the problem
vanishes:

```
template<class T> class Pointer {
public:
        // T, not T&
        T operator*() const {
                if (ap == 0)
                        throw "* of unbound Pointer";
                return (*ap)[sub];
        }
};
```

Unfortunately, this rewrite creates a new problem. What we did here was to say
that `operator*` returns a `T`, rather than a `T&`. But now we can't assign to it! In
other words, if p is a `Pointer<T>`, this change would allow

```
t = *p;
```

but would prohibit

```
*p = t;
```

The point is that it is difficult to allow

```
*p = t;
```

without also allowing

```
T* tp = &*p;
```

It is this latter usage that we want to prohibit.

But we cannot simply bar the use of a `Pointer` to update an element of its corresponding `Array`. How, then, might we achieve an equivalent effect?

The simplest possibility is to introduce a new operation into our `Pointer` class, called `update`. Instead of saying

```
*p = t;
```

we will say

```
p.update(t);
```

It is easy to define such an operation; with it, our `Pointer` class now looks like this:

```
template<class T> class Pointer {
public:
        Pointer(Array<T>& a, unsigned n = 0):
                ap(&a), sub(n) { }
        Pointer(): ap(0), sub(0) { }

        T operator*() const {
                if (ap == 0)
                        throw "* of unbound Pointer";
                return (*ap)[sub];
        }

        void update(const T& t) {
                if (ap == 0)
                        throw "update of unbound Pointer";
                (*ap)[sub] = t;
        }
        // ...

private:
        Array<T>* ap;
        unsigned sub;
};
```

Of course, there is little point in using an `update` function in class `Pointer` if class `Array` still lets the user obtain the address of an element. Thus, we'll want to use an `update` function or something like it for `Array`s as well. So we'll need to change our `Array` class:

```
template<class T> class Array {
public:
        T operator[](unsigned n) const {
                if (n >= sz)
                        throw "Array subscript out of range";
                return data[n];
        }
```

```
void update(unsigned n, const T& t) {
        if (n >= sz)
                throw "Array subscript out of range";
        data[n] = t;
}
// ...
};
```

Unfortunately, this approach introduces problems of its own. Recall that, in Section 12.4 (page 138), we discussed using an update function to modify values stored in a container. In that discussion, we saw that using update rather than operator[] effectively precluded Arrays of Arrays.

Thus, we face one of those nasty convenience-versus-safety decisions. By using update, we make it possible to hide our implementation and to protect users from errors resulting from dangling pointers. But we do so at the cost of prohibiting the useful ability to form types such as Array< Array<int> >.

Which approach we choose will hinge on how we believe our class will be used. Because arrays of arrays are such a useful data structure, it's likely that our users will similarly want to make Arrays of Arrays. Furthermore, when we're done, our Pointer class will provide careful users with the ability to ban pointers (as opposed to Pointers) from their programs. Given this, we will go with convenience over safety, and will abandon our attempt to provide different functions to read and write elements:

```
template<class T> class Pointer {
public:
        Pointer(Array<T>& a, unsigned n = 0):
                ap(&a), sub(n) { }
        Pointer(): ap(0), sub(0) { }

        T& operator*() const {
                if (ap == 0)
                        throw "* of unbound Pointer";
                return (*ap)[sub];
        }
private:
        Array<T>* ap;
        unsigned sub;
};
```

13.3 Remaining problems

So far, we've managed only to add a level of indirection for things to go awry. Now, when an Array goes away, there may still be a Pointer, rather than pointer, to one of its elements. Using that Pointer will cause chaos, just as using a pointer would have. We need to look more deeply at this problem to see whether it is possible to find a more general solution. The following program fragment illustrates the problem:

```
Array<int>* ap = new Array<int> (10);
Pointer<int> p(*ap, 5);
delete ap;
*p = 42;
```

Here, we dynamically allocate an Array<int>, create a Pointer<int> called p that points at one of the elements in the Array, delete the Array, and then try to assign a value to the element. Is it possible to do anything about this misbehavior? Is it even desirable?

We have stated a simple problem. Might there be a similarly simple solution? What if we just make sure that an Array object never goes away as long as there exists a Pointer object that refers to it?

Of course, that is not quite trivial. Consider, for example, our problematic case. There, we explicitly allocated an Array, and then explicitly deleted it. How can we arrange things such that deleting an Array doesn't really make that Array go away?

The way to solve problems of this kind is to apply what I sometimes call the *fundamental theorem of software engineering,* even though it isn't really a theorem: *We can solve any problem by introducing an extra level of indirection.* We apply the "theorem" to this example by noting that, if we want to keep the data around after the Array object is deleted, we can do so by making the Array point to the data rather than contain it.

That means that instead of two classes we will have three: Array, Pointer, and one more that we will call Array_data. The Array and Pointer classes will look the same to their users as they do now, but each Array object will point to an Array_data object.

What about Pointers? Because it is still possible to delete an Array—indeed, that is the whole point of the exercise—evidently each Pointer object will now point to an Array_data object, rather than to an Array.

The main problem that remains is figuring out when to delete the Array_data objects. It looks like we'll want to delete one as soon as there are no Array or Pointer objects referring to it. The easiest way to do that is to keep track of the number of such objects, so each Array_data object will contain a use count. This count will start out at 1 when the Array_data object is created (because each Array_data object will be created only as part of constructing an Array), will be incremented each time an Array or Pointer is created that refers to the particular Array_data, and will be decremented each time that an Array or Pointer to it is destroyed. If decrementing the use count causes it to reach 0, that is the time to destroy the Array_data object itself.

13.3.1   *Filling in the details*

We now know enough to write class `Array_data`. It will contain the actual data, the number of elements in the `Array` and a use count. We'll need `operator[]` to get at the data, a constructor to allocate space and set the use count, and a destructor to free the space. We want there to be only one instance of an `Array_data` object for any memory, so we'll prevent copying and assigning of `Array_data` objects by declaring, but not implementing, the copy constructor and assignment operator. Because this class is not intended for direct user consumption, all its members are private. Looking ahead, we will nominate `Array` and `Pointer` as friends:

```
template<class T> class Array_data {
        friend class Array<T>;
        friend class Pointer<T>;

        Array_data(unsigned size = 0):
                sz(size), data(new T[size]), use(1) { }
        ~Array_data() { delete [] data; }

        const T& operator[](unsigned n) const {
                if (n >= sz)
                        throw "Array subscript out of range";
                return data[n];
        }

        T& operator[](unsigned n) {
                if (n >= sz)
                        throw "Array subscript out of range";
                return data[n];
        }

        // unimplemented, no copies allowed
        Array_data(const Array_data&);
        Array_data& operator=(const Array_data&);

        T* data;
        unsigned sz;
        int use;
};
```

Now we must write class `Array`. Essentially, instead of a `T*`, it will have an `Array_data<T>*`, and it will simply forward most operations to the corresponding `Array_data` object:

```
template<class T> class Array {
        friend class Pointer<T>;

public:
        Array(unsigned size):
                data(new Array_data<T>(size)) { }
```

```
~Array() {
        if (--data->use == 0)
                delete data;
}

const T& operator[](unsigned n) const {
        return (*data)[n];
}

T& operator[](unsigned n) {
        return (*data)[n];
}
private:
        Array(const Array&);
        Array& operator=(const Array&);
        Array_data<T>* data;
};
```

Now we come to the heart of the matter: We also define class `Pointer` to refer to an `Array_data` object, rather than to an `Array` object, and we make sure to handle the use counts properly:

```
template<class T> class Pointer {
public:
        Pointer(Array<T>& a, unsigned n = 0):
                ap(a.data), sub(n) { ++ap->use; }

        Pointer(): ap(0), sub(0) { }

        Pointer(const Pointer<T>& p): ap(p.ap), sub(p.sub) {
                if (ap)
                        ++ap->use;
        }

        ~Pointer() {
                if (ap && --ap->use == 0)
                        delete ap;
        }

        Pointer& operator=(const Pointer<T>& p) {
                if (p.ap)
                        ++p.ap->use;
                if (ap && --ap->use == 0)
                        delete ap;
                ap = p.ap;
                sub = p.sub;
                return *this;
        }

        T& operator*() const {
                if (ap == 0)
                        throw "* of an unbound Pointer";
                return (*ap)[sub];
        }
```

```
private:
        Array_data<T>* ap;
        unsigned sub;
};
```

As before, we have allowed for the possibility of a `Pointer` that doesn't point anywhere, as long as no one tries to use it.

Here, we have to provide explicit versions of the copy constructor, assignment operator, and destructor to manage the use counts. Note that copying a `Pointer` does not involve copying the elements of the associated `Array_data`. This is only proper: A class called `Pointer` should act like a pointer!

As usual, it is important to make sure that nothing goes wrong when assigning a `Pointer` to itself. Trace through the code to convince yourself that it handles self assignment properly.

With this definition of `Array` and `Pointer`, our problem example finally works:

```
Array<int>* ap = new Array<int> (10);
Pointer<int> p(*ap, 5);
delete ap;
*p = 42;
```

When we delete `ap`, the use count of the associated `Array_data` object is still nonzero, because the `Pointer` object `p` is still around. Therefore, the dereference of `p` is still valid.

13.4 **Pointer** to **const Array**

Unfortunately, there's still one remaining snag: We can't make a `Pointer` to an element of a `const Array`. One might argue that `const Array`s aren't terribly useful, so it might be tempting to ignore them and live with this restriction. After all, declaring an `Array` as `const` means that we cannot give its elements any values other than those they had when the `Array` was first initialized.

However, even though there may be few actual variables of type `const Array`, our users will surely want to pass `Array`s by reference to functions. Those functions will often operate on `const Array&` parameters, both so that the function can't change them and, more important, so that expressions and other nonconst values can be passed to them. So it looks like we need to allow for `const Array` objects.

This implies that we'll need another class that looks a lot like `Pointer`, but that can be bound to a `const Array` and that will return a `const T&` from `operator[]`. In addition, to mimic behavior of built-in pointers, we'll want to allow a conversion from `Pointer` to this new class, but not vice versa. We could define a new, independent class and provide a conversion operator to that class in class `Pointer`. However, it is simpler and more convenient to use inheritance to capture the similarities between these two types.

Because we want to allow for conversion from `Pointer`, but not from our new class, we'll make the new class the base:

```
template<class T> class Ptr_to_const {
public:
        // const Array&, not Array&
        Ptr_to_const(const Array<T>& a, unsigned n = 0):
                ap(a.data),
                sub(n) { ++ap->use; }

        Ptr_to_const(): ap(0), sub(0) { }
        Ptr_to_const(const Ptr_to_const<T>& p):
                ap(p.ap), sub(p.sub)
        {
                if (ap)
                        ++ap->use;
        }

        ~Ptr_to_const() {
                if (ap && --ap->use == 0)
                        delete ap;
        }

        Ptr_to_const& operator=(const Ptr_to_const<T>& p) {
                if (p.ap)
                        ++p.ap->use;
                if (ap && --ap->use == 0)
                        delete ap;

                ap = p.ap;
                sub = p.sub;
                return *this;
        }

        // return const T&, not T&
        const T& operator*() const {
                if (ap == 0)
                        throw "* of unbound Ptr_to_const";
                return (*ap)[sub];
        }

private:
        Array_data<T>* ap;
        unsigned sub;
};
```

This class looks remarkably like our previous version of class `Pointer`. The comments mark the only differences. Perhaps the most interesting change is one that isn't there: member `ap` still points to a `Array_data<T>`, rather than to a `const Array_data<T>`. Because we want class `Pointer` to inherit from `Ptr_to_const`, it will simplify things if we store the pointer to the underlying

Array_data as though that object were not const. Our operations in
Ptr_to_const won't let users get at these data, and making ap nonconst
saves doing the casts in the Pointer operations.

Class Pointer has to redefine (only) those operations where the constness
of the Array matters:

```
template<class T> class Pointer: public Ptr_to_const<T> {
public:
        Pointer(Array<T>& a, unsigned n = 0):
                Ptr_to_const<T>(a,n) { }
        Pointer() { }

        T& operator*() const {
                if (ap == 0)
                        throw "* of unbound Ptr_to_const";
                return (*ap)[sub];
        }
};
```

13.5 Useful additions

At this point, our Array class is almost as useful as a built-in array, and even has
some nice improvements. We can defer setting the size of an Array until the
object is created, and subscripting off the end of an Array will throw an exception. This will ensure that unchecked errors immediately terminate the program,
rather than leading to the mystifying behavior that is characteristic of trying to
read off the end of an array.

In addition to providing this extra degree of safety, we also wanted to use
class Pointer to let users change the size of an Array. Let's see how that might
be defined.

First, recall from Section 12.5 (page 139) that we need to think about our strategy for resizing the Array. We'd like to avoid growing or shrinking the Array
one element at a time.

Users will be likely to grow or shrink the Array in two ways: Either they'll
know the new size to which they want to change or they won't. In the former
case, the user has a way of determining how many more or fewer elements are
needed. In this case, we can let the user tell us how big to make the Array.

In the latter case, however, the user doesn't know the size that's needed.
Imagine reading new input from a keyboard and storing the results in the
Array. We'd like to avoid adding one element at a time in this case. One way
to handle this would be to provide a function that ensures that the Array is as
big as some value. This function could grow the Array in large chunks rather
than an element at a time, which would reduce the frequency with which memory is acquired.

But what about shrinking the `Array` one element at a time? It's hard to see how a chunk-at-a-time strategy can work for reducing the size of the `Array`. Fortunately, we can leave this to the user to manage. When growing the `Array`, the user needs a place to store elements. When shrinking it, the user just has to avoid looking at elements that have been removed. Once the final size is known, the user can call the resize operation.

This analysis implies that we want to add two new functions to class `Array`.

The `resize` function will allocate space of the requested size, and will copy the existing elements into this new space. As usual, the function on `Array`s forwards the request to the `Array_data`:

```
template <class T> class Array {
public:
        void resize(unsigned n) {
                data->resize(n);
        }
        // ...
};
```

And class `Array_data` does the real work. We have to remember to save the old elements before allocating new space for `data`, and to `delete` them after we've copied them. We also must take care to copy only as many elements as are in the new array if we're shrinking the `Array`, or only as many as were in the old array if we're growing it:

```
template <class T>
void Array_data<T>::resize(unsigned n)
{
        if (n == sz) return;

        T* odata = data;
        data = new T[n];
        copy(odata, sz > n ? n: sz);
        delete [] odata;
        sz = n;
}
```

Here, we assumed the existence of a utility function `copy`:

```
template <class T>
void Array_data<T>::copy(T* arr, unsigned n)
{
        for (int i = 0; i < n; i++)
                data[i] = arr[i];
}
```

Given a pointer to an array (small a) of type `T`, `copy` copies n elements from the array into `data`.

The other operation will be used when the user doesn't know how much to grow the `Array`. Because its intended purpose is to "reserve" space for some new element, we'll call this function `reserve`.

Before writing this operation, it will be useful to think a bit about how the user is likely to call it. Recall that reserve is intended to be used when the user needs to add elements one at a time to the Array. We'll require that the user call this function to ensure that the Array is big enough to hold that element. So we'll have something like

```
Array<some_type> a;
//...
while (/* some condition */) {
        a.reserve(n+1);
        a[n] = // some value
}
```

Note that, to ensure that there's room for element a[n], we need to make sure the Array is at least as big as n+1. A little reflection should convince us that this is a rich source of user error. It's much more likely that the user will in fact write

```
a.reserve(n);
a[n] = // some value
```

This suggests that we should have reserve(n) ensure that the Array is strictly bigger than n:

```
template <class T> class Array {
public:
        void reserve(unsigned new_sz) {
                if (new_sz >= data->sz)
                        data->grow(new_sz);
        }
        // ...
};
```

If we need to grow the underlying array, we'll use a strategy that keeps doubling the space allocated until it's strictly bigger than the size that was requested:

```
template <class T>
void Array_data<T>::grow(unsigned new_sz)
{
        unsigned nsz = sz;
        if (nsz == 0)
                nsz = 1;
        while (nsz <= new_sz)
                nsz *= 2;
        resize(nsz);
}
```

Conveniently, once we know the new size, we can call resize to do the work.

It may not be obvious, but being able to resize an Array effectively requires us to be able to assign and copy it as well. To see this, note that resizing an Array requires us to be able to copy its elements. And, when we have an Array of Arrays, those elements are Arrays.

This means that it's time to implement copy and assignment for `Array`s. As suggested in Section 12.2 (page 134), we'll arrange for copying an `Array` to copy its elements. Both the copy constructor and assignment operator will need to allocate space and then do the copy. The copy constructor does just that:

```
template <class T> class Array {
public:
        Array(const Array& a):
                data(new Array_data<T>(a.data->sz))
        {
                data->copy(a.data->data, a.data->sz);
        }
        Array& operator=(const Array&); // ???
        // ...
};
```

It's tempting to define `operator=` to call `Array_data::operator=`. The only problem is that we do not want to allow `Array_data` objects to be assigned! If we did allow assignment, we wouldn't be able to manage the use counts correctly. Instead, we'll define a `clone` operation in `Array_data` that will reallocate the underlying `data` array and do the copy. As usual, it's important to check for self assignment:

```
template <class T> class Array {
public:
        Array& operator=(const Array& a) {
                if (this != &a)
                        data->clone(*a.data, a.data->sz);
                return *this;
        }
        // ...
};

template <class T>
void Array_data<T>::clone(const Array_data& a, unsigned n)
{
        delete [] data;
        data = new T[sz = a.sz];
        copy(a.data, sz);
}
```

With this, our `Array` class is more useful: Not only can we defer until run time saying how big the `Array` should be, but also we can change the size of an `Array` after the `Array` has been created. Safety is improved, because subscript bounds are checked.

There's but one remaining problem: We haven't completely eliminated the need for pointers. Users who are willing to restrict themselves to subscript notation can navigate through the `Array` confident that out-of-bounds subscript errors will be caught. But they can't use `Pointer`s to move through the `Array`.

If they want to do pointerlike operations on the `Array`, they have to use built-in pointers, not `Pointer`s, with all the potential for dangling pointers.

We'd like to let users ban the use of pointers into `Array`s altogether. To do so, we'll have to support all the operations on built-in pointers. The issue of pointer arithmetic is a special case of a more general container-class issue commonly called iterators; we'll deal with this question in Chapter 14.

14

Iterators

In Chapters 12 and 13, we designed and implemented a set of classes `Array<T>`, `Pointer<T>`, and `Ptr_to_const<T>`, which let the following program fragment work:

```
Array<int>* ap = new Array<int> (10);
Pointer<int> p(*ap, 5);
delete ap;
*p = 42;
```

Here, dereferencing p after ap has been deleted will succeed, because the Array class has not deleted the underlying storage associated with ap.

Given this safety, we'd like users to use only `Pointer`s to access the Array. But to entice users to give up pointers, we must ensure that `Pointer`s support all the operations that pointers do. In particular we need to support arithmetic and comparisons on `Pointer`s to enable users to navigate through the Array. First, we'll look at the issue of iteration by implementing the rest of the pointer operations for `Pointer`s. Then we'll make some observations about iterators in general.

14.1 Completing the `Pointer` class

Because our objective is to ban pointers, we should start by looking at how pointers can be used, so that we will know what operations we must supply. We'd like to allow programs that are analogous to

```
void f()
{
        int a[10];
        int* pa = a;
        int* end = pa + 10;
        while (pa != end)
                *pa++ = 0;
}
```

Here, we define a pointer, pa, to the beginning, and another pointer, end, to the end of the array. We then use operator++ to move the pointer pa one element at a time through the array, and use operator* to dereference pa when it points to each element and set the element's value to 0. We know we're done when operator!= says that pa has reached end.

From this example, it appears that we'll need to provide the addition, subtraction, and relational operators for Pointers and Ptr_to_consts. We'll need to define these operators in both the base and derived classes (that is, in both Ptr_to_const and Pointer), because the return types will differ. Operations in the Pointer class will return Pointers, and those in Ptr_to_const will return Ptr_to_consts. For brevity, we'll show only the derived class here:

```
template <class T> class Pointer: public Ptr_to_const<T> {
public:
        // prefix operators
        Pointer& operator++() {
                ++sub;
                return *this;
        }

        Pointer& operator--() {
                --sub;
                return *this;
        }

        // postfix operators
        Pointer operator++(int) {
                Pointer ret = *this;
                ++sub;
                return ret;
        }

        Pointer operator--(int) {
                Pointer ret = *this;
                --sub;
                return ret;
        }

        Pointer& operator+=(int n) {
                sub += n;
                return *this;
        }

        Pointer& operator-=(int n) {
                sub -= n;
                return *this;
        }

        // ...
};
```

Each of these operators works by modifying the value sub appropriately. We'll define the compound assignment and the prefix ++ and -- operators to return a reference, so that operations such as *p++ will work properly.

So that they will behave like the built-in C and C++ operators, we'll define the postfix operations to return an rvalue, rather than an lvalue. Because the postfix operations return their operands' original values, we'll need to remember the old state of the Pointer before adjusting sub.

As usual, we'll define the other arithmetic operations as nonmember functions. We'll need to take a bit of trouble to mirror properly the semantics of built-in pointers. Subtracting two pointers yields a (signed) int value. Because we can freely convert a Pointer to a Ptr_to_const, we can define a single version of these operations:

```
template <class T> int operator-
    (const Ptr_to_const<T>& op1, const Ptr_to_const<T>& op2)
{
        return (int)op1.sub - (int)op2.sub;
}
```

We'll also need to go back to class Ptr_to_const and add friend declarations for the operator- functions.

Adding (subtracting) an integer to (from) a pointer yields a new pointer. As with the increment and compound assignment operators, we'll have to define addition (subtraction) of Pointers or Ptr_to_consts separately to ensure the correct return type. As before, we'll show the version for Pointers. Here, we define only addition. Subtraction is similar; we leave it as an exercise:

```
template <class T> Pointer<T> operator+
    (const Pointer<T>& p, int n)
{
        Pointer<T> ret = p;
        return ret += n;
}

template <class T> Pointer<T> operator+
    (int n, const Pointer<T>& p)
{
        Pointer<T> ret = p;
        return ret += n;
}
```

That takes care of arithmetic, but we also need the comparison operators. For completeness, we'll need to implement all six of them. Because all these operators can be expressed in terms of equality and the less-than operator, we'll define only those here. We can convert between Pointers and Ptr_to_consts, so we can define these operations in the base class.

Before writing these functions, we need to think a bit. A Pointer encapsulates the notion of a pointer into a particular Array. Therefore, what will the

comparison operators do when invoked on Pointers to *different* underlying
Arrays? For == and !=, the answer is straightforward: Two Pointers are
equal if and only if they point to the same element of the same Array (or both
point to no Array at all). But the answer is less clear for the other comparison
operators, because there is no way to define it that does not depend on an accident of implementation. We will therefore throw an exception when comparison
operators other than == and != are asked to compare Pointers to elements of
different Arrays:

```
template <class T> int operator==
    (const Ptr_to_const<T>& op1, const Ptr_to_const<T>& op2)
{
        if (op1.ap != op2.ap)
                return 0;
        return (op1.sub == op2.sub);
}

template <class T> int operator<
    (const Ptr_to_const<T>& op1, const Ptr_to_const<T>& op2)
{
        if (op1.ap != op2.ap)
                throw "< on different Arrays";
        return op1.sub < op2.sub;
}
```

These operators will also need to be friends to class Ptr_to_const.

Finally, we may wish to allow users to add (subtract) an integer to (from) an
Array to yield a Pointer. The conversion from Array to Pointer that
already exists isn't good enough to make this work. The reason is that in an
expression like a+1, where a is an Array, the compiler doesn't know whether to
convert a to Pointer or to Pointer_to_const. Solving this problem
involves defining operator+ on all the relevant combinations of Array&,
const Array&, and int.

We might also decide to offer a way of testing whether a Pointer points at
an element of an Array or not, analogously to comparing a built-in pointer to
zero.

We will leave both these extensions as exercises.

14.2 What is an iterator?

The class Pointer that we have just seen is a member of a family of classes
known as *iterators*.

In general, each container class will have one or more associated iterator
types. Iterators let us access container elements without exposing the internal
structure of the container.

Note that iterating through a container is rarely so simple as it was to iterate through `Arrays`. For `Arrays`, there is a straightforward way to get from one element to the next: Add `1` to the index. For more complicated containers, however, there may be no index (a `List` or `Set` class), or the index may not support addition (an associative array where the index can be any ordered type, such as a `String`).

We can think of iterators as a family of types, because they all hold the same kind of data and offer the same kind of operations. An iterator will mark a place in a container, and provide operations to walk through the container. The set of operations may be as simple as allowing the user to get from one element to the next element. Or, the iterator could be as fully functional as our `Pointer` class, which offered a number of ways to navigate through the `Array`, as well as supporting the relational operators. Not surprisingly there are several questions to ask when designing an iterator. These will be the topic of the rest of this chapter.

14.3 Deleting an element

We said that an iterator will mark a place in a container. For example, in class `Pointer`, we stored a pointer to some `Array_data` object, along with a subscript that indicated which element in the underlying array this `Pointer` addressed. Because our `Array` class did not support deleting a single element, we did not have to worry about what to do if the element marked by a `Pointer` went away. In general, when we are designing an iterator, we have to decide what to do if elements can go away.

For example, assume that we have a container and its associated iterator class:

```
Container<T> c;
Iterator<T> it(c);
```

We now insert an element into `c`, and position the iterator to refer to that element:

```
c.insert(some_obj);
// position it to refer to some_obj
```

Suppose that we next remove that element from the container:

```
c.remove(some_obj);
```

What will happen when we now try to use the iterator? For example, what if we use the iterator to advance to the next element

```
it++;
```

If our container is implemented as a listlike structure, where `operator++` follows a pointer from the current element to the next one, chaos will surely result.

There are several ways that we might deal with this issue. As usual, knowing how the class will be used is the best basis for deciding which way to go.

We could simply prohibit deleting elements from the container. If we expect our users to build up the container, but not to need to eliminate individual elements, then this will work. For example, our container might represent a dictionary to which words can be added, but from which they are never removed. As long as we can discard entire containers, removing individual elements is not as essential as it seems at first.

If we think that users will need to remove elements from the container, then we have to find some way to let them do so. One way we might do this is to keep, in each container object, a list of active iterators. Then, when we remove an element, we can use the list to find and move any iterator that happens to point to the element being removed.* We might also put use counts along with each element in the container, and defer deleting any element until the final reference to it (either from an iterator or from the container) goes away. We might even solve this problem more easily by associating each iterator with a copy of the container. When we allocate an iterator we'd make a copy of the container and use the iterator on that copy. At first glance, this might seem to waste space, but there are schemes that can ensure that we make the copy only when we're going to change the container. More important, however, this scheme will surprise users who expect the iterator to address the real—possibly changing—container.

Another approach is to have iterators act like they point between elements in the container. This finesses the problem of what to do when the user deletes an element—at least from the user's viewpoint. It isn't any easier to implement, though: It's equivalent to moving every iterator that happens to point to an element that is deleted. Moreover, it doesn't end up helping the user. The problem with this approach is that it has a surprisingly pervasive effect on code that uses the iterator. Looking at the element indicated by the iterator requires the user to think about whether the *next* or *previous* element is the right one to retrieve. This becomes especially tricky when the iterator is positioned at the beginning or end of the container.

14.4 Deleting the container

A question closely related to what to do about deleting a single element is what to do when the container itself goes away while there are active iterators. For Arrays, we arranged to defer deleting the Array until the final iterator (that is, the final Pointer) went away as well.

---

* Of course, that assumes that we know where to move the iterator. What if we just deleted the only element?

Alternatively, we might use many of the ideas just discussed for dealing with deleting single elements. For example, we could keep a list of active iterators in the container. Then, the destructor for the container could use that list to set the iterators into an "invalid" state as part of deleting the container itself. The approach of associating a copy of the container with each iterator would also protect against the container being deleted while the iterator was live. Each of these approaches to deleting an entire container has the same drawbacks and advantages as does the corresponding approach to deleting a single element, although the single-element case is often harder to implement efficiently.

Another alternative is to make it the user's problem to ensure that iterators are not used once the associated container is deleted. This approach is the one used for built-in arrays; it has the same pitfalls for containers as dangling pointers provide in C.

We could prohibit deletion of the container itself as long as there are live iterators. Before deleting a container, we could check whether there are any iterators attached to it and throw an exception if there are. The problem with this approach is that it may turn a harmless oversight into a fatal error. A user who has lost track of an iterator may call `delete` on the container assuming that doing so will be safe. The program will be terminated even though, had it run, the offending iterator might never have been used.

14.5 Other design considerations

When designing an iterator class, it is important to think about how to create iterators and what copying and assigning them will mean. Creating iterators presents the most interesting design decisions.

Should it be possible to create an iterator that is not bound to a particular container? Should it be possible to create an iterator that is bound to a container, but not to a particular element? For `Arrays`, we answered these questions "yes" and "no", respectively. We said that the user could create an unbound `Pointer`. If the user didn't give us a position in the `Array` when creating a `Pointer`, we arbitrarily positioned the iterator to point to a nonexistent element. If we allow unbound iterators, we also need to decide what, if anything, to do if an unbound iterator is used. In `Array`, we checked for this case and threw an exception.

Remember that it probably will be convenient to define containers or arrays of the iterator class that you are defining. This implies that you'll need to define the default constructor. The need to support containers of iterators may influence what to do about unbound iterators.

As with any class, you need to think as well about copy, assignment, and the destructor. If the iterator is simply a pointer to the container and some way of marking a position in that container, then the default definitions for these operations probably will suffice. However, if the iterator relies on some kind of use-counted memory, as was the case for `Pointers`, you'll need to define these operations to manage the use count appropriately.

Often, it is useful to provide some way of testing whether an iterator is at the end of its associated container. We did not provide this test with our `Pointer` class. Instead, we required the user to get a `Pointer` to the end of the `Array`, and then to test each time through whether the iterator was equal to the `Pointer` to the end. We might have provided a separate function that would test whether the `Pointer` pointed to the end of the `Array`. It might be even more convenient to return an "end of iterator" signal as a side effect of iterating past the end of the container.

14.6 Discussion

This has been a lot of detail—so much that some readers will surely be asking themselves: "Is all this necessary?"

The answer is "Yes and no." To define an abstract data type, you must decide how it should behave. There is no escaping it. If you don't think about it, the class will still behave somehow; you will merely have given up control over how.

If you know you're not going to use that undefined behavior, and you never let anyone else use your class, then there's no problem. If you do wind up using it, though, your program is likely to do things you hadn't anticipated, at which point you are going to have to figure out why it did what it did. It may well be more trouble to debug an inadvertent use of undefined behavior than it would have been to define the behavior in the first place. At the very least, you should take the trouble to make your copy constructor and assignment operator private if you don't want to think about what they should do.

Once you have put in the effort to design an abstraction that does what you want, you have effectively added a new word to your vocabulary. What you gain in exchange for the trouble of defining classes carefully is the ability to understand and predict what objects of these classes will do in practice. Once you have learned a new word, you can use it whenever the occasion arises.

15

Sequences

Over the past several years, a canonical style has evolved for C++ container classes: A container holds objects, whereas an object of an iterator class marks a place in the container. Chapters 12 through 14 explored this style of containers and iterators.

Experience with container classes suggests that a simpler approach can be useful. This chapter describes a reduced instruction set container class called Seq, which is patterned after lists in vintage-1960 pure Lisp. Although it does not offer all the functionality of other, widely available list classes, it is surprisingly useful. Moreover, it is much smaller and simpler than conventional classes.

15.1 The state of the art

The kind of container and companion iterator class that we developed for Arrays and Pointers is an example of the usual way of building C++ containers. A container holds the user's objects; iterators mark places in the container.

This strategy is similar to how arrays work in traditional languages: An array holds values, and an auxiliary value—usually an integer or a pointer—marks a place in the array. Thus, when we write a C program fragment such as

```
int a[N];
int i;

for (i = 0; i < N; i++)
        a[i] = i;
```

we are using a as a container and i as an iterator.

Because the iterator idea fits well with data structures in traditional programming languages, C++ programmers find iterators easy to adopt. However, iterators are less simple in practice than they are in theory. For example, because containers might be const, each container needs two kinds of iterators: one that can only read the container and one that can both read and write it. This is analogous to the two kinds of pointers that might point to an object of type T—namely, T* and const T*.

In addition to requiring three classes for each kind of container, the traditional approach calls for lots of features. Aside from yielding to the usual social pressure to include everything in a library that every user might want, library designers need to make containers and iterators work in all combinations.

For example, the list class from the USL Standard Components* library supports the following operations:

- Create a list from zero, one, two, three, or four elements.
- Copy and assign a list.
- Determine the length of a list.
- Concatenate two lists.
- Determine whether two lists are equal.
- Add, access, or delete an element at either end.
- Access the nth element.
- Sort a list.
- Print the list using the output operation defined on the list elements.

In addition, there are list iterators that support the following operations:

- Create, copy, assign, and compare iterators.
- Find the list associated with a given iterator.
- Determine whether the iterator is at the end of its list.
- Search for an element with a given value.
- Advance the iterator to refer to the next (or previous) element in the list.
- Access the element before or after the iterator (iterators point "between" elements).

The operations add up: The USL list class has 70 members and one friend function, divided as follows:

- List: 27 members, one friend.
- Const_listiter: 28 members.
- Listiter: 15 members.

The implementation is more than 900 lines of source code.

15.2 A radical old idea

All this is nice, but it sometimes leaves one wishing for less. If we can have lightweight processes and reduced instruction set computer (RISC) chips, why not a RISC (reduced instruction set container) class? For inspiration, I went back more than a third of a century and looked at Lisp.

---

* Not to be confused with the C++ Standard Library, the USL Standard Components was the work of AT&T people, including the authors, in the late 1980s.

Lisp has grown greatly over the years, but it originally defined a list in terms of just five operations:

- `nil`: A list with no elements.
- `cons(a,b)`: A list whose first element is a, and whose subsequent elements are those of the list b.
- `car(s)`: The first element of s, which must be a list with at least one element.
- `cdr(s)`: All the elements of s except the first; s must be a list with at least one element.
- `null(s)`: True if s has no elements, false otherwise; s must be a list.

Note that none of these operations modifies the list or any element in the list. We can build lists and extract values from them, but we cannot mutate them.

There is a *very* large body of theory and practice that shows that these operations are useful. Moreover, this kind of list is easy to implement in C++ if we add the restriction that all the elements of a list must have the same type. Using templates, we can then define a class Seq<T> that represents a list of objects of type T. I called it Seq, rather than List, to avoid confusing it with any of the other List classes out there.

Suppose that we start by implementing the five primitive Lisp operations. How might those look in C++? Assume that t has type T and s has type Seq<T>. Then the following C++ operations suggest themselves:

- `Seq<T>()`: Create and return a sequence with no elements.
- `Seq<T>(t,s)`: Create and return a sequence with first element t and subsequent elements those of s.
- `s.hd()`: Return the first element of s; s must have at least one element.
- `s.tl()`: Create and return a sequence containing all but the first element of s; s must have at least one element.
- `(bool)s`: Return false if s has no elements; otherwise, return true.

The names hd and tl are there because they are easier to explain to nonLispers than are car and cdr. The conversion to bool is intended for use in if and while statements.

So, let's start by writing down what we know so far:

```
template<class T> class Seq {
public:
        Seq();
        Seq(const T&, const Seq&);
        T hd() const;
        Seq tl() const;
        operator bool() const;
};
```

Next, how will we represent a Seq? Well, it is a list, after all, so we'll probably need another, private class to hold an element value and a pointer to the next element in the list. It's also worth thinking here about the implications of the fact that `Seq` objects are immutable. One immediate realization is that it might be possible to avoid copying `Seq`s or subsequences, and instead to arrange for `Seq`s to share the underlying sequence when appropriate. This insight suggests that we give the element class a use count. Let's do that, and see how it plays out:

```
template <class T> class Seq_item {
        friend class Seq<T>;

        int use;
        const T data;
        Seq_item* next;

        Seq_item(const T& t, Seq_item* s);
        Seq_item(const T& t): use(1), data(t), next(0) { }
};
```

The only tricky part of implementing this class is what to do when creating a new `Seq` from a value and an existing `Seq`. After this operation, the two `Seq`s can share the common tail represented by `s`. This means that we have to increment the use count properly:

```
template <class T>
Seq_item<T>::Seq_item(const T& t, Seq_item<T>* s):
        use(1), data(t), next(s)
{
        if (s)
                s->use++;
}
```

It is important to understand this use-count strategy thoroughly. For example, after executing

```
Seq_item x = Seq_item(t, s);
```

the use count of the first `Seq_item` in `s` will be one more than it was, but the use count of the first `Seq_item` in `x` will be 1. Note that the use count of the first item of the sequence stored in `x` will be less than the use count of the second item in that *same* sequence. The importance of this will become more evident as we continue building the class.

Because we're using use counts, we will surely have work to do each time that a `Seq` object is created, destroyed, or assigned. Thus, we need a copy constructor, destructor, and assignment operator. Taking that need into account, and making the `Seq` class contain a pointer to the `Seq_item` that represents the first element of its sequence, we have

```
template<class T> class Seq {
public:
        Seq();
        Seq(const T&, const Seq&);
        Seq(const Seq&);                // added
        ~Seq();                         // added
        Seq& operator=(const Seq&);     // added
```

```
T hd() const;
Seq tl() const;
operator bool() const;
```
```
private:
        Seq_item<T>* item;                       // added
};
```

Now we can start working on implementation. The default constructor is straightforward. We'll set the item pointer to 0 for an empty sequence:

```
template<class T> Seq<T>::Seq(): item(0) { }
```

Our next constructor—the one that makes a Seq from a reference to T and another Seq—is not much harder. It allocates a Seq_item object to contain the value, and makes the given Seq into the tail of the result:

```
template<class T>
Seq<T>::Seq(const T& t, const Seq<T>& x):
        item(new Seq_item<T>(t, x.item)) { }
```

The conversion operator is trivial:

```
template<class T> Seq<T>::bool() const
{
        return item != 0;
}
```

The copy constructor is scarcely less trivial; all we have to do is to remember to increment the use count:

```
template<class T> Seq<T>::Seq(const Seq<T>& s): item(s.item)
{
        if (item)
                item->use++;
}
```

The destructor and assignment operator must potentially free a whole list of Seq_items, so we'll return to them after implementing a few of the other, easier member functions.

The hd operation, for example, returns the value in the first Seq_item. The only nontrivial decision is what to do when someone tries to take the hd of an empty sequence. We'll throw an exception:

```
template<class T> T Seq<T>::hd() const
{
        if (item)
                return item->data;
        else
                throw "hd of an empty Seq";
}
```

What about tl? It has to return a new Seq formed by the tail of this Seq; how do we create such a beast? The information that we need is sitting right there in `item->next`, but it's a `Seq_item`, and we need a `Seq` to hold it. It looks like we'll need to define another (private) constructor first:

```
template<class T>
Seq<T>::Seq(Seq_item<T>* s): item(s)
{
        if (s)
                s->use++;
}
```

Now, it's easy to implement `tl`:

```
template<class T>
Seq<T> Seq<T>::tl() const
{
        if (item)
                return Seq<T>(item->next);
        else
                throw "tl of an empty Seq";
}
```

As we did for `hd`, we take exception to a request for the `tl` of an empty sequence.

Now, let's return to the destructor and assignment operator. They will need to destroy the underlying sequence if and only if this object is the only one sharing the sequence. To figure out how to determine whether the sequence is shared or not, we must think about how our use-count strategy works. Remember that some other object may be sharing the tail of this sequence. This means that the use count of the head of this sequence may be less than the use count of some item further on in the sequence. For example,

```
Seq<T>* sp = new Seq<int>;
// put some values in sp
Seq<T> s2 = sp->tl();
delete sp;
```

Here, we dynamically allocate a `Seq` and put some elements in it. Now we set `s2` to the tail of the sequence pointed to by `sp`. We need to make sure that the elements in the tail are still around for `s2` to refer to after we `delete sp`. Thus, when deleting a sequence, we may be able to delete only some of the elements before we are stopped by reaching a shared tail. The elements in the tail will stick around until it comes time to delete all the sequences that share that tail. The destructor and assignment operator will have to deal with this appropriately.

It will be simpler if we define a function to manage the use counts, as well as deleting the `Seq_item` elements as appropriate. Assuming that we've got such a function, say `destroy`, then the assignment operator and destructor are easy:

```
template<class T>
Seq<T>& Seq<T>::operator=(const Seq<T>& s)
{
        if (s.item)
                s.item->use++;
        destroy(item);
        item = s.item;
        return *this;
}

template<class T> Seq<T>::~Seq()
{
        destroy(item);
}
```

We have to make sure we guard against self assignment in operator=; we do so by incrementing the use count of the right-hand side before calling destroy.

Now, the only thing we have left to do is to implement destroy:

```
template<class T>
void Seq<T>::destroy(Seq_item<T>* item)
{
        while (item && --item->use == 0) {
                Seq_item<T>* next = item->next;
                delete item;
                item = next;
        }
}
```

15.3 Well, maybe a few extras...

This class was easy to implement. Moreover, it is useful as it stands. However, it is hard to resist the temptation to add a few additional operations to make it easier to use. Some of this ease of use comes from differences in typical style between Lisp and C++ programs.

For example, the way that we put a new value onto the beginning of a sequence is to construct a new sequence explicitly, so, if t is a value of type T and s is of type Seq<T>, then Seq<T>(t, s) is a sequence whose first element is t and whose subsequent elements are those of s.

Aside from being ungainly, using the constructor has the disadvantage of forcing us to state the type T explicitly in Seq<T>—a type that we might not know. We can solve both of these problems by taking a cue from Lisp and defining a cons function explicitly:

```
template<class T> Seq<T> cons(const T& t, const Seq<T>& s)
{
        return Seq<T>(t, s);
}
```

Now we can write cons(t, s), instead of Seq<T>(t, s), and make no explicit mention of the type T.

As another example, suppose that we want to compute the number of elements in a sequence. A Lisp programmer might write it this way:

```
template<class T> int length(const Seq<T>& s)
{
        if (s)
                return (1+ (length (s.tl())));
        return 0;
}
```

A C++ programmer, however, would be prone to do it this way:

```
template<class T> int length(Seq<T> s)
{
        int n = 0;
        while (s) {
                s = s.tl();
                n++;
        }
        return n;
}
```

The second version relies on iteration instead of recursion, which means that it also relies on variables that can change value—in this case, n and s. Note particularly that the second version picks elements off the front of s one at a time and throws them away, eventually destroying s completely. It can get away with this because s is a copy of the argument to length.

Because n has type int, we can use the good old ++ operator to mutate it. What about s?

That statement

```
s = s.tl();
```

seems to cry out for abbreviation, just as

```
n = n + 1;
```

can be abbreviated as

```
n++;
```

What about taking

```
s = s.tl();
```

and defining

```
++s;
```

as an abbreviation for it? That may look a little weird, but is it really? An object of class Seq<T> is implemented in terms of a pointer; the only difference between applying ++ to a Seq<T> and applying ++ to a raw pointer is that the latter operation assumes that the pointer is pointing to an element of an array.

Indeed, we can carry this analogy still further. Lisp programmers are used to car as an explicit function (even if it is called hd), but C++ programmers are more likely to be familiar with using operator* to access container elements.

This suggests adding a couple of operators to make this class more comfortable for C++ programmers:

- operator*(), which will be a synonym for hd()
- operator++(), which will abbreviate the assignment s = s.tl();

These additions will allow the economy of expression familiar to C++ programmers. For example, in finding some value val in a Seq named s,

```
while (s && *s != val)
        ++s;
```

is more likely to be familiar to a C++ veteran than is

```
while (s && s.hd() == val)
        s = s.tl();
```

Furthermore, we can implement the abbreviated operations more efficiently than users could do by themselves, by exploiting knowledge of the underlying Seq_items. These operators can deal with the use counts explicitly, getting rid of the original first element if appropriate. Here is the prefix operator++:

```
template <class T> Seq<T>& Seq<T>::operator++()
{
        if (item) {
                Seq_item<T>* p = item->next;
                if (p)
                        p->use++;
                if (--item->use == 0)
                        delete item;
                item = p;
        }
        return *this;
}
```

The postfix version is

```
template <class T> Seq<T> Seq<T>::operator++(int)
{
        Seq<T> ret = *this;
        if (item) {
                --item->use;
                item = item->next;
                if (item)
                        item->use++;
        }
        return ret;
}
```

The postfix operator saves a copy of the old value in ret, and then increments it. When the smoke clears and we return ret, we know that there will be at least one user—namely ret—of the first element in the sequence. Hence, we can decrement that element's use count without checking whether or not it might have become 0.

Of course, operator* is merely a synonym for hd:

```
template<class T> T Seq<T>::operator*()
{
        return hd();
}
```

Another common operation is to put a new value at the head of a list. Using the primitives, that operation looks like this:

```
s = cons(s, x);
```

Again this is sufficiently common to warrant a faster, built-in operation:

```
template <class T>
Seq<T>& Seq<T>::insert(const T& t)
{
        item = new Seq_item<T>(t, item);
        return *this;
}
```

At this point, we've added operations to make the class feel more natural to a C++ programmer. These added operations are also more efficient than ones users could write for themselves, because they exploit the internal structure of class Seq. Of course, it is a hard judgment call where to stop adding things, but we've done enough that it's time to stop and see how we might use this class.

15.4 Example of use

The best way to give a feel for how this class works is to work through a complete example. We will begin with a function to merge two sequences, each assumed to be in ascending order:

```
template<class T>
Seq<T> merge(const Seq<T>& x, const Seq<T>& y)
{
        // if one Seq is empty, return the other
        if (!x) return y;
        if (!y) return x;

        // both are nonempty; extract the first elements
        T xh = x.hd();
        T yh = y.hd();
```

```
        // compare them
        if (xh < yh)
                return cons(xh, merge(x.tl(), y));
        return cons(yh, merge(x, y.tl()));
}
```

Next, is a function that splits a sequence into two piles, much as one would deal a deck of cards. We will assume either that the piles are empty to start, or that our caller doesn't mind our piling the elements on top of the ones already there. The elements are reversed in the process, as they are when dealing cards:

```
template<class T> void split(Seq<T> x, Seq<T>& y, Seq<T>& z)
{
        while (x) {
                y.insert(x.hd());
                if (++x) {
                        z.insert(x.hd());
                        ++x;
                }
        }
}
```

Finally, we can use these two functions to make a simple sort function:

```
template<class T> Seq<T> sort(const Seq<T>& x)
{
        if (!x || !x.tl())
                return x;

        Seq<T> p, q;

        split(x, p, q);
        return merge(sort(p), sort(q));
}
```

Simple as it is, this merge sort has $O(log\ n)$ performance, even in the worst case. Perhaps a measure of the utility of the Seq class is how rare it is to find a sort that novices can understand and that also has good worst-case performance.

Programmers who aren't used to recursion might prefer merging this way:

```
template<class T> Seq<T> merge2(Seq<T> x, Seq<T> y)
{
        Seq<T> r;

        while (x && y) {
                if (x.hd() < y.hd()) {
                        r.insert(x.hd());
                        x++;
                } else {
                        r.insert(y.hd());
                        y++;
                }
        }
}
```

```
while (x) {
        r.insert(x.hd());
        x++;
}

while (y) {
        r.insert(y.hd());
        y++;
}

r.flip();
return r;
}
```

Aside from the primitives, and `insert` and `operator++`, this second implementation requires one more operation on Seqs, which we must now implement: `r.flip()` reverses the elements of r in place.

Which of these two versions is easier to understand probably depends on
where you were brought up. But because we're trying to cater to C++ users, and
because this version of `merge` is more natural to that community, it looks like the
`flip` operation should be part of our class, rather than being an auxiliary function for `merge`.

The first thing to note is that, if we are to reverse a Seq in place, this Seq
must "own" all the elements in the sequence that it holds. That is, the use count
of every Seq_item must be 1. Once we have our own copy of the sequence,
reversing the elements is just a matter of manipulating pointers.

So, first we'll need a function to ensure that we have our own, changeable
copy of the sequence. We'll call this function `owntail` because we can no longer
share a tail with any other Seq. The first thing that `owntail` has to do is to find
the first Seq_item, if any, in its sequence that has a use count greater than 1.
Then, it will create a new copy of the sequence from that point to the end of the
sequence. Finally, it will splice that new copy into the existing sequence, replacing the old tail with the new copy, and adjusting the use count of the old tail
appropriately. It turns out to be useful for `owntail` to return a pointer to the
last item in the new tail.

First, note that there's nothing to do if this sequence is empty, so we can
return:

```
template<class T> Seq_item<T>* Seq<T>::owntail()
{
        if (item == 0)
                return 0;
```

Now, we declare some local pointers to use in iterating through the sequence and
use these to find the first Seq_item, if any, with a use count greater than 1. Of
course, if we hit the end of the sequence, then there's no further work to do—we
already have our own copy of the tail:

```
Seq_item<T>* i = item;
Seq_item<T>** p = &item;
while (i->use == 1) {
        if (i->next == 0)
                return i;
        p = &i->next;
        i = i->next;
}
```

If we get this far, i points to the first item with use!=1, and p points to the pointer we must overwrite to splice in the new tail. That pointer might be the next member of some Seq_item, or it might be the item member of the Seq itself. We'll make that pointer point to a new Seq_item that will be the first item on our new copy of the old tail, and we'll reset the use count of the old tail:

```
*p = new Seq_item<T> (i->data);
--i->use;
i = i->next;
```

Next we have to walk down the rest of the old tail, allocating new Seq_items for the copy that we're creating, and initializing those new nodes with a copy of the old values. Here, we use i to march through the old sequence, and j to point into the new copy:

```
Seq_item<T>* j = *p;
while (i) {
        j->next = new Seq_item<T> (i->data);
        i = i->next;
        j = j->next;
}
return j;
}
```

Now, flip is just a matter of manipulating pointers. After getting our own copy of the tail, we change the next pointer of each Seq_item to point at the *previous* Seq_item, instead of at the next one. This requires that we keep three pointers into the sequence, which point to the current Seq_item, the one behind it, and the one ahead of it:

```
template<class T> Seq<T>& Seq<T>::flip()
{
        if (item) {
                Seq_item<T>* k = owntail();
                Seq_item<T>* curr = item;
                Seq_item<T>* behind = 0;

                do {
                        Seq_item<T>* ahead = curr->next;
                        curr->next = behind;
                        behind = curr;
                        curr = ahead;
                } while (curr);
```

All that's left is to reset the `item` pointer in `Seq`, and return `*this` (because `flip` returns a reference):

```
            item = k;
    }

    return *this;
}
```

15.5 Maybe a few more...

The operations that we have added so far either have provided a more natural syntax for one of the primitives, (`operator*`), or have provided useful functionality that the user could not provide as efficiently, (`operator++` and `flip`). There are a few more operations that fall into this latter category. One is to concatenate two sequences. Once we use `owntail` to ensure that the left-hand-side sequence doesn't share with any other sequence, we can splice the right-hand side onto the end. The user can't do this directly, of course. To add concatenation, we need to define a member `operator+=` and a nonmember `operator+`; we'll leave this as an exercise.

A more interesting addition might be to support testing for (in)equality. Note first that if we want to do this efficiently, we should probably add a `length` operation first. Two sequences of different lengths are surely unequal, and it is much easier to discover this if we can find the lengths without having to compute them. Assuming that we can find the length, then the test for equality starts by seeing whether both sequences are the same length:

```
template<class T>
bool operator==(const Seq<T>& op1, const Seq<T>& op2)
{
        if (op1.length() != op2.length())
                return 0;
```

If they're the same length, then we need to walk the two sequences. If the `Seq_items` are the same node, then we know that the sequences are identical. If the nodes are different but hold the same values, then we need to keep checking:

```
        Seq_item<T>*p = op1.item;
        Seq_item<T>*q = op2.item;

        while (p != q) {
                assert (p != 0 && q != 0);
                if (*p++ != *q++)
                        return true;
        }

        return false;
}
```

Note that, once we get to the `while` loop, we already know that both sequences have the same number of elements. The `assert` is there to detect any bugs in the implementation that might have misled us in our reliance on this fact.

The `length` function requires that we go back and reimplement our `Seq` class to store the length and to update each of the `Seq` operations that change the length of the sequence to keep the length up to date.

It turns out that we have a choice of two plausible places in which to store the length: We might store the length with each `Seq` object, or with each `Seq_item` object. Each alternative has advantages and disadvantages, but it is probably best to store the length in the `Seq`, on the basis that, because the average length of a sequence is likely to be greater than 1, there are likely to be more `Seq` objects than `Seq_item` objects in existence.

Assuming that we store the length in the `Seq` object, it is then easy to make the `length` function return the stored value:

```
template<class T> class Seq {
public:
        unsigned length() { return len; }

private:
        unsigned len;
        // ...
};
```

The constructors, assignment operator, increment operators, concatenation operators, `insert`, and `tl` functions will all have to be updated to manage `len`. Only one of these functions is interesting: the `private` constructor that takes a `Seq_item`. Because we can't directly obtain the length of the (sub)sequence pointed to by any `Seq_item`, we'll need to give this constructor another argument:

```
template<class T>
Seq<T>::Seq(Seq_item<T>* s, unsigned l):
        item(s), len(l)
{
        if (s)
                s->use++;
}
```

We'll also pass the length of the (sub)sequence when we use this constructor:

```
template<class T>
Seq<T> Seq<T>::tl() const
{
        if (item)
                return Seq<T>(item->next, len-1);
        else
                throw "tl of an empty Seq";
}
```

The reader may find it useful to go back over the rest of the Seq class and retrofit the code necessary to keep len up to date for all the other Seq operations.

15.6 Food for thought

Even with the extra operations and optimizations, the class has only 16 members and two nonmember operations. The complete implementation is less than 200 lines of source code; the manual page fits on one (double-sided) sheet of paper. For the operations that it supports, it runs about as fast as the USL list class.

More generally, it would be interesting to apply the RISC approach to other data structures. It works well for sequences because we can afford to tell our users that they cannot modify the elements after a sequence has been created. This restriction is harder to maintain for more general data structures, but the functional-programming community has shown that it is possible. The interesting question is whether that style can be transplanted into C++ and, if so, whether people will find it worthwhile to use. This is an open question that deserves an answer.

16

Templates as interfaces

Chapters 12 through 15 looked at a classic use for templates: building container classes. Templates can also be a general way of describing the interface to a program or collection of programs.

In this chapter, we'll see how to use templates to provide abstract interfaces. We can then write functions that are independent of any actual types by writing them to operate on these abstract interfaces.

This difficult chapter is based on an article from mid-1991, and uses ideas from ML (a language with good support for generic and functional programming—see, for instance, Chris Reade: *Elements of Functional Programming*, Addison-Wesley 1989) and elsewhere. Many of these ideas found their way into the Standard Template Library (STL), which we'll explore in Chapters 17 through 22. Because this use of abstraction is a bit slippery, it seems worthwhile to go over this ground a couple of times to cement our understanding of these ideas.

16.1 The problem

Consider an on-line student-registration system. Part of that system will implement the registration logic. Another part will be there because it is an on-line system. Still other code will talk to the underlying database.

It would be nice if the parts of the system that deal with conceptually different characteristics were themselves kept carefully separate. Doing so, for example, would make it possible for us to use the on-line and database parts of the system in building, say, an on-line library-circulation system.

To understand how the parts of such a system might be kept separate, we will write a tiny program and separate it into pieces. When studying those pieces, think about how the techniques used there might apply to larger programs.

16.2 The first example

Here is a function that adds the elements of an array of integers:

```
int sum(int* p, int n)
{
        int result = 0;
        for (int i = 0; i < n; i++)
                result += p[i];
        return result;
}
```

We can use it to find the sum of the nonnegative integers less than 10:

```
#include <iostream.h>

int main()
{
        int x[10];
        for (int i = 0; i < 10; i++)
                x[i] = i;
        cout << sum(x, 10) << endl;
}
```

The sum function knows about three things:
1. it is adding a bunch of numbers together,
2. the numbers that it is adding are integers, and
3. the integers that it is adding are stored in a particular way.

Let's see how we can partition the program so that each one of these characteristics is contained in a different part. Clearly, the first thing that the sum function knows—that it is doing addition—is intrinsic to this function. The idea, therefore, is to rewrite the sum function such that it makes minimal extra assumptions about what it is adding up.

16.3 Separating the iteration

The first thing that we will remove from the sum function is the knowledge that elements being added are contained in an array. To do this, we follow the standard C++ technique: Make this knowledge into a class.

What kind of class might encapsulate the notion of iterating over a collection of integers? An object of that class evidently would have to represent the state of the iteration, so the relevant operations are
- A constructor, which establishes the data to be handled
- A way of asking for the next element in sequence
- A way of telling when the iteration is complete
- An assignment operator, copy constructor, and destructor to enable one of these objects to be used as a value

We have already encountered such objects, called iterators, in Chapter 14. There are many possible kinds of iterators; what we have just seen is a fundamental outline of how they work.

Let's write down what we know so far about our iterator:

```
class Int_iterator {
public:
        Int_iterator(int*, int);      // address, length
        ~Int_iterator();

        int valid() const;
        int next();

        Int_iterator(const Int_iterator&);
        Int_iterator& operator=(const Int_iterator&);
};
```

This class is called `Int_iterator`, rather than `Iterator`, because it expresses an iteration through a sequence of `int` values. We will generalize it later to values of arbitrary type.

The constructor takes two arguments: the address of the initial element of the sequence, and the number of elements. The `valid` member returns a nonzero value if there are still elements left in the sequence; the `next` member fetches the next element in the sequence if there is one. We will assume that `next` is called only if there is known to be a value remaining in the sequence.

Before we even fill in the definition of our iterator, we can already rewrite the sum function:

```
int sum(Int_iterator ir)
{
        int result = 0;
        while (ir.valid())
                result += ir.next();
        return result;
}
```

This version no longer relies on knowing *directly* how the elements it is adding are stored. That knowledge is encapsulated in `Int_iterator`, and is inaccessible to sum.

Notice that this function does indeed use the `Int_iterator` copy constructor and destructor, because its formal parameter is an `Int_iterator`, rather than a `const Int_iterator&`. Because an iterator contains a state, iteration necessarily changes the iterator's value. Thus, making the parameter a `const` is out of the question. Moreover, if the parameter were an `Int_iterator&`, that would restrict the arguments to being lvalues, because only an lvalue argument can be passed to a nonconst reference parameter. The sum function does not use the iterator assignment operator.

A main program that uses this sum function might look like this:

```
#include <iostream.h>
int main()
{
        int x[10];
        for (int i = 0; i < 10; i++)
                x[i] = i;
        cout << sum(Int_iterator(x, 10)) << endl;
}
```

The only difference is that instead of calling sum(x, 10), we now must call
sum(Int_iterator(x, 10)). Of course, it is possible to write an overloaded
sum function that preserves the original interface:

```
int sum(int* p, int n)
{
        return sum(Int_iterator(p, n));
}
```

It is time to return to the definition of the Int_iterator class. What information is necessary in an object of that class? We need to be able to locate the next
element in the sequence, presumably through an int*, and we need to know
when the sequence is finished. We could obtain this latter information by
remembering either how many elements are left or the address that is one past
the last element. If we arbitrarily choose to remember how many elements are
left, the private members of the Int_iterator class then look like this:

```
        int* data;
        int len;
```

The constructor is straightforward. All it has to do is to initialize the data and
len members from its corresponding parameters.

The destructor, assignment operator, and copy constructor are even easier.
Because their actions are equivalent to the corresponding actions on the data
members, we can omit these three member functions altogether. The compiler
will automatically insert appropriate definitions for them.

Finally, we must define valid and next. After doing so, our class looks like:

```
class Int_iterator {
public:
        Int_iterator(int* p, int c): data(p), len(c) { }

        int valid() const { return len > 0; }
        int next() {
                --len;
                return *data++;
        }

private:
        int* data;
        int len;
};
```

16.4 Iterating over arbitrary types

The name `Int_iterator` is a dead giveaway that we have missed an opportunity for abstraction. We can readily turn the `Int_iterator` class into a general `Iterator` template:

```
template<class T> class Iterator {
public:
        Iterator(T* p, int c): data(p), len(c) { }

        int valid() const {
                return len > 0;
        }

        T next() {
                --len;
                return *data++;
        }

private:
        T* data;
        int len;
};
```

The only thing the least bit difficult about this rewrite is figuring out which instances of `int` in the `Int_iterator` class should become `T`, and which should remain `int`.

The rest of our program can remain completely unchanged, provided that we make the type `Int_iterator` equivalent to `Iterator<int>`:

```
typedef Iterator<int> Int_iterator;
```

Alternatively, we can change the rest of the program by simply substituting `Iterator<int>` everywhere that `Int_iterator` appeared formerly:

```
int sum(Iterator<int> ir)
{
        int result = 0;
        while (ir.valid())
                result += ir.next();
        return result;
}

int main()
{
        int x[10];
        for (int i = 0; i < 10; i++)
                x[i] = i;
        cout << sum(Iterator<int>(x, 10)) << endl;
}
```

16.5 Adding other types

Now that we can iterate over arrays of arbitrary type, let's use that new capability to find the sum of values of arbitrary type. We can do this easily by making the sum function into a template:

```
template<class T> T sum(Iterator<T> ir)
{
        T result = 0;
        while (ir.valid())
                result += ir.next();
        return result;
}
```

With this rewrite, it is possible to calculate the sum of arrays of objects of other classes. What classes? Any class for which
- It is possible to convert 0 to an object of that class
- The += operator is defined on objects of that class
- The objects have valuelike semantics so the sum function can return them as its value

All the numeric types meet this requirement, of course, and it is easy to define other classes that do so as well.

16.6 Abstracting the storage technique

At this point, the only knowledge sum has about the values that it is adding is that its argument is of type Iterator. But the logic in sum doesn't rely on much from the Iterator class: It uses just the valid and next operations. How might we exploit this to be able to use sum on types other than those stored in an array?

What we need are different kinds of iterators to reflect different data structures. So far, we have only one type of iterator, which lets us access values stored in arrays. But what if our values are in a linked list? What if they are in a file? Is it possible to abstract those as well?

The standard way to solve this problem is to turn the Iterator class into an abstract base class that can represent any one of a number of different kinds of iterator classes:

```
template<class T> class Iterator {
public:
        virtual int valid() const = 0;
        virtual T next() = 0;
        virtual ~Iterator() { }
};
```

Next, we could say that an Array_iterator<T> is a kind of Iterator<T>:

```
template<class T> class Array_iterator: public Iterator<T> {
public:
        Array_iterator(T* p, int c): data(p), len(c) { }

        int valid() const { return len > 0; }
        T next() {
                --len;
                return *data++;
        }
private:
        T* data;
        int len;
};
```

Finally, we could define the sum function to take a *reference* to an Iterator as its argument, to allow dynamic binding:

```
template<class T> T sum(Iterator<T>& ir)
{
        T result = 0;
        while (ir.valid())
                result += ir.next();
        return result;
}
```

Then, to add the elements of an array, we merely create an appropriate Array_iterator to describe it, and pass that iterator to sum:

```
#include <iostream.h>

int main()
{
        int x[10];
        for (int i = 0; i < 10; i++)
                x[i] = i;
        Array_iterator<int> it (x, 10);
        cout << sum(it) << endl;
}
```

The difference in this code and the version of main from Section 16.4 (page 195) is that we have explicitly created an Array_iterator<int> object named it to express the iteration over the elements of x. We cannot simply say

```
cout << sum(Array_iterator<int>(x, 10)) << endl;
```

because the subexpression Array_iterator<int>(x, 10) is not an lvalue, and therefore cannot have a nonconst reference attached to it.

That is a minor inconvenience. Another, somewhat less minor, inconvenience is that, because dynamic binding is used, every iteration of the inner loop in the sum function requires a virtual function call. This could be expensive compared to the inline expansion of our previous examples, especially if the objects being added are simple things such as integers.

We will deal with both of those objections by dispensing with dynamic binding. That means that when we want to add the elements of some collection, we will have to know at compile time what kind of collection it is, but this restriction probably will not impose a major hardship.

Rather than using inheritance, we'll make the sum function take *two* type parameters: the type of the iterator and the type of the objects being added. Unfortunately, this doesn't work, if we try to define the sum function in the straightforward way:

```
template<class Iter, class T> T sum(Iter it)
{ /* ... */ }
```

We now find that we have defined a function whose return type is unrelated to its argument type. That is, the type of sum(x) is independent of the type of x. This is illegal in C++*, because otherwise there would be no way to determine the type of an expression without examining a potentially unbounded amount of context.

Fortunately, there is a traditional way out of this corner: We'll define sum to take a reference to its result. Because that involves giving it a second argument, which makes it easier to confuse with our original sum function, we will call it sum2:

```
template<class T, class Iter>
void sum2(T& result, Iter ir)
{
        result = 0;
        while (ir.valid())
                result += ir.next();
}
```

We'll need to rewrite our main program to work with this version of sum2:

```
int main()
{
        int x[10];
        for (int i = 0; i < 10; i++)
                x[i] = i;
        int r;
        sum2(r, Iterator<int>(x, 10));
        cout << r << endl;
}
```

Of course, as before, we can preserve the interface to our original sum making it call sum2:

---

* The standards committee has approved a way to allow the return type to differ from any of the argument types, but few compilers support it yet.

```
template<class T> T sum(T* p, int n)
{
        T r = 0;
        sum2(r, Iterator<T>(p, n));
        return r;
}
```

This then allows the original main program to work:

```
int main()
{
        int x[10];
        for (int i = 0; i < 10; i++)
                x[i] = i;
        cout << sum(x, 10) << endl;
}
```

16.7 The proof of the pudding

To illustrate the flexibility of this approach, let's use sum2 to add a potentially unbounded collection of numbers read from an istream.

First, we need a class that we can use as an iterator. Because its behavior is markedly different from that of our previous Iterator class, we'll call it a Reader. In other words, a Reader<T> object will read a sequence of T values from an istream in such a way that sum2 can use a Reader<T> as an iterator.

This design presents a small problem. The way that we defined iterators, we have to be able to test whether there are data left before reading any. That's not how istreams work, however; the way to tell whether data are left in an istream is to read from it and to see if the read worked.

We will solve this problem by reading ahead one element in the Reader class, and remembering whether the read was successful. Because we must do the read and test both in the constructor and in the valid member function, we'll make that operation a separate, private member function called advance:

```
template<class T> class Reader {
public:
        Reader(istream& is): i(is) { advance(); }
        int valid () const { return status; }
        T next() {
                T result = data;
                advance();
                return result;
        }

private:
        istream& i;
        int status;
        T data;
```

```
            void advance() {
                    i >> data;
                    status = i != 0;
            }
    };
```

Each `Reader` object binds a reference to an `istream` that is given to its constructor. Thus, `Reader<double>(cin)` is a `Reader` object that will fetch a sequence of `double` values from `cin`.

With this class and `sum2` from the previous example, we can now add numbers read from the input:

```
int main()
{
        cout << "Enter numbers:" << endl;
        double r = 0;
        sum2(r, Reader<double>(cin));
        cout << r << endl;
}
```

The remarkable thing about this example is that `sum2` is precisely the same function that we used to add the elements of an array.

16.8 Summary

The key to building a system of any significant size successfully is to break it up into pieces on which people can work independently. The key to that, in turn, is to define clear interfaces between those pieces.

This chapter has illustrated how we can use C++ class definitions as interfaces, to reduce the amount of information that one part of a system has to know about another. Specifically, we took a simple `sum` function and split off each of its three parts into an independent piece of code.

Consider again the on-line student-registration system mentioned at the beginning of this chapter. How might we apply these ideas to that kind of application?

First, we must decide on the abstract interface that we wish to use to handle the on-line part of the system. The idea here is to think about what *this* application needs from its window system(s), rather than to define a generic interface for all uses of a window system.

Once we know what operations we'll need, we have defined a set of requirements for whatever window system(s) we'll use in developing this application. Because no two window systems use the same operations to perform the same abstract actions, we'll probably also need to encapsulate the window system by providing a class that forwards window requests from our abstract interface to the operations provided by the windowing system. We will have one such inter-

face class per window system we support. Of course, this abstract interface can
be developed independently from the development of the registration system
and from the on-line library circulation system.

To maintain database independence, we should go through the same steps to
abstract our use of the database. First, we define the requirements that we need
from our database; then we provide classes that implement those requirements
for each database that we use.

Now, we can write our registration system as a template parameterized by
these window and database interfaces:

```
template <class W, class DB> class Registration {
public:
        // whatever operations we need to register students
};
```

Operations in class `Registration` that manipulate the window will use only
those window operations that are in our abstract window interface. Similarly for
uses of the database.

Finally our main function instantiates a `Registration` object for whatever
window and database system we're using:

```
int main()
{
        Registration<whizzy_window, dazzling_DB> r;
        // ...
}
```

As long as `whizzy_window` meets our specification for windowing systems and
`dazzling_DB` meets our database specification, everything works correctly.

17

Templates and generic algorithms

At the Kitchener, Ontario C++ standards meeting in July 1994, the committee voted to adopt a proposal by Alex Stepanov to include, as part of the standard C++ library, a collection of generic algorithms that he and his colleagues had developed at Hewlett-Packard Laboratories. Collectively, the classes and algorithms included in this library are known as the *Standard Template Library* (STL). These classes and algorithms are themselves a useful addition to the C++ library. More fundamentally, the STL provides a conceptual framework that makes it easy for users to add their own algorithms and data structures.

Rather than providing a reference manual for the STL, I want to concentrate on the underlying ideas. Those ideas are interesting, and can be used by C++ programmers independently of the library itself, so they are worth describing on their own merit.

A generic algorithm, in this context, is an algorithm expressed in a way that assumes as little as possible about the data structure on which it is acting. Of course, templates make a certain degree of genericity easy:

```
template<class T>
void sort(T* ptr, int size)
{
        // ...
}
```

is a typical way of writing a program—in this case presumably a sort function— that does not depend on the exact type of the values being sorted.

But there is much more to the idea of genericity than just writing functions that handle arguments of diverse types. For example, there exist sorting algorithms that work efficiently regardless of whether the elements to be sorted are stored in arrays or, say, doubly linked lists. Wouldn't it be nice if it were possible to write a *single* program that would express such an algorithm and yet would work on both data structures? Wouldn't it be even nicer if that algorithm worked efficiently? Alex's design does precisely that.

Of course this approach builds on earlier work. This library is at least the fourth such library Alex has developed, and the second in C++ (his earlier efforts were in Ada and Scheme). Its sources include the article on which Chapter 16 was based. In addition, I have seen generic libraries in Smalltalk, and ML, and probably in other languages that I've forgotten to mention. What makes Alex's approach particularly interesting, aside from the fact that it is in C++, is how cleanly it meshes with the built-in types. That means that people who wish to use programs written with the STL have to be aware of remarkably little extra stuff. Moreover, programs written this way can be as fast as are hand-coded algorithms designed for single types.

Because this chapter is not intended as a treatise on sorting algorithms, the examples that follow will be based on a much simpler problem. It is left to the reader to expand the approach to suit more complicated algorithms.

17.1 A specific example

Suppose that we want to find the first element of an array of integers that is equal to some given value. We might write something like this:

```
const int*
find1(const int* array, int n, int x)
{
        const int* p = array;
        for (int i = 0; i < n; i++) {
                if (*p == x)
                        return p;
                ++p;
        }
        return 0;
}
```

This is very nearly a C program: All that keeps it from being one is the declaration of the local variable i inside the for statement. We will call it find1 because there will be several revisions to come.

What must we know about the data structures that find1 uses?
- We are looking for some value of type int
- We are looking in an array of int objects
- We know in advance how many elements there are
- We know the address of the first element

All this required knowledge makes the algorithm less useful. In the examples that follow, we will generalize the algorithm by removing as many assumptions as possible.

17.2 Generalizing the element type

The obvious place to start is to remove the dependency on int. This will eliminate the first two of the requirements that the function places on its data types.
Of course, the way to do that is with a template:

```
template<class T>
T* find2(T* array, int n, const T& x)
{
        T* p = array;
        for (int i = 0; i < n; i++) {
                if (*p == x)
                        return p;
                ++p;
        }
        return 0;
}
```

Note first that the consts in find1 have disappeared, because if we call find2
with a pointer to const, then T will include const appropriately as part of its
type. There is therefore no need to cater to const explicitly as a special case.

Aside from that, and aside from using the template to remove the int dependency, the only other alteration is to change the formal parameter x from int to
const T&. This last change is partially for efficiency reasons: Although it's
cheap to copy an int, it might be expensive to copy an object of unknown type.
More important, we might not be allowed to copy T objects at all. Perhaps class
T has a private copy constructor. Our caller might be a friend or member of T,
and therefore might be allowed to copy T objects, but we might not be so privi-
leged. Dealing with this kind of detail quickly becomes second nature when
writing template libraries.

These small changes have already changed what we need to know about type
T. We still need to know how many elements to search, and we still need a
pointer to the first element. But now we can use find2 on any data structure
that supports operator==. More precisely, we need to know that, if t1 is of
type T and t2 is of type const T, then t1==t2 must be defined to yield a type
that can stand as the condition in an if statement. In particular, we do not need
to know whether t1==t2 involves a conversion, or whether it calls a member
function, or any other such details.

17.3 Postponing the count

In the next few examples, we will try to avoid having to know that the data are
stored in an array. Our ultimate goal will be to produce a function that can
search an array, or a linked list, or even a file. Producing such a function all at

once, however, would be hard to follow. We will therefore proceed one step at a time.

First, we will avoid having to know in advance how many elements there are. The main reason to eliminate this dependency is that with more general data structures, it might be expensive to compute the number of elements in advance. For some data structures it might even be impossible—consider, for example, using this function to look for a particular record in a file.

Instead of having it take a count, we can change our function to accept pointers to the first and last elements. Having read *C Traps and Pitfalls* (Addison-Wesley, 1989), however, we know the hazards of referring directly to "the last element" in a data structure. What if there aren't any elements at all? Then, there will be no last element. In such a case, the pointer to the "last element" would wind up having to point *before* the first element—a strange state of affairs, and one that might not even be legal in some implementations.

For these reasons, it is better to accept as an argument a pointer to *one element beyond* the last element. Our next version then looks like this:

```
template<class T>
T* find3(T* array, T* beyond, const T& x)
{
        T* p = array;
        while (p != beyond) {
                if (*p == x)
                        return p;
                ++p;
        }
        return 0;
}
```

The use of != instead of < to tell when the loop is done is no accident. In one sense, there is no difference between the two: If the input to find3 makes any sense, then p will be less than beyond until it becomes equal to it. However, types for which < imposes a total ordering can always be compared with !=. On the other hand, it is possible to imagine types, which we might later want to substitute for pointers, for which != is perfectly well defined, but < is not. In that sense, using < is a gratuitous assumption, and we will therefore avoid it.

Another assumption that we are making about pointers is that it is possible to convert 0 to a pointer value that is distinct from all others. Although this is an entirely legitimate assumption for pointer types, our desire for generality argues that we should stop making it in this program. We can avoid the assumption by changing slightly the behavior of the program: If the value sought is not found, we can return beyond instead of 0. If the reason for doing the search is that we want to replace the element that has the value we sought, this definition might even be more useful: We might be able to avoid a special check to see whether the element was found.

```
template<class T>
T* find4(T* array, T* beyond, const T& x)
{
        T* p = array;
        while (p != beyond) {
                if (*p == x)
                        return p;
                ++p;
        }
        return beyond;
}
```

Of course, properly rigorous software engineers may raise their eyebrows in disapproval. Change the specification once implementation has begun? Horrors! To them, we say that we are developing a prototype and are using the function itself as a design tool. We can always write the specification after we're done. That happens more often than people admit anyway.

This change also lets us simplify the code. We note that when we leave the loop, p==beyond, so we are always returning the value of p. Thus, we never need to return from the middle of the loop:

```
template<class T>
T* find5(T* array, T* beyond, const T& x)
{
        T* p = array;
        while (p != beyond && *p != x)
                ++p;
        return p;
}
```

17.4 Address independence

If we look at our program again, we see that we still rely on being passed a pointer to the beginning of the data to be searched. But if we look carefully, we see that we depend on only a few remaining properties of pointers:

- We can accept them as arguments and return them as results
- We can compare them for (in)equality
- We can dereference them to get a value: *p is a value
- We can increment them, thereby getting to the next element

And that's it! In particular, although the code declares variables of type T*, there is no reason why the variables should have to be (built-in) pointers, as long as they satisfy these few assumptions.

Suppose that we remove our dependence on pointers as such by making the type T* into a template parameter? Then, we have this:

```
template<class P, class T>
P find6(P start, P beyond, const T& x)
{
        while (start != beyond && *start != x)
                ++start;
        return start;
}
```

We have stripped our function completely of any knowledge of concrete types! In particular, there is no requirement that P be a (built-in) pointer type at all. P can be any type that meets the four properties outlined at the beginning of this section. Indeed, we could write the function this way:

```
template<class S, class T>
S find6a(S a, S b, const T& x)
{
        while (s != b && *s != x)
                ++s;
        return s;
}
```

This function is now so general that it would be a nice exam question to figure out what it does.

Still, from the user's viewpoint, we haven't changed much. The only changes are that find6 now takes a pair of pointers as arguments, instead of a pointer and a count, and it returns its second argument, instead of a null pointer. We can still use this function to search for elements of integer arrays, so that

```
int x[100];

// ...
int* p = find6(x, x + 100, n);
```

will place in p a pointer to the first element of x that is equal to n, or x + 100 if no such element exists. What is different is that find6 makes no assumptions about its arguments beyond those that are absolutely necessary for the algorithm to work. It has become generic, in the sense that it can be applied to much more than searching in arrays.

17.5 Searching a nonarray

Suppose that we have a naive implementation of a singly linked list that contains elements of class String:

```
struct Node {
        String value;
        Node* next;
};
```

This data structure is not particularly abstract, but it will serve for illustration purposes. In practice, we would hope to have a library available with a list class already in it.

Suppose further that we want to find whether one of these lists contains a particular value. Then, a naive approach would be:

```
Node* listfind(Node* p, const String& x)
{
        while (p && *p != x)
                p = p->next;
        return p;
}
```

This function looks remarkably like find6. That should not be surprising, as it solves the same problem; the only difference is that it uses a different data structure. Because find6 is generic, though, it should be possible to use it directly, instead of reinventing the algorithm. Indeed, by defining an auxiliary class, we can do just that. All we need to do is to make * and ++ work appropriately, and to define a bit of other scaffolding:

```
class Nodep {
public:
        Nodep(Node* p): pt(p) { }
        String& operator*() { return pt->value; }
        void operator++() { pt = pt->next; }
        friend int operator==(const Nodep&, const Nodep&);
        friend int operator!=(const Nodep&, const Nodep&);
        operator Node*() { return pt; }
private:
        Node* pt;
};

int operator==(const Nodep& p, const Nodep& q)
{
        return p.pt == q.pt;
}

int operator!=(const Nodep& p, const Nodep& q)
{
        return p.pt != q.pt;
}
```

Now we do not need to define a separate listfind operation at all. We can use the existing find6 function on Nodeps directly. Given that p is a pointer to some Node and x is some String, we can write

```
find6(Nodep(p), Nodep(0), x);
```

Of course, if we already have users of listfind, we can redefine it in terms of Nodep and find6:

```
Node* listfind(Node* p, const String& x)
{
        return find6(Nodep(p), Nodep(0), x);
}
```

The only unusual thing that we did here was to make the `Nodep` class return a `String&` when "dereferenced," instead of returning a `Node&`. This is consistent with the notion that a `Nodep` "points" to the value contained somewhere within the data structure.

17.6 Discussion

As we have shown it, this example doesn't seem to be worth the trouble. After all, it was much more work to define `Nodep` than it was to write `listfind` in the first place. Why bother?

One reason is that `Nodep` needs to be written only once—namely, for the `Node` structure. Then, we can use `Nodep` not only for the `find` algorithm, but also for whatever other algorithms we might invent. In effect, the `Nodep` structure makes it possible for us to adapt whatever generic algorithms we have to the particular linked-list structure we're using. This is true *even if the author of the generic algorithms has never seen the list structure*. In other words, if we have m data structures and n algorithms, then we may well be able to apply each of those algorithms to each of those data structures with only $O(m+n)$ effort rather than $O(m{\times}n)$ effort. A substantial gain indeed!

Another reason is that we deliberately chose both the `Node` class and the `find` function to keep the presentation simple. As we saw in Chapters 12 through 14, container classes like a list class would, in practice, include semantics much richer than those in this simple `Node` class. In particular, any realistic list class would have a companion iterator class. A large part of the contribution of the STL is its intellectual framework for building classes and their iterators. Classes that use this framework can immediately use any of the generic algorithms supplied with the STL. New algorithms written in terms of the STL framework can operate on any classes that provide the appropriate iterators.

It's worth noting that, because we took care to model container behavior accurately, many existing container classes either already provide iterators that match this framework or can be made to do so easily. For example, not surprisingly, the `Array` and `Pointer` classes that we developed in Chapters 12 through 14 can be used as is with the `find6` function. After all, that function started out to search an array, and those classes were designed to provide arraylike behavior. More interesting, the lightweight list class developed in Chapter 15 also works with `find6`. The initial version of that class had used `next`, rather than `operator++`, to advance through the container and provided only the `hd` function; we added the `operator*` synonym. But with those simple additions, these *existing* classes can be readily used with the STL algorithms.

Of course, we have glossed over many details. For example, if we have a library of algorithms, those algorithms are not all going to have the same assumptions about the types on which they act. Our `find` function does not require the ability to back up in the input, but other algorithms might well have such a requirement. Algorithms that produce complicated data structures as output have still other requirements. For example, we must know when a value is known, so that we can be write it into a file (assuming that the data structure does describe a file). A good deal of the work Alex and his colleagues have done on this library deals with details like this. We will look at some of these details in Chapter 18.

18

Generic iterators

In Chapter 17,* we discussed a series of examples that led up to the following:

```
template<class P, class T>
P find(P start, P beyond, const T& x)
{
        while (start != beyond && *start != x)
                ++start;
        return start;
}
```

Chapters 16 and 17 explored how we can use templates to write functions that allow us to vary the data structures on which the function operates, as well as the argument types. Thus, in this example, by defining an appropriate class to use as P, we can use the same find function to search an array, a linked list, a file, or any of a number of other data structures.

There is one other thing, however, that we might vary—namely the algorithm being used. When we do that, we find that the particular algorithm that we are using determines the behavior that we expect from our template parameters. Thus, the find example makes assumptions about type P that are different from those that other algorithms might make.

To explore this relationship between iterator types and algorithms, we will look at a few other algorithms, and will see the behavior that they impose on their corresponding template parameter types.

18.1 A different algorithm

The example that we've been using so far is a linear search. What if, instead, we wrote a function to reverse the elements of a sequence? Such a function might look like this:

---

* We called the function find6 because it was the sixth version that we presented; the function presented here is identical aside from the name change.

213

```
// first try—not quite right
template<class P, class T>
void reverse(P start, P beyond)
{
        while (start < beyond) {
                T t = *start;
                --beyond;
                *start = *beyond;
                *beyond = t;
                ++start;
        }
}
```

This function is only slightly more complicated than find. Using it is straightforward too; for example, if x is an array with n elements, then calling

```
reverse(x, x+n);
```

will reverse those elements. As we did with find, we adopt the convention that
the arguments represent the first element in the sequence to be reversed and
"one past" the last element.

Despite its apparent simplicity, this function reveals several new questions
about generic algorithms that must be answered before we can build useful generic libraries. By far the most important observation is that reverse requires
operations that find did not. If type P does indeed represent some kind of
built-in pointer type, that is no problem, but if P represents a user-defined type,
then the user who defined it might have to meet additional requirements.

The find function requires only that, if p is of type P, then ++p,
p != beyond, and *p be appropriately defined. The reverse function also
requires a definition for p < beyond and --p, and insists that *p be an lvalue.

These differences between find and reverse are important, because they
affect the kind of data structures to which we can apply reverse. For example,
because reverse changes the value of *p, reverse requires that the data structures passed to it allow modification of their elements. This limitation should
come as no surprise. What may come as a surprise is the requirement for
p < beyond.

There is an important difference between the ability to tell whether two values are equal and the ability to tell which one comes first. Consider, for example,
what happens if the things to be reversed are stored in some kind of linked list.
Then, it will generally be fast to tell if two elements are the same, even though it
might be hard to determine which one comes first. Similarly, the ability to evaluate --p as well as ++p seems to rule out singly linked lists and similar data structures.

If we want to reverse a data structure in place, it is hard to see how we can do
so without requiring the ability to change the value of *p. What about the other
requirements? It turns out to be fairly easy to replace the p < beyond requirement with one for p != beyond, as follows:

```
template<class P, class T>
void reverse2(P start, P beyond)
{
        while (start != beyond) {
                --beyond;
                if (start != beyond) {
                        T t = *start;
                        *start = *beyond;
                        *beyond = t;
                        ++start;
                }
        }
}
```

We have replaced one order test by two (in)equality tests. Because one of these tests always follows every change to start or beyond, there is no possibility that start and beyond will somehow pass each other without ever having been equal—assuming, of course, that the input wasn't garbage to begin with. It may seem inefficient to do two tests instead of one, but the test is likely to be cheap compared with the cost of interchanging elements. Moreover, careful examination of the initial version of reverse will reveal that, if it is reversing a data structure with an odd number of elements, it will exchange the element in the middle with itself. In other words, although the double test isn't free, it doesn't cost much, and it might potentially allow the algorithm to be used with a wider range of data structures.

What about the requirement that we be able to decrement values of type P? That can be bypassed also, albeit at a considerable cost. One way is to allocate an auxiliary array of T, copy the data into the array, then copy them back in reverse order. Another is to allocate an auxiliary P array. There are recursive techniques as well. All these techniques, however, require auxiliary storage proportional to the size of the data structure being reversed, so having the decrement operation available saves a lot of time and space.

18.2 Categories of requirements

We have seen two different algorithms, find and reverse, that logically impose different requirements on the classes that they use. Someone who designs a data structure to be used with find will have to solve a problem that is different from the one faced by the designer of a data structure to be used with reverse. If we have 50 different algorithms, will we have to have 50 sets of requirements? That would be intolerable.

Yet it seems that we can't get by with just one set of requirements. If we want to be able to reverse the elements of a sequence, we effectively have to be able to visit them in reverse order. But the requirement to support operator-- will be too restrictive if we want to be able to find a particular record in a sequential file that can't be read backwards. Therefore, we can't use the same requirements for both purposes.

These remarks imply that we must somehow classify our requirements—we must find a single set of requirements, which fits each of a collection of algorithms reasonably well, a second set that fits another collection, and so on. If we're lucky (or careful), we'll have few enough sets of requirements that we can remember them, while still being able to use a wide variety of algorithms.

18.3 Input iterators

The find function imposes what seem to be the simplest requirements that still make it possible to do anything useful. If an object p is to behave at all like a pointer into a sequence, then it must be possible to use p to fetch an element of the sequence, to make p point at the next element of the sequence, and to see whether we've reached the last element that we wish to use. That gives us the requirements that *p, ++p, and p!=q must work appropriately.

To avoid violating the principle of least surprise, we must add two other operations: p++ and p==q. After all, it seems unreasonable to expect the author of an algorithm to remember which of two usually equivalent forms is right and which is wrong. Finally, of course, we must make it possible to copy p.

A type that meets these requirements lets us read (but not write) the elements of a sequence in a single, prescribed order. For that reason, we call such a type (or sometimes an object of that type) an *input iterator*.

It is important to remember that an input iterator is neither a specific type nor an object. Instead, it is a concept that refers to any member of a whole set of types: the types that meet these specific requirements. The simplest example of an input iterator type is a pointer type such as int*, when such a pointer points to an element of an array. Not surprisingly, the class Pointer, developed in Chapters 13 and 14, which was designed to act like a built-in pointer, also qualifies as an input iterator. More interesting, so does class Seq, our lightweight container class and iterator all rolled into one, which we built in Chapter 15.

18.4 Output iterators

If we can read a sequence, we should also be able to write one. That is, there should be output iterator types that behave analogously to input iterators.

What must an output iterator do? Evidently, the only difference between input and output iterators lies in the behavior of *p. If p is an input iterator, then *p is a value that we can read, but that we are not necessarily allowed to modify. If p is an output iterator, then we should be allowed to modify *p, but not necessarily to read it. After all, the storage that p addresses before modification might contain a garbage value that cannot be copied legitimately.

Using input and output iterators, we can write a generic copy function:

```
template <class In, class Out>
void copy(In start, In beyond, Out result)
{
        while (start != beyond) {
                *result = *start;
                ++result;
                ++start;
        }
}
```

Of course, most experienced C or C++ programmers will want to condense the function:

```
template <class In, class Out>
void copy(In start, In beyond, Out result)
{
        while (start != beyond)
                *result++ = *start++;
}
```

Thus, we must be certain that our requirements include giving the normal meaning to the postfix operators: If p is an input or output iterator, the value of p++ should be the old value of p.

18.5 Forward iterators

So far, we have iterators that allow us to read or write the elements of a sequence. What about one that allows both? For example, consider an algorithm that marches through the elements of a sequence, modifying each element in some way, but never visits an element again after it has touched that element. That operation calls for an iterator that combines the operations of input and output iterators and does no more. We call it a *forward iterator*; we might use one this way:

```
template<class Iter, class Function>
void apply(Iter start, Iter beyond, Function f)
{
        while (start != beyond) {
                *start = f(*start);
                ++start;
        }
}
```

Here, we use `*start` both to read and to write. It is clear that neither an input iterator nor an output iterator would do the trick, but a forward iterator is exactly right.

Type `Function` is interesting too: It can be any type whose objects can be made to behave as though they were functions. Objects of such types are called *function objects*. Essentially, a function object encapsulates a function and any values that should be passed to that function. In the case of `apply`, the function object `f` is assumed to provide an overloaded function-call operator, `operator()`, that takes a single argument of the type returned by `operator*`. Therefore, the call

```
f(*start)
```

normally will involve passing `*start` to the function encapsulated by `f`.

Chapters 21, 22, and 29 explore function objects in detail.

18.6 Bidirectional iterators

Let's look again at our `reverse` function. Evidently, not even a forward iterator is good enough there, because `reverse` expects to be able to apply `operator--` to its arguments. Suppose that we add the requirement for `operator--` to one of our sets of existing iterator requirements. Which set should it be? What does it do for us?

A little reflection should convince us that the only sensible requirements to use as a basis are those for forward iterators. Being able to back up in a data structure already rules out things such as printers and keyboards, so restricting reading or writing provides little gain. Moreover, building on top of forward iterators means that we need only one kind of additional iterator, instead of two.

A *bidirectional iterator*, then, is like a forward iterator, except that it supports `operator--` in addition to its other operations. It is evident that the `reverse` function needs a bidirectional iterator.

18.7 Random-access iterators

Suppose that `p` points to the initial element (that is, element number 0) of a sequence, and we want to get to the next element. That's easy: execute `++p`. What if we want element number 1000? Then, the problem becomes more interesting: Must we execute `++p` 1000 times, or is there a more efficient way?

If `p` were a pointer to an array element, there would be no problem: We would say `p += 1000` and be done with it. However, `p` might be a class that behaves like a pointer to an element of a linked list, in which case it is impossible to implement p += 1000 except by executing ++p 1000 times. It usually does no service to users to give them an easy, convenient way of doing something slowly. For that reason, the iterators that we have seen so far do not support +, or –, or their variants +=, –=, or [ ].

On the other hand, some algorithms absolutely need to be able to get at arbitrary elements of a data structure efficiently. Consider, for example, a binary search:

```
template <class P, class X>
P binsearch(P start, P beyond, X x)
{
        P low = start, high = beyond;

        while (low != high) {
                P mid = low + (high - low) / 2;
                if (x == *mid)
                        return mid;
                if (x < *mid)
                        hi = mid;
                else
                        low = mid + 1;
        }

        return beyond;
}
```

The key to the binary-search algorithm is the ability to compute a pointer to the middle element of a sequence. Here, that computation is done by

```
P mid = low + (high - low) / 2;
```

If that computation requires stepping through the elements of the sequence, the whole point of having a binary search is lost.*

To allow binary searches and other inherently random-access algorithms, we must add another kind of iterator. A *random-access iterator* adds +, –, +=, –=, and [ ] to the bidirectional iterator operations, with the meanings that one would expect.

Both built-in pointers and Pointers (Chapters 13 and 14) are random-access iterators.

---

* To test your understanding, explain why
   P mid = (low + high) / 2;
wouldn't work. Then, try rewriting binsearch so that it uses only operator< on container elements, not operator==.

18.8 Inheritance?

We have defined five categories of iterators. Input and output iterators have several operations in common, but neither can substitute for the other. A forward iterator can always serve as an input or an output iterator. Similarly, a bidirectional iterator can act as a forward iterator, an input iterator, or an output iterator, and a random-access iterator can act as any of the others. Shouldn't we be using inheritance to relate them?

People often ask that question, and are surprised to hear that the answer is no. Inheritance is a way of relating types, but iterator categories aren't types. Rather, they're collections of requirements that types might or might not meet. How, then, could inheritance relate them?

Suppose, for example, that we wanted to say that forward iterators inherit the properties of input and output iterators. What would that claim mean? Evidently it would add more requirements: A forward iterator would have to be a class, rather than a built-in type, and would have to have a particular base class. We would lose the ability to use pointers as iterators. Moreover, these additional requirements wouldn't gain anything: The algorithms we've seen certainly don't need them, and neither do the ones in the STL.

So what we have here isn't really inheritance, even though it looks a little like it. Perhaps we should call it *conceptual inheritance*. Neither it nor the iterator requirements are part of the C++ language or the library; instead, they are part of the conceptual framework that makes the library possible.

18.9 Performance

We use random-access iterators to allow operations that work efficiently on certain data structures but not on others. We would not bother with them if we did not care about efficiency in general, but efficiency is one of the reasons that people use C++. C++ users are likely to appreciate efficiency guarantees in their libraries. For example, we would be surprised to see a bidirectional iterator implemented to require $O(n)$ time to go from element n to element $n-1$ of a sequence.

In fact, the STL accepted by the standards committee imposes on iterators stronger performance requirements than that: For each operation that a particular kind of iterator is required to support, that operation must be fast—its amortized execution time must be $O(1)$. This requirement makes it possible to make performance claims about all the algorithms in the library. For example, it allows the claim that applying `reverse` to an n-element sequence requires $O(n)$ amortized time.

18.10 Summary

A generic algorithm is one that incorporates as little knowledge as possible of the details of the data structures on which it acts. The ideal, of course, would be to require no knowledge at all, but life isn't like that. As a compromise, the STL categorizes data structures according to the operations that they support efficiently. Then, for each algorithm, it says what categories that algorithm requires.

What is categorized is neither the algorithms nor data structures directly, but rather the types used to access the data structures. Objects of these types are called iterators. Iterator types fall into five categories: input, output, forward, bidirectional, and random access. Conceptual inheritance relates the categories; it is conceptual because the categories are themselves concepts, rather than types or objects.

The effect of the whole structure is to make it easy to know which algorithms will work with which data structures. Moreover, that structure provides a framework that others can use to contribute algorithms that might not be part of the library itself.

19

Using generic iterators

In Chapter 18, we explored a classification scheme for iterators that let us build iterators that provided operations needed by various kinds of algorithms. In this chapter, we'll concentrate on a single small program and demonstrate how we can make that program do dramatically different things by giving it different types of iterators to use. Our program copies sequential data structures:

```
template<class In, class Out>
Out copy(In start, In end, Out dest)
{
        while (start != end)
                *dest++ = *start++;
        return dest;
}
```

This function copies the sequence delimited by the iterator values `start` and `end` into a sequence beginning at the position indicated by the iterator `dest`. In addition to copying the data, it returns as its result an iterator that indicates the first place in the sequence beginning at `dest` that was *not* used for output. That information is potentially useful, and might be hard to compute were it not returned as a result.

We can see how this function works by giving it some (built-in) pointers:

```
int main()
{
        char* hello = "Hello ";
        char* world = "world";
        char message[15];
        char* p = message;

        p = copy(hello, hello+6, p);
        p = copy(world, world+5, p);
        *p = '\0';

        cout << message << endl;
}
```

Here, the first call to `copy` copies `Hello` (followed by a space) to the first six character positions of `message`, the second call to `copy` copies `world` to the next five characters of `message`, and `p` winds up pointing to the character immediately following the `d` of `world`. The assignment to `*p` puts a null character after the `d`, to follow the normal C convention of using null characters to terminate strings. Finally, we print the message on `cout`.

19.1 Iterator types

Our program uses the template parameter types `In` and `Out` as input iterator (Section 18.3 (page 216)) and output iterator (Section 18.4 (page 216)) types, respectively. Saying that a type is an input or output iterator implies that it supports comparison for equality (both `==` and `!=`) and the `++` increment operator (both prefix and postfix). It must also be possible to copy and assign input and output iterator objects, so that they can be passed as function arguments, returned as results, stored in data structures, and so on.

Where input and output iterators differ from each other is in how one accesses the data that those iterators represent. Both kinds of iterators are required to support indirection via the unary `*` operator, but an input iterator is required only to yield a value whereas an output iterator is required only to allow a value to be assigned to it. Thus, for example, if `in` is an input iterator and `out` is an output iterator, then

        *out = *in;

must work as expected but

        *in = *out;

need not.

There is one additional restriction on using output iterators: Each location represented by an output iterator must have a value assigned to it once and once only. Similarly, input iterators have the restriction that after an iterator has been incremented past a particular input value, that value must not be accessed again. We will see why these restrictions exist shortly.

19.2 Virtual sequences

Clearly, the type `int*` can serve as both an input and an output iterator when a value of that type points to an element of an array. Let's see whether we can create other types that also can serve as such iterators.

Suppose, for example, that we wanted to create an input iterator that would appear to be reading a sequence of identical constant values. Such an iterator might be useful, for example, for setting the elements of an array to a particular value:

```
int x[100];
Constant_iterator c(0);

copy(c, c+100, x);
```

Here, we are using c as a "pointer" into an "array" of 100 values, all of which are 0. Indeed, we shall see that c can behave as a "pointer" into an "array" of unbounded size; we must merely add some integer to c to obtain an appropriate upper bound.

Here is a declaration of class Constant_iterator that behaves appropriately:

```
class Constant_iterator {
public:
        Constant_iterator(int=0);
        int operator*() const;
        Constant_iterator& operator++();
        Constant_iterator operator++(int);

private:
        int n;
        int count;
        friend int operator==(const Constant_iterator&,
                              const Constant_iterator&);
        friend int operator!=(const Constant_iterator&,
                              const Constant_iterator&);
        friend Constant_iterator operator+
                (const Constant_iterator&, int);
        friend Constant_iterator operator+
                (int, const Constant_iterator&);
};
```

Aside from the copy constructor and assignment operator, which we get by default, these are all the operations we need. The idea is that the member count will keep track of how many values have been produced so that the comparison operators can tell when we've reached the end of the "sequence." The following member-function definitions will do the trick:

```
Constant_iterator::Constant_iterator(int k): n(k) { }

int Constant_iterator::operator*() const { return n; }
```

As expected, the constructor remembers what value the iterator generates, and the dereference operator returns that value.

The increment operators increment the count of how many values we've iterated through. As usual, we maintain consistency with the built-in pre- and postfix conventions and return a reference to the iterator itself.

```
Constant_iterator& Constant_iterator::operator++()
{
        ++count;
        return *this;
}

Constant_iterator Constant_iterator::operator++(int)
{
        Constant_iterator r = *this;
        ++count;
        return r;
}
```

Now we must tend to the nonmembers. The idea here is that applying + to a Constant_iterator and an int will add the int to the count to produce a new Constant_iterator, which can act as a sentinel.

```
Constant_iterator
operator+(const Constant_iterator& p, int n)
{
        Constant_iterator r = p;
        r.count += n;
        return r;
}

Constant_iterator
operator+(int n, const Constant_iterator& p)
{
        return p + n;
}
```

Two iterators will be equal if and only if they have generated the same number of values and the values themselves are the same.

```
int operator==(const Constant_iterator& p,
               const Constant_iterator& q)
{
        return p.count == q.count && p.n == q.n;
}

int operator!=(const Constant_iterator& p,
               const Constant_iterator& q)
{
        return !(p == q);
}
```

If you follow through these definitions, you will see that our previous example

```
int x[100];
Constant_iterator c(0);

copy(c, c+100, x);
```

will indeed set the elements of x to zero.

Thus we've created an iterator that pretends to represent an array of identical values that aren't really there. It is, of course, a trivial matter to arrange for these imaginary values to differ from one another. For example, we could create an arithmetic sequence iterator, which represents a sequence of steadily increasing or decreasing values, such as $1, 3, 5, 7, \ldots$. The constructor for such an iterator would take the starting point and the distance between values as arguments. Another useful exercise is to use templates to generalize this example to work with types other than `int`.

19.3 An output-stream iterator

Now that we've defined an input iterator that can create values, let's make an output iterator that can print them. We will say such an object is of class `ostream_iterator`.

How might this class work? We can imagine giving an `ostream` as a constructor argument, after which "storing" into it would cause the value "stored" to be written on the `ostream`. That is, if `out` is an iterator of this type

```
ostream_iterator<int> out(cout);
```

then

```
*out++ = x;
```

should print x on `cout`. Looking a little deeper, though, reveals a subtle problem. Consider printing a sequence of values. The obvious way to do this with an `ostream_iterator` is:

```
for (int i = 0; i < 10; i++)
        *out++ = i;
```

But, this is equivalent to

```
for (int i = 0; i < 10; i++)
        cout << i;
```

which prints

```
0123456789
```

This output probably isn't what we intended.

More generally, when we want to write a sequence of values directly to an `ostream`, we'll also want to put something between adjacent values. Therefore, we will design our `ostream_iterator` class to take *two* constructor arguments: an `ostream` and a `const char*` that represents a string to write after each value written. Thus, for example, we would like

```
ostream_iterator<int> out(cout, "\n");

*out++ = 42;
```

to print 42 followed by a newline.

If we want to use `ostream_iterator` as an output iterator we need to implement the rest of the operations that will make it an output iterator. We'll need increment, dereference and assignment, as well as the comparison operators.

Here is where we exploit the earlier requirement that the user must dereference and assign through each particular value of an output iterator type only once. If `out` is an output iterator, we will want

```
*out = x;
```

to print x without waiting for the user to increment `out`. If assignment to `out` is what triggers the output, then there is no real work left for the increment operators to do. We can therefore implement `out++` and `++out` as null operations. Now, how shall we define `*out`? We know that `*out` must be an object of some class whose assignment operator prints its right-hand-side operand; beyond this requirement, `*out` can be of any type. In fact, we already have a useful type available to us: We can use the `ostream_iterator` class itself for this purpose, effectively making `*out` and `out` equivalent!

With that trick, we can define `ostream_iterator` this way:

```
template<class T>
class ostream_iterator {
public:
        ostream_iterator(ostream& os, const char* s):
                strm(&os), str(s) { }

        ostream_iterator& operator++() { return *this; }
        ostream_iterator& operator++(int) { return *this; }
        ostream_iterator& operator*() const { return *this; }
        ostream_iterator& operator=(const T& t)
        {
                *strm << t << str;
                return *this;
        }

private:
        ostream* strm;
        const char* str;
};
```

Because we don't need `==` or `!=` for `ostream_iterator` to work with our `copy` program, we'll leave the definitions of `==` and `!=` as an exercise.

With these definitions of `ostream_iterator` and `Constant_iterator`, we can use `copy` to print 42 to the standard output 10 times, each time on a separate line, as follows:

```
int main()
{
        ostream_iterator<int> oi(cout, "\n");
        Constant_iterator c(42);

        copy(c, c+10, oi);
}
```

19.4 An input-stream iterator

We've seen that, by defining appropriate iterators, we can use copy to write a generated sequence of values to an ostream. Now, let's create an input iterator that reads values from some istream, so that we can use copy to read a stream and write to some other stream.

As so often happens, input is harder than output. The difficulty in this case comes from several sources:

- It is rarely necessary to compare output iterators. For example, we could use ostream_iterators in copy even though we hadn't implemented comparison. For input iterators, however, we need comparison so that we can determine when we have reached end of file.

- It is not possible to tell whether we have reached end of file without first trying to read something. Reading a value consumes it, however, so we do not want to read until we absolutely have to do so.

These two constraints together force us to adopt a lazy-evaluation strategy. Each istream_iterator object will hold a one-element buffer, and a flag that indicates whether the buffer is full. In addition, each istream_iterator will have a second flag that says whether end of file has been reached. Because we've determined the structure of our class, let's begin with that:

```
template<class T>
class istream_iterator {
private:
        T buffer;
        istream* strm;
        int full;
        int eof;
        // ...
};
```

The structure gives us enough that we can next write down the constructors. In doing so, we must answer one question: Should it ever be possible for full and eof both to be true at once? There are arguments for both answers, but it seems easier to say that full is true if and only if buffer holds a useful value. That's all we need to know in order to write our constructors:

```
template<class T>
class istream_iterator {
public:
        istream_iterator(istream& is):
                strm(&is), full(0), eof(0) { }

        istream_iterator():
                strm(0), full(0), eof(1) { }
        //...
};
```

Now we can look at the operations that `istream_iterator` must support. Recall that to allow class `istream_iterator` to act as an input iterator, we'll need the assignment, dereference, increment, and equality operators.

Assignment is easy: We don't need to define it; we can use the default.

When we define the increment operators, we must ensure that once we increment the iterator past a value, we won't attempt to read that value again. We do that by manipulating `full`:

```
template<class T>
class istream_iterator {
public:
        istream_iterator& operator++()
        {
                full = 0;
                return *this;
        }

        istream_iterator operator++(int)
        {
                istream_iterator r = *this;
                full = 0;
                return r;
        }
        //...
};
```

While looking at the dereference and equality operators, we should think a bit about our strategy for actually reading data from the `istream`. We said that we'd adopt a lazy-evaluation strategy, in that we'd read values only when forced. Dereferencing clearly forces us to read the stream. More interesting, so do the equality operators!

To see this, we need to understand what it means for two `input_iterators` to be equal. We will adopt a restricted definition of equality, for the purpose of this discussion: Two `istream_iterators` will be equal only if they are the same object, or if both of them are at end of file. We can get away with this definition, because in practice, the only use for such comparisons will be to see whether we have reached the end of the file. Note, that even with this restricted definition, it may be necessary for comparison on an `istream_iterator` to fill the buffer—as usual, we have to read ahead to determine whether the stream is

at end of file. This means that the comparison operators will have to take an
`istream_iterator&`, instead of a `const istream_iterator&` as one might
expect. Similarly, our lazy-evaluation strategy implies that `operator*` might
modify its object as well. Evidently a `const istream_iterator` object won't
be good for much.

So, now we know that we'll need to read into `buffer` in several places,
which suggests a private function to do so. Our lazy-evaluation strategy first
checks if input is needed, and, if so, reads data and sets the status appropriately:

```
template<class T> class istream_iterator {
private:
        void fill() {
                if (!full && !eof) {
                        if (*strm >> buffer)
                                full = 1;
                        else
                                eof = 1;
                }
        }
        // ...
}
```

Given this function, `operator*` becomes a simple matter:

```
template<class T> class istream_iterator {
public:
        T operator*() {
                fill();
                assert(full);
                return buffer;
        }
        // ...
};
```

The `assert` is here to trap attempts to find out the value referred to by an
`istream_iterator` after it has reached end of file.

All that's left are the comparison operators. They too are straightforward—
provided that we adopt the earlier, deliberately incomplete, strategy that two
`istream_iterators` are equal only if they are the same object or both are at
end of file.

```
template<class T>
int operator==(istream_iterator<T>& p, istream_iterator<T>& q)
{
        if (p.eof && q.eof)
                return 1;
        if (!p.eof && !q.eof)
                return &p == &q;
        p.fill(); q.fill();
        return p.eof == q.eof;
}
```

```
template<class T>
int operator!=(istream_iterator<T>& p, istream_iterator<T>& q)
{
        return !(p == q);
}
```

With these definitions of `istream_iterator` and `ostream_iterator`, it is indeed possible to use our `copy` function to copy values from an input file to an output file:

```
int main()
{
        ostream_iterator<int> output(cout, "\n");
        istream_iterator<int> input(cin);
        istream_iterator<int> eof;

        copy(input, eof, output);
}
```

19.5 Discussion

When using something that looks like a pointer, it is tempting to imagine that it can be nothing more than a mere pointer. However, looking carefully at the pointer operations that a particular algorithm uses may reveal that it is possible to simulate pointers for other data structures.

Not all of these data structures need to exist. Thus, for example, our `Constant_iterator` class makes it possible to pretend that we have an infinite sequence of values through which we can iterate. More interesting, the `istream_iterator` and `ostream_iterator` classes make it possible to treat files as if they were sequences of values.

The `istream_iterator` and `ostream_iterator` classes are part of the standard template library. The `Constant_iterator` class is not, which is why I spelled it with an uppercase C. The interested reader may enjoy inventing other kinds of iterators that traverse imaginary data structures.

20

Iterator adaptors

Chapters 17 through 19 talked about iterators and related concepts in the Standard Template Library (STL). Here, we continue that discussion with the idea of *iterator adaptors*—templates that take iterators as parameters and convert them to other iterators. We'll see that by transforming iterators, we can extend the range of programs that can be used with the underlying iterator. This notion can be tricky to understand, so we will lead up to it a step at a time in the context of a few key examples.

20.1 An example

Chapter 17 developed the following generic function:

```
template<class T, class X>
T find(T start, T beyond, const X& x)
{
        while (start != beyond && *start != x)
                ++start;
        return start;
}
```

This function does a linear search in a (more or less) arbitrary data structure, which is characterized only by the types of the template parameters `start` and `beyond`. We use `start` and `beyond` as input iterators. That is, we require that they support only those operations that are necessary to read the contents of the data structure that we are searching.

Ordinary pointers can act as input iterators. Thus, for example, if we have declared

```
int x[100];
```

and we want to find the first place 42 appears in x, we can say

```
int* p = find(x, x+100, 42);
```

after which p will either point to the first element of x that is equal to 42, or will be equal to x+100 if no element of x is 42.

Suppose that instead of finding the first instance of some particular value, we wanted to find the last instance. How can we do that?

We want to write a function that will find the last element equal to x in a sequential data structure characterized by a pair of input iterators called start and beyond. Clearly that function is easy to implement if we find the element we seek. What if it isn't there? Then, we must return some value that refers to none of the elements of the data structure; the only such value that we have available is beyond. Evidently, both forward and reverse searching must return the same value on failure; this requirement breaks what would otherwise be complete symmetry.

Once we've decided what to do, we can do it. The straightforward way is to keep searching until we reach the end:

```
template<class T, class X>
T find_last(T start, T beyond, const X& x)
{
        T result = beyond;
        while (start != beyond) {
                if (*start == x)
                        result = start;
                ++start;
        }
        return result;
}
```

Indeed, if all we can assume about T is that it is an input iterator, we have little choice about how to implement find_last. But this strategy has a serious dis-advantage: It always looks at all the elements of the data structure that it is searching, even if the value being sought is at the very end of that structure.

If, instead of input iterators, we have bidirectional iterators, that opens up new possibilities. Now we do not need to rely only on ++; we can use -- as well. That means that we can scan the data structure starting from the end and moving toward the beginning:

```
template<class T, class X>
T rfind(T start, T beyond, const X& x)
{
        if (start != beyond) {
                T p = beyond;
                do {
                        if (*--p == x)
                                return p;
                } while (p != start);
        }
        return beyond;
}
```

Why is this function so much more complicated than the original `find`? The fundamental reason is that the value returned when x is not found is less natural than it is when searching forward.

In the original `find`, we could use `start != beyond` as our loop termination, destroying the initial value of `start`, secure in the knowledge that, regardless of whether or not x was found, `start` would be pointing at the right place. In `rfind`, we do not have that luxury. Instead, we must save the value of `beyond` so that we can return it later if x is not found. Moreover, we must make a special test for an empty array, because if the array is empty, there is no guarantee that we will be able to compute the value of `--start` successfully.

20.2 Directional asymmetry

We have seen an important point in algorithm construction: It is not always possible to preserve symmetry exactly when we are reversing the direction of an algorithm. In the case of `rfind`, the asymmetry stems from a characteristic of iterators that, in turn, comes from the C language definition: Although iterators generally guarantee that there is an off-the-end value available, there is no comparable guarantee for any off-the-beginning value.

To illustrate this more directly, consider a simple loop that sets the elements of a 10-element array a to 0:

```
int a[10];
for (int i = 0; i < 10; i++)
        a[i] = 0;
```

At the end of this loop, i will be 10—which value, of course, causes no particular problem. If we want to zero the elements of a in reverse order, there is still no problem:

```
for (int i = 9; i >= 0; i--)
        a[i] = 0;
```

At the end of this loop, i will be -1—which is certainly a plausible value for i to have.

If, however, we change this loop to use pointers instead of subscripts, we begin to see the source of the asymmetry:

```
for (int* p = a; p < a+10; p++)
        *p = 0;
```

At the end of this loop, p will be equal to a+10, which is the address of an "element" of a that does not exist. This program works only because the C and C++ languages guarantee the ability to form the address of what would be the element that is one past the end of any array. In other words, a+10 is legal but a+11 is not—and neither is a-1.

That means that if we want to rewrite the backward loop to use pointers, we must be careful never to form the address of a-1. In particular, we cannot write

```
// this does not work
for (int* p = a+9; p >= a; p--)
          *p = 0;
```

This fails because the loop will terminate only when we reach a state where p < a, and there is no assurance that such a thing can ever happen. Evidently, we must contrive to use p > a as our comparison instead and assign to *p *after* we have decremented p:

```
// this works
int* p = a+10;
while (p > a)
          *--p = 0;
```

This way we guarantee that p never takes on a prohibited value.

20.3 Consistency and asymmetry

We have learned so far that we can search data structures both forward and backward, but with a catch: The value returned in case of failure must always be the off-the-end value. This restriction can be a nuisance, especially if we use find or rfind to search portions of sequential structures.

For example, it is common to look for an element with a particular value in a data structure, and then to append one with that value if none is found. It is convenient that find returns a pointer to the place to put the element if the value was not already in the structure. The rfind function is not similarly considerate: If the value sought is not found, it returns a pointer that, although it is an off-the-end pointer in a strict sense, must really be treated as an off-the-beginning pointer, because we are searching backward. This puts us at exactly the wrong end of the data structure for appending a new value. Is there anything we can do about this?

At first glance, one would think not. An *n*-element data structure makes available only *n*+1 distinct iterator values: those referring to the *n* elements, and the off-the-end value. But what if we offset everything by 1? What if, instead of using the iterator values directly, we pretend that each iterator points to the spot in the data structure immediately *after* the element that we were seeking?

Then, we would use the off-the-end value to point at the last element of the structure, a pointer to the last element to refer to the next-to-last element, and so on. We would thus free up the pointer to the first element to use as an off-the-beginning value.

This is easier to demonstrate than to describe. The following function, called rnfind (for *reverse neighbor find*) searches a sequential data structure from end to beginning, and returns an iterator that points to the element *after* (one element closer to the end than) the one sought. If the value is not found, it returns an iterator that refers to the first element (that is, one past the nonexistent off-the-beginning element):

```
template<class T, class X>
T rnfind(T start, T beyond, const X& x)
{
        while (beyond != start && beyond[-1] != x)
                --beyond;
        return beyond;
}
```

Of course, this function cheats a bit by using `beyond[-1]`, as a way of abbreviating `*(beyond-1)`, because `beyond` happens to point one element past the one that `rnfind` needs to compare with `x`. Doing so, instead of using `--x`, means that `T` must be a random-access iterator and not just a bidirectional iterator. Of course, we can rewrite `beyond[-1]` in terms of `--`, but that would obscure the important point: `rnfind` looks much more like `find` than any of the previous reverse find functions.

It is the neighbor technique that has allowed `rnfind` to look that way. Indeed, it appears that, in general, we can reverse the direction of sequential algorithms if we swap starting and ending values, swap `++` and `--`, and adopt the convention that iterators point to the element after the one that we really want.

20.4 Automatic reversal

The argument so far has involved a lot of hand waving. It is time to make it more precise. Suppose that type `T` is a bidirectional iterator. Then, we can imagine creating a new type—called, say, `TR` (for `T` *reversed*)—that behaves just like `T`, but goes in the opposite direction.

Our neighbor convention says that converting a `T` to a `TR` must result in something that appears to point to the element before (or is it after? —we'll see) the one to which `T` pointed. Also, the senses of `++` and `--` must be exchanged, and the usual copy, assignment, comparison, and dereferencing must work too.

Can we do all that as a template? Well, almost. Dereferencing causes the one significant problem. For example, suppose that we said

```
template<class T> class Rev<T>
{
        // ...
        ??? operator*();
};
```

We would not know what type to return from `operator*`. That implies that we need an extra template parameter for the type of the objects that the iterator yields, as well as the usual parameter for the type of the iterator. After that observation, we can declare the template:

```
template<class It, class T> class Rev {
        friend bool operator==
                (const Rev<It, T>, const Rev<It, T>);
        friend bool operator!=
                (const Rev<It, T>, const Rev<It, T>);
public:
        Rev();
        Rev(It i);
        operator It();
        Rev<It, T>& operator++();
        Rev<It, T>& operator--();
        Rev<It, T> operator++(int);
        Rev<It, T> operator--(int);
        T& operator*();
};
```

Nothing here is particularly difficult. We declare exactly the operations that we need for a bidirectional iterator: construction, dereferencing, (in)equality, and prefix and postfix increment and decrement. We do not explicitly declare destruction, copying, and assignment, because we anticipate that the corresponding operations on our iterator type will handle those correctly.

Implementation also is straightforward. The only point to remember is that dereferencing must look at the element immediately before the one at which our private data member points. The following implementation includes that data member, as well as definitions for all the operations:

```
template<class It, class T> class Rev {

        friend bool operator==
                (const Rev<It, T>&, const Rev<It, T>&);
        friend bool operator!=
                (const Rev<It, T>&, const Rev<It, T>&);

public:
        Rev() { }
        Rev(It i): it(i) { }
        operator It() { return it; }

        // here is where we reverse the sense of the argument iterator
        Rev<It, T>& operator++() { --it; return *this; }
        Rev<It, T>& operator--() { ++it; return *this; }

        Rev<It, T> operator++(int) {
                Rev<It, T> r = *this;
                --it;
                return r;
        }
```

```
Rev<It, T> operator--(int) {
        Rev<It, T> r = *this;
        ++it;
        return r;
}

T& operator*() {
        It i = it;
        --i;
        return *i;
}
```

private:
```
        It it;
};
template<class It, class T>
bool operator==(const Rev<It, T>& x, const Rev<It, T>& y)
{
        return x.it == y.it;
}
template<class It, class T>
bool operator!=(const Rev<It, T>& x, const Rev<It, T>& y)
{
        return x.it != y.it;
}
```

The neighbor rule appears as part of operator*:

```
T& operator*() {
        It i = it;
        --i;
        return *i;
}
```

How can we convince ourselves that --i and not ++i, is correct here? We note first that variable i, of type It, is the original iterator type. Its value might refer to any element in the (original) structure, or might be an off-the-end value. If we wrote ++i, there would be no way to get at the first element of the structure because there would be no value to which we could apply ++ and make the result refer to that first element. As written, on the other hand, --i translates the off-the-end value into a pointer to the last element of the original structure, so it must be right.

Now that we have the iterator adaptor, we can use it to transform a bidirectional iterator from one that iterates forward into one that iterates backward through the iterator's associated container. This let's us use the same find function to look for some value starting at the beginning or at the end:

```
typedef Rev<int*, int> R;

int* p = find(x, x+100, 42);
R r = find(R(x+100), R(x), 42);
```

Here we have introduced R as a convenience; we could also have written

```
Rev<int*, int> r =
        find(Rev<int*, int>(x+100),
            Rev<int*, int>(x), 42);
```

After this, p points to the first place 42 occurs in x and r "points" to the last place.

20.5 Discussion

What we have achieved is the ability to use a single algorithm to search a data structure forward and backward, subject only to the availability of a bidirectional iterator type that describes that data structure. In effect, we have written a template that does interface matching: We have one interface, we need a different one, and so we make what we have into what we want.

This particular task is a little more complicated than we might have thought at first. This is because of the asymmetrical nature of C arrays: We are guaranteed an off-the-end value, but not an off-the-beginning one. It is tempting to argue that C++ should allow off-the-beginning values as well, but that would not solve the problem, because this whole technique is intended to work with arbitrary data structures and not just with arrays. Insisting on off-the beginning values would therefore require implementors of all kinds of data structures to complicate them to take into account the off-the-beginning convention. Instead, we solve the problem once in the reverse-iterator adaptor and then don't worry about it any more.

STL has a template called `reverse_bidirectional_iterator` that is a slightly more general version of the `Rev` template that we developed in this chapter. In addition, if you have a random-access iterator, instead of just a bidirectional iterator, you can use `reverse_iterator`. It requires full random-access-iterator semantics from its argument, in return for which it presents random-access-iterator semantics to its user.

Iterator adaptors obviously have applications beyond just reversing the direction of an iterator. For example, we could create a bounds-checking adaptor. Given an iterator type, it might yield another iterator type that has the ability to confine iterator values to be within a pair of bounds given when creating an object of that type. Used carefully, iterator adaptors can greatly reduce the number of variations of an algorithm one must write, or increase what one can accomplish with a fixed amount of effort.

21

Function objects

In addition to iterators and adaptors, the STL offers a concept called *function objects*. Function objects, like adaptors, are a tricky concept; simply put, function objects provide a way to bundle together a function to call and implicit arguments to pass to that function. This allows us to build up complicated expressions using surprisingly simple syntax.

A function object represents an action. By combining function objects, we can obtain compound actions. We obtain compound actions in ordinary programs by writing loops and conditionals, calling functions, and combining statements into blocks. Such combinations, however, are cast in stone during compilation. Function objects allow us to combine actions as part of running a program. This combination comes from the ability to treat functions as values, with all the flexibility that that implies.

Because function objects are so flexible that they make unfamiliar things possible, they can be hard to understand at first. Thus, we'll start with an example of how we might use such objects, and then we will explore how they work.

21.1 An example

The standard library contains a function called `find_if` whose arguments are a pair of iterators and a *predicate*—a function that yields a truth value. The `find_if` function returns the first iterator value, in the range bounded by the pair, for which the predicate is true. Suppose, for example, that we have an object v of type `vector<int>`, and we wish to find the first element of v that is greater than 1000. We can do that by constructing a predicate function—called, say, `greater1000`—which tests whether its argument is greater than 1000:

```
bool greater1000(int n)
{
        return n > 1000;
}
```

We can then use this function as the third argument to `find_if`, so

```
find_if(v.begin(), v.end(), greater1000)
```

either returns an iterator that points to the first element in `v` that is greater than `1000`, or returns `v.end()` if there is no such element.

Function objects and function-object adaptors let us write an expression that achieves the same effect as `greater1000`, without actually defining a function. We'll eliminate the need for `greater1000` step by step in the rest of this section.

We begin by noting that the library includes a template class called `greater`. Objects of class `greater` act as predicates that take two arguments and determine whether the first is greater than the second. We can use that class to rewrite `greater1000`:

```
bool greater1000(int n)
{
        greater<int> gt;
        return gt(n, 1000);
}
```

Here, we create a function object called `gt`, of type `greater<int>`, which compares two integers, and we use it to see whether `n > 1000`.

The next step is where it gets interesting. The library has a function adaptor, called `bind2nd`, that, given a function object `f` that takes two arguments, and a value `v`, creates a new function object `g` such that `g(x)` has the same value as `f(x, v)`. The name `bind2nd` comes from the fact that this adaptor binds the value `v` to the second argument of `f`.

Applying `bind2nd` to our function object `gt` and to the value `1000`, by calling

```
bind2nd(gt, 1000)
```

gives us a new function object that will check whether its argument is greater than `1000`. Thus, for example,

```
(bind2nd(gt, 1000)) (500)
```

is `false`, and

```
(bind2nd(gt, 1000)) (1500)
```

is `true`.

We can use `bind2nd` to rewrite `greater1000` yet again:

```
bool greater1000(n)
{
        greater<int> gt;
        return (bind2nd(gt, 1000)) (n);
}
```

Next, we can get rid of the local variable gt, which is used only once, by remembering that the expression greater<int>() yields an anonymous object of type greater<int>. We can therefore create such an object, instead of using a local variable:

```
bool greater1000(n)
{
        return (bind2nd(greater<int>(), 1000)) (n);
}
```

At this point, we've reduced greater1000 applied to argument n as meaning a "call" of the expression

```
bind2nd(greater<int>(), 1000)
```

with argument n. That, in turn, means that the expression

```
bind2nd(greater<int>(), 1000)
```

is equivalent, for our purposes, to the predicate greater1000, and so we can (finally) eliminate the predicate altogether and call find_if this way:

```
find_if(v.begin(), v.end(),
        bind2nd(greater<int>(), 1000))
```

This may seem like a lot of complexity with little gain. However, suppose that we make our example slightly more realistic and search for the first value in v that is greater than x. It should be obvious that

```
find_if(v.begin(), v.end(),
        bind2nd(greater<int>(), x))
```

will do the trick. What may be less obvious is that the greater1000 technique doesn't work here.

The reason is that the value 1000 was built into the definition of greater1000. We will have a problem if we try to write a more general version of greater1000:

```
bool greater_x(int n)
{
        return n > x;
}
```

Where is the value of x set? We cannot pass x as a second argument, because find_if expects its predicate to take only a single argument. Apparently, then, we must make x into a global variable. Ouch!

Among the problems solved by function-object adaptors, then, is that of passing information from the program that uses a function object (here, the call to find_if) through another part of the program that doesn't know about that information (here, the body of find_if itself) to a third part that can retrieve it (here, the predicate expression involving bind2nd).

This kind of information hiding is subtle; this chapter and Chapter 22 are among the most difficult in the book and will repay close study. This chapter explores what a function object is; Chapter 22 will examine several of the function objects defined in the STL.

The ideas in these two chapters will help you understand Chapter 29. Based on an early paper in which I first broached some of these ideas, Chapter 29 looks at ways of using function objects to simplify syntax in the context of manipulations on streams.

21.2 Function pointers

In some programming languages, functions are first-class values. In such languages, it is possible to pass functions as arguments, to return them as values, to use them as components in expressions, and so on.

C++ is not quite one of those languages, although why not is not immediately obvious. After all, it is common for C++ programs to pass functions as arguments, and to store their addresses in data structures. Suppose, for example, that we want to apply a given function to all the elements of an array. If we know that the function takes an int argument and yields void, we can write something like this:

```
void apply(void f(int), int* p, int n)
{
        for (int i = 0; i < n; i++)
                f(p[i]);
}
```

Doesn't this show that C++ treats functions as first-class values?

The first subtlety in this example is that, despite appearances, f is not a function at all. Rather, it is a function pointer. As in C, it is not possible in C++ to have a variable of function type, so any attempt to declare such a variable is immediately converted into a declaration of a pointer to a function. Also as in C, an attempt to call a function pointer is equivalent to a call of the function to which that pointer points. So, the preceding example is equivalent to

```
void apply(void (*fp)(int), int* p, int n)
{
        for (int i = 0; i < n; i++)
                (*fp)(p[i]);
}
```

So what? What is the big difference between functions and function pointers? The difference is similar to the difference between any pointer and the object to which it points: It is not possible to create such objects merely by manipulating pointers. The total store of C++ functions is fixed before program execution begins. There is no way to create new functions once the program has started to run.* To see why the inability to create new functions dynamically is a problem, consider how one might write a C++ function to compose two functions, yielding a third function. Composition is one of the simplest ways imaginable to create a new function. To keep things simple for the moment, we will assume that each of our functions takes an integer argument and returns an integer result. Suppose, then, that we have a pair of functions f and g:

```
extern int f(int);
extern int g(int);
```

We want to be able to say something like:

```
int (*h)() = compose(f, g);
```

with the property that, for any integer n, h(n) (which you will recall is equivalent to (*h)(n)) will be equal to f(g(n)).

C++ offers no direct way to do that. We might imagine doing something like this.

```
// this does not work
int (*compose(int f(int), int g(int)))(int x)
{
        int result(int n) { return f(g(n)); }
        return result;
}
```

Here, compose is an attempt to define a function that takes two functions f and g, and yields a function that, when applied to x, yields f(g(x)); but this fails for two reasons. The first is that C++ does not support nested functions, which means that the definition of result is illegal. Moreover, there is no easy way of working around that restriction, because result needs access to f and g from the surrounding scope. Thus, we cannot simply make result global:

```
// this also does not work
int result(int n) { return f(g(n)); }

int (*compose(int f(int), int g(int)))(int x)
{
        return result;
}
```

The trouble with this example is that f and g are undefined in result.

---

* Of course, individual implementations may choose to modify this restriction, perhaps by offering some form of dynamically linked library. This does not apply to the language proper, though, and does not affect the discussion that follows.

The second problem is more subtle. Suppose that C++ did allow nested functions—after all, there are some C++ implementations that do so as an extension. Wouldn't that do the trick?

The answer, unfortunately, is "not really." To see why, let us rewrite our `compose` function a tiny bit:

```
//  this does not work either
int (*compose(int f(int), int g(int)))(int x)
{
        int (*fp)(int) = f;
        int (*gp)(int) = g;

        int result(int n) { return fp(gp(n)); }
        return result;
}
```

The change here has been to copy the addresses of f and g into two local variables fp and gp. Now, suppose that we call `compose` and it returns a pointer to `result`. Because fp and gp are local variables of `compose`, they will go away as soon as `compose` returns. If we now call `result`, it will try to use those local variables, even though they have already been deleted. The result probably will be a crash.

Why this program fails should be fairly easy to see from inspecting the last version of `compose` above. However, exactly the same problem exists in the first version. The only difference is that in the first version, instead of being ordinary local variables, f and g are were formal parameters. This difference doesn't matter: They still go away when `compose` returns; which means that when `result` tries to access them, disaster ensues.

Apparently, then, writing our `compose` function requires some kind of automatic memory management, beyond the usual stack-based implementations. Indeed, languages that treat functions as first-class values also usually support garbage collection. Although it would be nice in many ways for C++ to have garbage collection as a standard part of the language, there are enough difficulties involved that C++ isn't defined that way. Is there any way to circumvent this restriction, and to treat functions as values in a more general way?

21.3 Function objects

The difficulty is that our `compose` function tries to create new functions, and C++ does not allow that directly. Whenever we are faced with such a problem, we should think about using a class object to express the solution. If `compose` cannot return a function, then perhaps it can return a class object that acts like a function.

Such objects are called *function objects*. Typically, a function object is an object of some class type that includes an operator() member function. Having that member function lets us use the class object as though it were a function. So, for example, if we write

```
class F {
public:
        int operator() (int);
        // ...
};
```

then objects of class F will behave somewhat like functions that take integer arguments and return integer results. For example, in

```
int main()
{
        F f;
        int n = f(42);
}
```

the call of f(42) is equivalent to f.operator()(42). That is, f(42) takes the object f and calls its operator() member with argument 42.

We can use this technique as the basis for a class that we can use to compose functions:

```
class Intcomp {
public:
        Intcomp(int (*f0)(int), int (*g0)(int)):
                fp(f0), gp(g0) { }

        int operator() (int n) const {
                return (*fp)((*gp)(n));
        }

private:
        int (*fp)(int);
        int (*gp)(int);
};
```

Here, the constructor arranges to remember the function pointers f0 and g0, and the operator()(int) does the composition. First, operator() passes its int argument, n, to the function pointed to by gp, and then it passes the result returned by gp to fp. So, if we have our functions f and g as before, we can use an Intcomp to compose them:

```
extern int f(int);
extern int g(int);

int main()
{
        Intcomp fg(f, g);
        fg(42);                       // equivalent to f(g(42))
}
```

This technique solves the composition problem, at least in principle, because every `Intcomp` object has a place to store the identities of the functions being composed. However, it is still not a practical solution because it can compose only functions, and cannot compose function objects. Thus, for example, we cannot use an `Intcomp` to compose an `Intcomp` with anything. In other words, although we can use our `Intcomp` class to compose two functions, we cannot use it to compose more than two. What can we do about this?

21.4 Function-object templates

We would like to be able to create a class whose objects we can use to compose not only functions, but also function objects. The usual way in C++ of defining such a class is to use a template, which we shall call `Comp`. Template class `Comp` will have template parameters that include the types of the two things being composed. Looking ahead, we will also give `Comp` two more type parameters. When we call a `Comp` object, we will give it a value of one type, and it will return a value of another type. We will therefore make those two types into additional type parameters of the `Comp` template. That way, we will not be stuck dealing with only functions that return `int`:

```
template<class F, class G, class X, class Y> class Comp {
public:
        Comp(F f0, G g0): f(f0), g(g0) { }
        Y operator()(X x) const {
                return f(g(x));
        }
private:
        F f;
        G g;
};
```

The idea here is that an object of type `Comp<F, G, X, Y>` is capable of composing a function (or function object) of type `F` with another of type `G` to yield an object that takes an argument of type `X` and yields a result of type `Y`. Aside from that, the details are almost the same as the `Intcomp` class. We can use our `Comp` class to compose the integer functions `f` and `g` from before:

```
int main()
{
        Comp<int (*)(int), int (*)(int), int, int> fg(f, g);

        fg(42);              // calls f(g(42))
}
```

This works, after a fashion, but the need to specify the function type `int(*)(int)` twice is far from elegant. Indeed, if we wanted to compose, say, fg and f, the full type of fg would have to appear as the first template parameter. This would make the type truly awesome:

```
Comp<Comp<int (*)(int), int (*)(int), int, int>,
        int, int> fgf(fg, f);
```

Is there any way to simplify this enough to make it useful?

21.5 Hiding intermediate types

Let's think for a moment about where we are trying to go. At this point, we have a way of composing two functions or function objects, but the type of the function object that represents the composition is too complicated. Ideally, we would like to be able to write something like

```
Composition fg(f, g);          //  too optimistic
```

but that is too much to hope for. The reason is that later on, when we try to evaluate fg(42), the compiler won't know what type that expression should have. Whatever the type of fg(42) is, it must be implicit in the type of fg, and similarly for the argument type that fg expects. The best we can hope for, therefore, is something like

```
Composition<int, int> fg(f, g);
```

where the first int is the type of the argument that the function object fg expects, and the second one is the type of the result it will return when called. Given that definition, it is not hard to write at least part of the class definition:

```
template<class X, class Y> class Composition {
public:
        // ...
        Y operator() (X) const;
        // ...
};
```

But how do we implement it? For that matter, what does the constructor look like?

The constructor poses an interesting problem, because the Composition constructor must be capable of accepting any combination of functions and function objects—particularly Compositions. That suggests that the constructor must itself be a template,* so as to cater to all these possibilities:

---

* The standards committee approved this facility in 1994, which means that not all compilers will support it yet.

```
template<class X, class Y> class Composition {
public:
        template<class F, class G> Composition(F, G);
        Y operator() (X) const;
        // ...
};
```

But this just begs the question. Types F and G are not part of the type of class Composition, because they are not template parameters there. Yet presumably class Composition is going to work by storing an object of class Comp<F, G, X, Y>. How can it do that without making F or G a template parameter to class Comp itself? Fortunately, C++ has a mechanism for that, namely inheritance.

21.6 One type covers many

Suppose that we rewrite our class Comp such that Comp<F, G, X, Y> is derived from some other class that does not depend on F or G. We might call that class Comp_base<X, Y>. Then, in our class Composition, we will be able to store a pointer to Comp_base<X, Y>.

It is probably easiest to unravel this tangle from the inside out, by beginning with Comp_base. Conceptually, a Comp_base<X, Y> object will be something that will represent an arbitrary function object that takes an X argument and gives a Y result. We will therefore give it a virtual operator(), because the operator() in all classes derived from Comp_base<X, Y> will take an argument of the same type (namely, X) and will return a result of the same type (namely, Y). Because we do not want to define operator() specifically for a plain Comp_base, we will make it a pure virtual. Moreover, because inheritance is involved, Comp_base will need a virtual destructor.

Looking ahead again, we see that we will want to be able to copy Composition objects. Copying a Composition object will involve copying an object of some Comp type without necessarily knowing the exact type. So we will need a virtual function in Comp_base to make a copy of the derived class object.

Given all this, we have the following base class:

```
template<class X, class Y> class Comp_base {
public:
        virtual Y operator()(X) const = 0;
        virtual Comp_base* clone() const = 0;
        virtual ~Comp_base() { }
};
```

Now, we will rewrite class Comp to use Comp_base as a base class, and we'll add an appropriate clone function to Comp that will override the pure virtual in Comp_base:

```
template<class F, class G, class X, class Y>
                class Comp: public Comp_base<X, Y> {
public:
        Comp(F f0, G g0): f(f0), g(g0) { }

        Y operator()(X x) const { return f(g(x)); }
        Comp_base<X, Y>* clone() const {
                return new Comp(*this);
        }
private:
        F f;
        G g;
};
```

Now, we can make our `Composition` class contain a pointer to a `Comp_base`:

```
template<class X, class Y> class Composition {
public:
        template<class F, class G> Composition(F, G);
        Y operator() (X) const;

private:
        Comp_base<X, Y>* p;
        // ...
};
```

Whenever a class gains a member of pointer type, we should think about what to do with the pointer when we copy an object of that class. In this case, we want to copy the underlying object, making class `Composition` into a surrogate as discussed in Chapter 5—after all, that is why we put a `clone` function into class `Comp_base` in the first place. Thus, we must write an explicit copy constructor and destructor in class `Composition`:

```
template<class X, class Y> class Composition {
public:
        template<class F, class G> Composition(F, G);
        Composition(const Composition&);
        Composition& operator=(const Composition&);
        ~Composition();
        Y operator() (X) const;

private:
        Comp_base<X, Y>* p;
};
```

21.7 Implementation

At this point, implementing class `Composition` should be fairly straightforward. When constructing a `Composition<X, Y>` with a pair of objects of types F and G, we will create a `Comp<F, G, X, Y>` object, and will store its address in the pointer p. The following slightly weird syntax is the way to define a template member of a template class. For each variation of Composition<X, Y>, it defines the constructor Composition<F, G>, the full name of which is therefore

```
Composition<X, Y>::Composition<F, G>(F, G)
```

We define it as follows:

```
template<class X, class Y>
        template<class F, class G>
                Composition<X, Y>::Composition(F f, G g):
                        p(new Comp<F, G, X, Y> (f, g)) { }
```

This constructor initializes the member p, which has type Comp_base<X, Y>*, with a pointer to Comp<F, G, X, Y>. This initialization works because class Comp<F, G, X, Y> is derived from class Comp_base<X, Y>.

The destructor just deletes the object to which p points:

```
template<class X, class Y>
Composition<X, Y>::~Composition()
{
        delete p;
}
```

The copy constructor and assignment operator take advantage of the virtual clone function in class Comp_base:

```
template<class X, class Y>
Composition::Composition(const Composition& c):
        p(c.p->clone()) { }

template<class X, class Y>
Composition& operator=(const Composition& c)
{
        if (this != &c) {
                delete p;
                p = c.clone();
        }
        return *this;
}
```

Finally, operator() uses the virtual operator() in class Comp_base:

```
template<class X, class Y>
Y Composition::operator() (X x) const
{
        return (*p)(x);      // p->operator()(x)
}
```

At this point, we have our wish: We can say

```
extern int f(int);
extern int g(int);
extern int h(int);

int main()
{
        Composition<int, int> fg(f, g);
        Composition<int, int> fgh(fg, h);
}
```

and have `fg` and `fgh` be the same type, even though they do different things internally.

21.8 Discussion

One way of looking at this example is that it shows how much work we must do to get around a seemingly simple language restriction. Another viewpoint is that the example shows that extending the language to allow function composition is not quite as simple as it appears at first. Moreover, if we do the work of defining these function objects once, we can use them again later. Once we understand the concepts, we can use them in ways more straightforward than is shown in this convoluted example.

For example, there is a standard library function called `transform` that applies a function or function object to every element in a sequence, possibly yielding a new sequence. If `a` is an array with 100 elements, then

```
transform(a, a+100, a, f);
```

will apply `f` to each element of `a` in turn, and will store the result back into the same element of `a`.

Suppose that we want to use `transform` to add an integer `n` to every element of our array? Then, we could define a function object that adds an integer:

```
class Add_an_integer {
public:
        Add_an_integer(int n0): n(n0) { }
        operator() const (int x) { return x+n; }
private:
        int n;
};
```

We'd then call

```
transform(a, a+100, a, Add_an_integer(n));
```

But it is a nuisance to define a separate function-object class for this purpose.*

---

* To test your understanding, explain why we had to use a function object here instead of a function.

Indeed, it is possible to do even better. The library offers templates, called function adaptors, that we can use in combination to define classes such as `Add_an_integer` without actually having to write class definitions. The ideas on which these templates are based are the subject of Chapter 22.

22

Function adaptors

Chapter 21 described a function called `transform`, that is part of the standard library, and that applies a function or function object to every element in a sequence, possibly yielding a new sequence. So, for example, if `a` is an array with 100 elements, and `f` is a function, then

```
transform(a, a+100, a, f);
```

will apply `f` to each element of `a`, and will store the result back into that same element of `a`.

Chapter 21 also gave an example of how we can use `transform` to define a function object that adds an integer n to every element of our array:

```
class Add_an_integer {
public:
        Add_an_integer(int n0): n(n0) { }
        int operator() const (int x) { return x + n; }
private:
        int n;
};
```

We can use one of those function objects as an argument to `transform`:

```
transform(a, a+100, a, Add_an_integer(n));
```

Defining a class for this purpose is a bit of a nuisance, so the library provides classes and functions that simplify the job. The rest of this chapter will explain a few of them.

22.1 Why function objects?

Recall first that `Add_an_integer` is a function-object type rather than a function type because with function objects, we can combine a function and a value into a single entity. We could have used a function instead, had we been willing to put n temporarily into a variable with file scope:

```
static int n;
static int add_n(int x) { return x + n; }
```

After this, we would have been able to set n to the appropriate value, and to call

```
transform(a, a+100, a, add_n);
```

Having to use file-scope variables in this way is a nuisance, though, so we use function objects instead.

The nice thing about function objects is that they are objects, which means that in principle, we can do everything with them that we can do with any other kind of object. Indeed, the standard library gives us everything we need to obtain the same effect as Add_an_integer without having to define any auxiliary functions or objects at all. To add n to each element of a sequence, we merely need to write

```
transform(a, a+100, a, bind1st(plus<int>(), n));
```

It is probably not obvious at first glance, but the subexpression

```
bind1st(plus<int>(), n)
```

uses the library to create a function object with the same essential properties as

```
Add_an_integer(n)
```

that can then be used as the last argument of transform.

How does that subexpression work?

22.2 Function objects for built-in operators

To understand the expression

```
bind1st(plus<int>(), n)
```

we shall start with the subexpression

```
plus<int>()
```

Here, plus names a type, not a function, so plus<int>() is an expression that evaluates to a nameless object of type plus<int>. Such objects are function objects that, when given two values of type int, add them and yield their sum as result. So, for example, if we say

```
plus<int> p;
int k = p(3, 7);
```

then we have initialized k to the value 10. Similarly, we could say

```
int k = (plus<int>()) (3, 7);
```

which also gives k the value 10.

In addition to the `operator()` member that makes it a function object, class `plus<int>` has three other members that are the names of types. These three type members are `first_argument_type`, `second_argument_type`, and `result_type`; their meanings should be obvious from their names. So, for example, `plus<int>::first_argument_type` is an elaborate name for `int`. We shall see later why having access to these types is useful.

The standard library includes function objects for most of the built-in operators. The reason for their existence should be evident: In an expression like

```
bind1st(plus<int>(), n)
```

there is no way in C++ to name the built-in + operator directly.

22.3 Binders

We have seen how the library lets us create a function object that adds two values; now we need to be able to create a function object that remembers a value and adds that value to its (single) argument. Two library template functions called `bind1st` and `bind2nd` make that easier.

If `f` is a function object that, like `plus`, has an `operator()` that takes two arguments, and if `x` is a value that can stand as the first argument to `f`, then

```
bind1st(f, x)
```

is an expression that yields a function object that takes *one* argument, with the interesting property that

```
(bind1st(f, x)) (y)
```

has the same value as

```
f(x, y)
```

The name `bind1st` is intended to suggest a function that creates a function object that binds the first argument of a function. That is, the function object that results from a call to `bind1st` remembers some value, and supplies that value as the first argument to the user-supplied function that it calls.

The definition of `bind1st` implies that

```
(bind1st(plus<int>(), n)) (y)
```

is equal to y+n, which is what we wanted. But how does it work?

The easiest way to understand an expression like this is to take it apart and look at the pieces. To do that, we would like to be able to write

```
//  p is a function object that adds two integers
plus<int> p;
```

```
//  b is a function object that adds its argument to n
some_type b = bind1st(p, n);
```

```
//  initialize z to n + y
int z = b(y);
```

but what is the type of b?

The answer turns out to require another library-template type called binder1st, which takes as its template parameter the type of the first argument to bind1st (the function or function object that will be called). That is, to declare b above, we should write

```
//  p is a function object that adds two integers
plus<int> p;
```

```
//  b is a function object that adds its argument to n
binder1st< plus<int> > b = bind1st(p, n);
```

```
//  initialize z to n + y
int z = b(y);
```

Now it is easier to see what is happening: As before, p is a function object that adds together two numbers; b is a function object that binds the first of those numbers to the value of n, and z is therefore y+n.

22.4 A closer look

Suppose that we set out to write a declaration for binder1st. At first it is easy. We know that binder1st is a function object, so it will need an operator():

```
template<class T> class binder1st {
public:
        T1 operator() (T2);
        // ...
};
```

Here is our first problem: What are the right types for T1 and T2?

When we call bind1st with arguments f and x, we want to get a function object that can be called with the second argument of f (the one that is not bound) and return a result that is the same type of the result of f. But how do we figure out what those types are? We tried that with function composition in Chapter 21 and saw how hard it was.

Fortunately, our task is greatly simplified by the convention, mentioned in Section 22.2 (page 256), that the relevant function objects have type members whose names are first_argument_type, second_argument_type, and result_type. If we require that binder1st be used exclusively with classes that follow that convention, we can easily fill in the types for operator() and, for that matter, the constructor:

```
template<class T> class binder1st {
public:
        binder1st(const T&, const T::first_argument_type&);
        T::result_type operator()
                (const T::second_argument_type&);
        // ...
};
```

Taking advantage of the same convention, we can also write down the declaration for bind1st:

```
template<class F, class T>
        binder1st<F> bind1st(const F&, const T&);
```

We'll leave the definitions of bind1st and binder1st as exercises.

22.5 Interface inheritance

Template class plus is one of a family of function-object classes, each of which defines members first_argument_type, second_argument_type, and result_type. Whenever we have a family of classes with particular members in common, it is worth thinking about putting those members in a base class. The C++ library does exactly that. In fact, plus has a base class called binary_function, defined as follows:

```
template<class A1, class A2, class R>
class binary_function {
public:
        typedef A1 first_argument_type;
        typedef A2 second_argument_type;
        typedef R result_type;
};
```

This makes it much more convenient to define the other functions objects. For example, we can define plus this way:

```
template<class T> class plus:
    public binary_function<T, T, T> {
public:
        T operator() (const T& x, const T& y) const {
                return x + y;
        }
};
```

In addition to containing class binary_function, the standard library has a unary_function base-class template defined this way:

```
template<class A, class R> class unary_function {
public:
        typedef A argument_type;
        typedef R result_type;
};
```

This class is used, for example, as the base class for `negate`—a class whose objects apply unary - to a value:

```
template<class T> class negate:
    public unary_function<T, T> {
public:
        T operator()(const T& x) const {
                return -x;
        }
};
```

There are many more such functions; the full details can be found in any book on the STL or on the forthcoming C++ standard library.

22.6 Using these classes

Suppose that `c` is some kind of standard-library container, and `x` is a value that might be in the container. Then,

```
find(c.begin(), c.end(), x);
```

yields an iterator that refers to the first element of `c` that is equal to `x`, or refers to 1 past the end of the container if no element is equal to `x`. We can use function adaptors to obtain the same result in a slightly more elaborate way:

```
find_if(c.begin(), c.end(),
    bind1st(equal_to<c::value_type>(), x));
```

In addition to using `bind1st`, this example uses the convention that all library containers have a member called `value_type` that denotes the type of an element of the container.

Similarly, we can look for an element that is greater than `x`:

```
find_if(c.begin(), c.end(),
    bind2nd(greater<c::value_type>(), x));
```

Here, we use `bind2nd`, because for each element `e`, we want to know whether `e>x`, rather than the other way around.

Suppose that `v` and `w` are containers, each holding the same number of elements. Then, we can add every element of `w` to the corresponding element of `v` by saying

```
transform(v.begin(), v.end(), w.begin(),
    v.begin(), plus<v::value_type>());
```

Here, we use the form of transform that has five arguments. The first two are iterators that delimit a range; the third is the beginning of a second range that is assumed to be the same size as the first. This version of transform takes elements in turn from each range, and uses those elements as the two arguments of whatever appears as the fifth argument to transform, placing each result in a sequence beginning wherever the fourth transform argument points. The fifth argument to transform in this example is a function object that adds two values of type v::value_type and yields a result of the same type.

More generally, there is nothing about this example that restricts it to numbers: As long as v and w are containers of types that allow +, it will apply + to each pair of elements appropriately.

The library includes function adaptors that can make function objects out of ordinary functions. As our last example, if we have an array of character pointers, such as

```
char* p[N];
```

then we can find every pointer that points at a null-terminated string containing the value "C" and can replace it by a pointer to the string "C++" as follows:

```
replace_if(p, p+N,
        not1(bind2nd(ptr_fun(strcmp), "C")), "C++");
```

This example uses the library function replace_if. Its first two arguments delimit a range, the third argument is a predicate that decides whether or not to replace a container element, and the fourth is a value to use for the replacement.

The predicate itself involves three function adaptors: not1, bind2nd, and ptr_fun. The adaptor ptr_fun creates a function object that is appropriate to hand to strcmp. bind2nd uses that object to create another function object that will compare its argument with "C". The call to not1 negates the sense of the predicate, which is necessary to accommodate the facts that strcmp returns 0 if its arguments are equal, and that 0 is ordinarily interpreted as false.

22.7 Discussion

Isn't this style of programming hard to understand? Why would anyone program this way?

One reason is that ease of understanding is often closely coupled to familiarity. Most people learning C or C++ encounter something like this at some point:

```
while ((*p++ = *q++) != 0)
    ;
```

The first few encounters with this kind of code can be puzzling, but soon enough, the compactness of the notation makes it possible to form mental chunks, and to understand the program at that level rather than in terms of its individual operations.

Moreover, these programs usually are no slower than their more conventional counterparts. In principle, they can be substantially faster: Because these function adaptors are part of the standard library, the compiler can recognize them and generate especially efficient code where appropriate.

This style of programming makes it possible to work with entire containers at once, instead of explicitly writing loops to deal with individual elements. That makes the programs smaller, more reliable, and, with familiarity, even easier to understand.

Part IV

Libraries

C++ is extensible. Users can't change the underlying language itself—they can't add new operators or change the syntax—but they can add new types to the language. In this way, C++ is similar to natural languages such as English, where people can coin new words, but cannot easily change the grammar. Saying that a language is extensible, however, is easier than extending it.

Most of the classes we've seen so far were designed to solve particular problems. We haven't worried about whether they'd be useful for all users in all situations. We've paid some attention to letting the class evolve gracefully, but we have concentrated on using classes in their original contexts. This is how most classes are designed and built. Sometimes, though, what we want to do is not only to add a type for our own use, but also to support that extension for other users. We call a collection of classes a library when it is meant for widespread use.

Designing a class for others to use requires taking on many of the responsibilities of a language designer. Users of a class will expect objects of that class to behave sensibly. The behavior they'll expect the class author to provide includes much of what we normally consider the compiler's responsibility: correctly creating, copying, assigning, or destroying an object. They will also expect reasonable semantics for the class: They'll want enough operations so that they can use the class in intuitive or natural ways. Chapter 25 covers these issues.

It's less often realized that the notion of *behaving sensibly* also includes designing an interface that reduces the number and kind of errors that users might make. Chapter 24 looks at this issue in the context of redesigning the interface to a common operating-system facility.

The flip side of letting users take on language design is that the C++ language itself had to be designed with the needs of library writers in mind. This ranges from supporting user-defined classes as full-fledged types to type-safe linkage. Chapter 26 looks at some of the language features that are in C++ primarily to support library authors.

To put these library issues in context, we'll start by seeing, in Chapter 23, how easy it can be to write programs when one has access to a well designed library.

23

Libraries in everyday use

In July 1993, I volunteered to become the project editor for the ISO C++ Standard. It did not take long to discover that it was too big a job to do by myself, which meant that I had to get others to help. Because the standards committee is a volunteer organization, I could not just tell people what to do; instead I had to accept what help people were willing to give me. If that help wasn't quite what I needed, sometimes I could use computers to bridge the gap between what I wanted and what I could get.

This chapter talks about one such use of computers. The specific problem that I needed to solve was merging two substantial pieces of text: the description of the proposed standard libraries and the list of open issues that the library working group maintains. The reason that it was a problem in the first place was that these two documents could not be merged once and for all: A different person maintained each one, and the respective maintainers weren't always in touch with each other.

23.1 The problem

To make the problem concrete, let's look at the (slightly simplified) beginning of one version of the text of the library description proper:

```
.H1 "Library" lib.library 17
.H2 "Introduction" lib.introduction
.P
A \*C implementation provides a
.I "Standard \*C library"
that defines various entities:
types, macros, objects, and functions.
```

The lines that begin with periods are formatting commands; the troff typesetting program, which I use to produce the document, interprets them. Thus, .H1 begins a first-level heading, .P begins a paragraph, .I precedes a word that is to appear in italics, and so on. The symbol *C translates to "C++," with the + symbols placed to look more attractive in print.

Most lines that start with .H contain a *symbolic name*, such as lib.library and lib.introduction in this example. These names make it possible to refer to a section of the text without knowing the actual section number, which might change in subsequent versions.

The library working group maintains the other file, which I call the *commentary file*. That file has lines in it that look like this:

```
### _lib.introduction_
The library working group needs to review this section.
```

Each line that starts with ### mentions the symbolic name of a section of the main text (surrounded by underscores, for uninteresting reasons), followed by commentary on that particular section. There is no requirement that the sections appear in the commentary file in the same order as in the main text. Moreover, several comments can apply to the same section.

The problem, then, is how to merge these two files mechanically. For example, given the two samples, I would like the result to be this:

```
.H1 "Library" lib.library 17
.H2 "Introduction" lib.introduction
.eN
The library working group needs to review this section.
.nE
.P
A \*C implementation provides a
.I "Standard \*C library"
that defines various entities:
types, macros, objects, and functions.
```

Here, the text identified by

```
### _lib.introduction_
```

has been inserted immediately after the header line for the section with the symbolic name lib.introduction, surrounded by .eN and .nE directives. These directives are defined as part of the macro package that I use for producing the working drafts; they tell troff to place the text thus surrounded into a rectangular box, so that the text stands out in the printed document.

This is a good example of the kind of problem that programmers face so often in practice: prosaic, somewhat messy, and with much more of a premium on getting a reasonably good solution quickly than on getting a gorgeous solution slowly. It is the kind of problem that is ideally suited to pattern-matching languages such as Awk, Perl, or Snobol, and, at least at first glance, does not appear terribly well suited to C++. However, given that the purpose of this program was to produce part of the C++ standard, I thought that it would be wise to use C++ unless I could find an overwhelming reason not to do so.

Using C++ turned out to be easier than I expected, mostly because I used a general-purpose library instead of relying solely on raw C++. The particular library that I used was the "Standard Components," once sold by USL and since discontinued. I chose it because I personally contributed to its development while it was under the AT&T umbrella. I have no doubt that one could write a similar program using any of several other available libraries as well. From here on in this chapter, I will refer to this library as "the library."

23.2　Understanding the problem—part 1

Because the commentary file can mention sections in any sequence, we cannot read it and the main text in parallel and simply merge them. Instead, we must store one of the files in a way that allows us to jump around in it. The commentary file is much smaller than the main text, so we'll store that one and then process the main file sequentially.

We must store the commentary file in such a way that, each time that we encounter a header line in the main file, we can discover whether any comments apply to the section that uses that symbolic name. The most direct way to do that is with an *associative array*: an arraylike data structure that allows arbitrary values as subscripts. Fortunately, the library has such a data structure.

To store the commentary file by sections, we need a way to tell where those sections are. We therefore need to be able to determine easily whether a line in the commentary file begins a new section. The library contains a regular expression matcher, which makes this problem easy too.

We'll also want to ignore the details of reading variable-length character strings and of storing the lines of the commentary file. We'll use the String and List classes provided by the library for these purposes.

23.3　Implementation—part 1

At this point, we can write code to solve the first part of our problem: Read the commentary file, split it into sections, and put each section into an element of an associative array. Because the details of creating and opening the particular commentary file that we want are not terribly interesting, we will omit them and assume that an input stream named comments has been opened and already refers to that file.

First, we declare the variables that we'll need:

```
String line;
String section;
Map<String, List<String> > map;
Regex pat("^###[ \t]*_(.*)_[ \t]*$");
Subex substrings;
```

The variables `line` and `section` will hold successive lines of the commentary file and corresponding symbolic names of sections, respectively. The variable `map` is an associative array, as described earlier. Given a symbolic name x, the value of `map[x]` will be a list that contains all the commentary associated with that symbolic name. We'll store each line of the commentary as an element in this list.

The value of the variable `pat` may look a little intimidating. Briefly, it is a *regular expression* that describes what kind of string is to be sought. In this particular case, it describes the line that begins a commentary section.

The first character in the regular expression is a ^, which constrains whatever follows to match starting at the first character of the subject string. The three # characters stand for themselves, so ^### is a request to match ### at the beginning of the line.

After that, we see [\t]*, which is a request to match any number of spaces or tabs. Next comes an underscore, which is the first character of a symbolic section name. The (.*) matches any characters at all; the parentheses make it possible to determine later what characters were matched, as we shall see. Then comes another underscore, more spaces or tabs, and finally a $ that represents the end of the line.

In other words, the declaration of `pat` describes a regular expression that matches any line that starts with ###, then white space, then any characters surrounded by underscores, then more white space, and finally the end of the line. We said that we could get at the parenthesized subexpression (the characters) matched by the regular expression `pat`. We'll use the variable `substrings` to extract that information, in a way that will become clear later.

The first line of the commentary file is supposed to be a ### line. In case it isn't, we'll discard any stuff that precedes the first ### line with appropriate diagnostics. Throughout this program, we will observe the convention that `line` contains the current line of the input file, so we begin by establishing that convention:

```
line = sgets(comments);     // read a line
```

Now, as promised, we discard any junk at the beginning of the comments file:

```
while (comments && !pat.match(line, substrings)) {
        cerr << "skipping leading junk: " << line << endl;
        line = sgets(comments);
}
```

Using comments in this way in a while condition is a shorthand way of saying "while we have not yet reached the end of the file." More interesting is the expression !pat.match(line, substrings). Recall that pat is the variable that holds the regular expression. It has a member function called match, which accepts a String as its first argument. If the regular expression successfully describes the String, the result is nonzero; otherwise, it is zero. We can therefore read this loop as saying, "As long as there is still input, and the current line doesn't look like a ### line, print an error message and discard the line." As a side effect, the match function stores information in substrings about what part of the input it matched.

At this point, either we're at a ### line or we've reached end of file. Here begins the main loop of this section of the program: For each ### line, it reads the corresponding text, and puts that text into map.

```
while (comments) {
        String key;
        substrings(1, key);
        List<String>& contents = map[key];

        if (contents) {
                contents.put(".nE");
                contents.put(".eN");
        }

        line = sgets(comments);
        while (comments && !pat.match(line, substrings)) {
                contents.put(line);
                line = sgets(comments);
        }
}
```

The previous call to match(line, substrings) stored in substrings information about each parenthesized subexpression that matched. This was the point of putting the .* in parentheses inside the regular expression. In this case, there is only one—namely, the (.*). We can then declare a local variable key, and can have the pattern-matching library store the substring matched by (.*) into key by saying

```
substrings(1, key);
```

Next, we look in map for the List<String> that represents the commentary corresponding to the key we have just found. For convenience, we create a local reference variable called contents, and bind it to that list. If this key was not yet in the map, it will be created automatically with an empty list as its value.

We take advantage of this design by checking whether contents refers to an empty list. If the list is not empty, we know that we are working on the second or subsequent comment referring to the same symbolic name, so we insert an end delimiter .nE and a start delimiter .eN to put the two comments in separate boxes. We don't have to worry about the first .eN or the last .nE, because we'll insert these when we generate the output.

This is not the cleanest possible way to deal with the first- and last-directive problem. If I were writing this program as an example for a software-engineering course, I would probably find a way to abstract out all knowledge of .eN and .nE into a separate class. However, the purpose of this program is to get the right answer with a minimum of effort, and yet to write a program that is not too hard to change later. The program is small, so the extra abstraction mechanism might add more complexity than it saves. Sometimes, the best way to get a job done is just to do it.

Anyway, at this point, we read lines from the commentary file until we find another ### line. All the lines that we read go into contents. When this loop terminates, either we're back at a ### line, or we've reached the end of file. If we're at a ### line, the surrounding loop will pick it up. Otherwise, we've read the entire commentary file, and it's time to deal with the main text.

23.4 Understanding the problem—part 2

We now have a data structure, in variable map, that tells us, for each section of the main text, whether there is any commentary for that section. We must then do two things.

First, as we read the main text, we must determine when we have reached a section header, so that we can print the commentary, if any.

Second, as we print commentary sections, we must note ones we have printed, so that, when we're all done, we can look for ones we've missed. This would happen, for example, if a commentary section had its name misspelled; the misspelled name would match none of the symbolic names in the main text.

23.5 Implementation—part 2

The most difficult part of the whole program to write or to read is the regular expression that recognizes section headers in the main text:

```
Regex cpat("^\\.H.*[ \t]+([^ \t]*[^ \t0-9][^ \t]*)"
           "([ \t]+[0-9]+)?[ \t]*$");
```

Because this string is so long, we have used the usual C and C++ convention that two or more character strings (enclosed in double quotes) separated only by white space (including a change to a new line) are concatenated into one during compilation. The idea of this big regular expression is to be able to pick out the symbolic names in section headers in either of the following forms:

```
.H1 "Library" lib.library 17
.H2 "Introduction" lib.introduction
```

Notice that one of them has a number—here 17—at the end. The regular expression caters to that optional number. Here is a detailed breakdown of how the pattern works:

`^`	the beginning of the line
`\\.H`	the characters `.H`; the `\` is needed before the `.` because a `.` in a regular expression ordinarily matches any character at all, and the other `\` is needed because, when writing a string literal as part of a C++ program, it is always necessary to say `\\` to represent a single `\`
`.*`	any string at all
`[ \t]+`	one or more spaces or tabs
`([^ \t]*[^ \t0-9][^ \t]*)`	zero or more characters that are neither spaces nor tabs, followed by a character that is neither a space, tab, nor digit, followed by zero or characters that are neither spaces or tabs
`([ \t]+[0-9]+)?`	one or more spaces or tabs followed by one or more digits (the + asks for one or more of whatever it follows), or nothing at all (the ? asks for zero or one of whatever it follows)
`[ \t]*$`	zero or more spaces or tabs followed by end of line

If you follow this logic closely, you will see that it is effectively looking in a line that begins with `.H` for a blank-delimited word that contains at least one nondigit, optionally followed by a numeral, and then the end of the line. This is exactly the way to pick out the symbolic name from a header.

After this regular expression, the rest is straightforward. First, we begin a loop that reads the entire text file. We always print each line that we read:

```
while (line = sgets(text), text) {
    cout << line << endl;
```

Next, we ask whether the line we printed is the beginning of a new section:

```
    if (cpat.match(line, substrings)) {
```

If it is, we extract the symbolic name (which corresponds to the first parenthesized part of the regular above) and place it in `s`:

```
        String s;
        substrings(1, s);
```

Then, we look in `map` to see whether that name is represented there:

```
if (map.element(s)) {
```

The call to map.element(s) effectively tests whether an element with subscript
s exists in map. If it does, we have a commentary section that we must write.
We do so and destroy it, so that we can know that it was printed. As before, we
use a local reference called contents for convenience:

```
List<String>& contents = map[s];
if (contents) {
        cout << ".eN" << endl;
        String line;
        while (contents.get(line))
                cout << line << endl;
        cout << ".nE" << endl;
}
                }
            }
        }
```

The only thing that may not be obvious here is what the get member does: It
tries to extract the first element of a list, places that element in its argument, and
returns a value indicating whether it was successful. Thus, get is destructive;
the side effect of executing it repeatedly is to set map[s] to the empty list.

   At this point, the program has done its main job. As we noted earlier, however, we should look through what is left in map to make sure that every symbolic name was used:

```
Mapiter<String, List<String> > it = map.first();
while (it) {
        if (it.value())
                cerr << "unmatched section: "
                        << it.key() << endl;
        ++it;
}
```

Here, we use a *map iterator* called it to visit all the elements of our associative
array. We ask whether each element is an empty list; if it isn't, we complain.

23.6 Discussion

This piece of program is neither very easy nor very difficult to write. Clearly,
however, writing it would have been a real nuisance without libraries. It relies
on four library facilities:
* Variable length character strings
* Lists (or at least lists of strings)
* Associative arrays
* Regular expressions

We could get by without lists. The easy way to do that would be simply to store the entire commentary for each symbolic name in one long string. The other three library facilities, though, appear essential for this particular application. Indeed, they are precisely the facilities that make languages such as Awk attractive for this sort of problem.

This example does require a good deal of specialized knowledge. However, that knowledge is not hard to acquire. Indeed, when I started writing the program, I had never used the regular expression classes. Nevertheless, it took me only a couple of hours to get the whole thing working, including my learning time.

If the library had not been available to me, I would not have attempted to solve this problem in C++. Instead, I would have used Awk, Perl, Snobol, or some other similar language. What is interesting is that C++ libraries make it possible to solve such problems without much more effort than using a much more specialized tool would require.

24

An object lesson in library-interface design

One thing that makes it a challenge to explain abstract data types to people unfamiliar with them is the difficulty of finding an example that's complicated enough to be realistic but small enough to understand. The purpose of data abstraction, after all, is managing complexity, so finding a simple example seems almost self contradictory.

A good example came along, though, in the form of a widely used collection of C library routines that made it possible to examine the contents of a file system directory. Although C programs can run on a wide variety of operating systems, most systems have similar notions of file and directory. Thus, we can talk about such notions without reference to a particular system.

What's especially useful about this example is that it concentrates on how we can use data abstraction to automate the conventions that are common in languages that don't directly support data abstraction. By hiding these conventions in the class, we can free our users from ever having to deal with them. Not only does that make using the class easier, but also it makes the class more robust.

It is easiest to see how the C library routines work by looking at a program that uses them:

```
/* This is a C program */
#include <stdio.h>
#include <dirent.h>

main()
{
        DIR *dp = opendir(".");
        struct dirent *d;

        while (d = readdir(dp))
                printf("%s\n", d->d_name);

        closedir(dp);
        return 0;
}
```

C programs communicate with the library through two types, called DIR and
struct dirent. Pointers to DIR objects are treated as *magic cookies*—that is,
small objects of mysterious nature that one gives to a program to entice it into
doing something.

We are not intended to know what is in a DIR object. Calling opendir yields
a DIR pointer, which we hand to readdir to read a directory entry, and which
we ultimately give to closedir to free the resources allocated by opendir.

Calling readdir returns a pointer to a struct dirent that represents the
directory entry just read. Again, we are not supposed to know the entire contents of a struct dirent, but one of its members is a null-terminated character
array called d_name that contains the name of the directory entry.

The way that this sample program works, then, is to call opendir to obtain a
magic cookie that represents the current directory; repeatedly call readdir to
fetch entries from that directory, printing the entries as it goes; and eventually
call closedir to clean up.

For completeness, I should mention two other library functions, although our
little program does not use them. The telldir function takes a DIR pointer,
which represents a directory, and returns a long that represents the current
position in that directory. The seekdir function takes a DIR pointer and a
value returned by telldir, and moves to the given point in the corresponding
directory.

24.1 Complications

This all seems very simple, but is it really? Our informal description fails to mention several questions that cause trouble for real programmers writing real programs. Here are the more important questions.

- *What happens if the directory does not exist?* When opendir is given the name
  of a nonexistent directory, it can't just crash—it must do something. The
  usual thing to do in such cases is to return a null pointer. Doing so makes it
  easy for programs to check whether or not the open worked. It does, however, lead to the next question

- *What happens when the argument to* readdir *is a null pointer?* This is exactly
  what would happen in the preceding program if the directory " . " did not
  exist. There are at least two possible answers to this question. Either readdir fails to check for a null argument, in which case we can reasonably
  expect a core dump or other disaster, or readdir does check and does something sensible. The latter case leaves a related question unanswered

- *What happens when the argument to* readdir *is neither a null pointer nor a value
  originally returned by the* opendir *function?* This kind of error is hard to
  check: Detecting it probably requires some sort of table of valid DIR objects,
  and a search through that table for every call to readdir. This is compli-

cated enough, and has enough associated overhead, that C library routines usually don't do it. A related question applies to the result of `readdir`

- *A call to* `readdir` *returns a pointer to memory allocated by the library. When is that memory freed?* In the example, each call to `readdir` returns a pointer value that is stored in d. What if the program did something like this?

```
d1 = readdir(dp1);
d2 = readdir(dp2);
printf("%s\n", d1->d_name);
```

How would we know whether the pointer d1 still points to a valid location after calling `readdir(dp2)`? Is d1 valid only when dp1!=dp2? Or does some other rule apply? The only way to know whether this code is correct is to know what operations might invalidate the value to which d1 points, and also to know whether or not we have done any of those things.

24.2 Improving the interface

Rather than answering these questions, let's redesign the interface in C++ to eliminate, where possible, the need to ask them. To do this redesign, we will replace magic cookies by objects, and will conceal the use of pointers.

The first magic cookie that we saw in the C version was the DIR pointer; let's make that pointer into a class called Dir. A Dir object represents a view into a directory; all the library functions but two that manipulate DIR pointers in the C version should logically become member functions of the Dir class. Those two are `opendir` and `closedir`, which must correspond to the constructor and destructor. The class definition then looks like this:

```
class Dir {
public:
        Dir(const char*);
        ~Dir();
        // declarations for read, seek, and tell
};
```

What are the argument and result types for the read, seek, and tell members? We'll tackle seek and tell first, because they're easiest: The C versions use magic cookies, so the C++ versions should use a little class to represent an offset. An object of this class represents an offset into a directory, so we'll call it Dir_offset:

```
class Dir_offset {
        friend class Dir;
```

```
private:
        long l;
        Dir_offset(long n) { l = n; }
        operator long() { return l; }
};
```

Note that this class has no public data. In particular, its constructor is private. Thus, the only way to create a `Dir_offset` object is to call a function—presumably a member of the `Dir` class—that knows how to create one. Once we have such an object, of course, we can copy it, but the way that this class is defined effectively makes it impossible for the user to peer into objects of this class directly.

The only data member of a `Dir_offset` object is a `long` that corresponds to the value returned by `telldir`.

Now we come to the `read` function. The C version returns a pointer to a `struct dirent` for an important reason: Doing so makes it possible to signal when the end of the directory has been reached by returning a null pointer. We won't bother to encapsulate the `dirent` structure here, but we will change how the `Dir` class reads it. Using C++ reference parameters, we can detect in a different way when we reach the end of the directory: Give `read` a parameter that represents an object into which to place its result, and have it return a "boolean" (really, an integer) that represents whether or not the read succeeded.

The discussion so far suggests that the public part of the `Dir` class should look like this:

```
#include <dirent.h>

class Dir {
public:
        Dir(const char*);
        ~Dir();
        int read(dirent&);
        void seek(Dir_offset);
        Dir_offset tell() const;
};
```

Given this interface, we can now rewrite our sample program as follows:

```
#include <iostream.h>
#include "dirlib.h"

int main()
{
        Dir dp(".");
        dirent d;

        while (dp.read(d))
                cout << d.d_name << endl;
}
```

Here, header `dirlib.h` contains declarations for `Dir` and `Dir_offset`.

24.3 Taking stock

We can't execute this program yet, because we haven't fleshed out our `Dir` class skeleton with member-function definitions. However, we can already say a few things about how our program has been improved.

First, note that the C version of the library injects seven names into the global name space: `DIR`, `dirent`, `opendir`, `closedir`, `readdir`, `seekdir`, and `telldir`. In contrast, the C++ version uses only `Dir`, `dirent`, and `Dir_offset`.

Second, we see that the C++ version of our program contains no pointer variables at all. In particular, d is an *object* that represents a directory entry, rather than a *pointer* to such an object as it was in the C version. We thus eliminate a whole class of possible problems: A program that doesn't use pointers can't crash because of an undefined pointer!

Third, because C++ does not require class names to be preceded by `struct` or `class` when they declare objects, the declaration of d has become more compact.

Finally, C++ version answers the the questions that the C version left open:

1. *What happens if the directory does not exist?* We still have to deal with this problem. In fact, using C++ has made it rather more obvious that we must deal with it, because a program that says

    ```
    Dir  d(some directory);
    d.read(somewhere);
    ```

    must do something sensible: d is an object even if the open fails. We will make a mental note to ensure that the `Dir` constructor leaves its object in a consistent state, even if the underlying call to `opendir` fails. If we do this once in the library, the people who use the library won't have to worry about the problem unless they want to.

    Another alternative would be to throw an exception if we are asked to create a `Dir` referring to a nonexistent directory. Still another possibility is to allow the `Dir` object to be created, but to raise an exception on an attempt to read it.

2. *What happens when the argument to* `readdir` *is a null pointer?* This becomes a nonquestion in the C++ version: We must call `read` on some object, and that object must have been constructed.

3. *What happens when the argument to* `readdir` *is neither a null pointer nor a value originally returned by the* `opendir` *function?* This is also a nonquestion, for the same reason.

4. *A call to* `readdir` *returns a pointer to memory allocated by the library. When is that memory freed?* Rather than having `read` return a pointer, we made it read into an object that the user supplies. This puts responsibility for memory allocation on the user's shoulders, but we can make the burden trivially light by using `read` to read into local variables.

Apparently, then, we've made these routines considerably more robust merely by translating them into C++, mostly because we tried to turn the underlying concepts in the C interface into explicit objects in the C++ interface.

24.4 Writing the code

Now that we have nailed down the interface, it shouldn't be hard to design an implementation. The `Dir` class encapsulates a `DIR` pointer, so we'll include that pointer in the private data of the `Dir` class. We'll also make it impossible to copy a `Dir` object, by making assignment and initialization private:

```
class Dir {
public:
        Dir(const char*);
        ~Dir();
        int read(dirent&);
        void seek(Dir_offset);
        Dir_offset tell() const;

private:
        DIR* dp;

        // copy control
        Dir(const Dir&);
        Dir& operator=(const Dir&);
};
```

We don't want to allow `Dir` objects to be copied, because reading from one would then affect the state of the other. Moreover, after we copied a `Dir` object, both the original and copy would have to be destroyed. We could design a more complicated `Dir` object that would cater to this possibility; doing so is left as an exercise.

Now, we can write the member functions. The constructor calls `opendir`:

```
Dir::Dir(const char* file): dp(opendir(file)) { }
```

Thus, we must ask what will happen if `opendir` fails. The answer, of course, is that dp will be null; we must remember to test for that case in the other member functions and do something sensible.

The destructor is easy—we call `closedir` unless the open failed:

```
Dir::~Dir()
{
        if (dp)
                closedir(dp);
}
```

If the open failed, dp will be 0. We test dp to see whether the open succeeded, so that we do not depend on whether the underlying C library correctly allows us to call closedir on a Dir pointer that is not pointing to an open Dir.

The seek and tell functions are also easy: We call seekdir or telldir. The only problem is what to return from tell if the open failed. Fortunately what we return doesn't matter much because any corresponding seek will do nothing anyway on discovering the failure:

```
void Dir::seek(Dir_offset pos)
{
        if (dp)
                seekdir(dp, pos);
}

Dir_offset Dir::tell() const
{
        if (dp)
                return telldir(dp);
        return -1;
}
```

Finally, we have the read member. This is the most complicated of them all, and it is still pretty simple:

```
int Dir::read(dirent& d)
{
        if (dp) {
                dirent* r = readdir(dp);
                if (r) {
                        d = *r;
                        return 1;
                }
        }
        return 0;
}
```

We follow the convention of returning 0 for failure and a nonzero value for success. This code first checks whether the open failed, and returns immediately in that case. It then calls readdir to read a directory entry; if it gets one, it copies the entry immediately into the dirent object that the caller supplied. Thus we have answered our earlier question: Reading a nonexistent directory will behave as if the directory has no entries at all.

Copying the value of *r into the user's space relieves the user of having to worry about the lifetime of *r, but only because when we read the description of struct dirent (the type of *r), we learn that it does not depend on any memory outside the structure itself. Were that not the case, it would be necessary to define a separate dirent class in C++, using a dynamic string class, instead of using the C version.

It might be nice to have a function to test explicitly whether a `Dir` object was successful in opening its underlying directory. That function—no harder than the ones we've seen here—is left as an exercise.

We note in passing that we can reduce the already small overhead of this interface by making the `Dir` member functions inline.

24.5 Conclusion

The C++ interface to this library improves on the C interface in small but telling ways. These improvements all stem from the notion of data abstraction: If each individual operation on a class object leaves the object in a sensible state, the object's state will always remain sensible.

The C interface has several hidden conventions that our earlier questions exposed. A program that fails to observe these conventions may well fail in strange ways at execution time. By making such conventions explicitly part of the interface, we can detect errors much earlier, and accordingly, programmers can work with greater confidence.

25

Library design is language design

One of the more important ideas in C++ (although the idea is certainly not unique to C++) is that user-defined types can be used as readily as built-in types. By defining new types, users can customize the language for their own purposes.

This is a powerful tool, and, like most such tools, it can be dangerous if misused. It is possible, for example, for the author of a type to make assignment work backwards for objects of that type, so that saying x=y would take the value of x and put it into y rather than vice versa. Doing so, however, would be certain to sow confusion among the users of that class.

Avoiding this kind of confusion is the responsibility of the author of any class intended to be used by others. In effect, designing a class library is like designing part of a programming language, and should be approached with commensurate respect.

25.1 Character strings

To make this discussion more concrete, let's look at a simple general-purpose class, intended to make it possible to have variable-length character strings. You most certainly have seen several similar examples elsewhere.

```
class String {
public:
        String(char* p) {
                sz = strlen(p);
                data = new char[sz + 1];
                strcpy(data, p);
        }

        ~String() { delete[] data; }

        operator char*() { return data; }
```

```
private:
        int sz;
        char* data;
};
```

This class definition is pretty much the simplest that is capable of behaving use-fully as though it were a string. Here is one example of how we might use it:

```
String s("hello world");
cout << s << endl;
```

This example initializes s, and then uses the conversion operator, operator char*(), to get a char* that we pass to the output operator defined in the stan-dard iostream library.

Although this particular example works as written, the class itself fails to address several subtle points. For instance, it neither accounts for all the opera-tions that might be performed on Strings, nor attempts to deal with all the error conditions that might come up. People who try to use objects of this class usually will be able to do so, but sometimes they will be in for a surprise. It is understanding when these surprises can occur, and deciding what to do about them, that makes the design of general-purpose classes a task that should not be attempted casually.

25.2 Memory exhaustion

One problem is that there may not be enough memory to contain the String being allocated. This might happen because the user has requested a huge String and there simply isn't enough memory.

What happens in such a case? The short answer is that the class definition didn't take that case into account, so we really don't know. The long answer is that the new expression in the constructor fails, and we must understand the con-sequences of that failure.

What it means for a new expression to fail differs from one implementation to another, and from time to time. In present implementations, one of three things usually happens: The library throws an exception, the whole program aborts with a suitable diagnostic message, or the new expression returns 0. If an excep-tion occurs or the whole program aborts, that is obvious enough that there's no mistaking it. Standard C++ will probably require the implementation to throw an exception. Nevertheless, it will be years before all implementations conform—many will offer a "compatibility mode" that will still return 0, and we will have to cater to that. We will therefore assume, in this chapter, that new returns 0.

What happens next is that the data pointer is set to 0. This probably leads to a crash inside strcpy when strcpy tries to write into data! Clearly, we need to check that data was allocated before doing the copy. What about the other operations? Applying delete to a zero pointer is a no-op, so there's no problems for the destructor. But what about operator char*()? Evidently, applying operator char*() to a String for which allocation has failed will return a zero pointer. What happens when the user tries to use this value? In most implementations, such operations are not really checked; the result may be garbage, or it may be a core dump.

Therefore, we see that memory exhaustion, while allocating a String, results in a String that can be freed normally, but any attempt to use it results in undefined behavior.

There are several ways to deal with this problem.

We could take the lazy way out, and say that the result of memory exhaustion is undefined: If you run out of memory, you get what you get.

We could explicitly shift the burden onto the user's shoulders, by saying that it is the user's responsibility to test that the value returned by operator char* is valid. For example, we could demand that every use of a String check that memory was available:

```
char* p;
String s(p);

if (s) {
        cout << s << endl;
}
```

Of course, what will happen is that almost all users will neglect to check at some point or another. Can we somehow force users to check?

The most straightforward approach to such enforcement is simply to check in the constructor whether or not the allocation succeeded, and to do something drastic if it failed:

```
class String {
public:
        String(char* p) {
                sz = strlen(p);
                data = new char[sz + 1];
                if (data == 0)
                        error();
                else
                        strcpy(data,p);
        }
        // ...
};
```

In effect, we are rendering user checks unnecessary by checking for memory exhaustion on the user's behalf. This approach seems sensible, but it has a serious problem: Can error return? If not, that leaves the poor user of this class with no way to detect memory exhaustion except to try to create a String—if the program is still running afterward, memory wasn't a problem!

If error *can* return, on the other hand, the problem still isn't solved: After error has returned, we have an invalid String, and we must still find out whether the user tries to use it without first checking. Therefore, it seems to be necessary to check inside operator char*() whether the object is valid. If we check before accessing the String for memory exhaustion, we will catch all cases of memory exhaustion without having to force users to validate their Strings explicitly:

```
class String {
public:
        operator char*() {
                if (data == 0)
                        error();
                return data;
        }
        // ...
};
```

The problem with this is that there is no way for the user to detect memory exhaustion without causing a call to error. Many users object to library functions that terminate the program unconditionally. This implies that we will need to add a function to test explicitly for memory exhaustion. For example, we could add another member function,

```
int String::valid() { return data != 0; }
```

which the cautious user could call before using operator char*(). This would allow programs written without explicit attention to memory exhaustion to do a reasonable thing: Such a program would be terminated by a call to error if memory exhaustion did occur but not otherwise. The cost of this strategy would be that users who wanted to test explicitly for memory exhaustion would be able to forget to do so without being told about it. This is a subtle tradeoff and class authors must consider their users carefully in making it.

Of course, this has a performance problem: Every time that a String is accessed, there is a check for data==0. It's hard to avoid this check if it is ever possible to create a String with data==0. Moreover, if error can return, it's hard to avoid creating such a String.

We can solve this problem by using exception handling:

```
class String {
public:
        String(char* p) {
                sz = strlen(p);
                data = new char[sz + 1];
                if (data == 0)
                        throw std::bad_alloc();
                else
                        strcpy(data,p);
        }
```

```
        ~String() { delete[] data; }

        operator char*() { return data; }
private:
        int sz;
        char* data;
};
```

Briefly, the idea is that the `throw` statement is a way of exiting unconditionally from the context in which the error was detected, while still allowing the author of the surrounding context to detect the error by writing something like this:

```
try {
        String s(p);
        // do something involving s
} catch (std::bad_alloc) {
        // handle memory exhaustion here
}
```

If s can't allocate enough memory, the `throw` statement causes control to be passed to the corresponding `catch` clause. Once control reaches that point, s is out of scope, and there's no way to access it. This code uses the `std::bad_alloc` exception defined in the standard library.

Using exceptions in this way can greatly simplify our programs, because the mere existence of a `String` guarantees that the memory for the `String` has been allocated successfully. Thus, it is never necessary to check for memory-allocation failure anywhere else in the `String` class.

25.3 Copying

Instead of continuing to explore alternative ways of dealing with memory allocation, let's look at what happens when someone tries to copy a `String`.

The definition of our little `String` class has no copy constructor or assignment operator. In such a case, the C++ implementation creates them on behalf of the programmer, and defines them recursively in terms of the corresponding operations on the class members. Thus, copying a `String` is equivalent to copying the values of the `sz` and `data` members of the `String`.

This causes a serious problem: After the copy, the `data` members of the original and the copy will point to the same memory! Thus, when the two `Strings` are freed, that memory will be freed twice.

As usual, there are several possible ways to deal with this problem. The easiest is to decree that `Strings` can't be copied at all, by making the copy constructor and assignment operator private:

```
class String {
private:
        int sz;
        char* data;
        String(const String&);            // copy protection
        String& operator=(const String&); // copy protection
        // ...
};
```

As long as these members aren't virtual (copy constructors can't be virtual, of course, but assignment might be), it's necessary only to declare them; there's no need to define them. It is a good idea, though, to use comments to make it plain that the reason that these members are declared is to prevent people from copying the objects.

However, it isn't nice to prohibit users from copying Strings, so perhaps we should think about how to allow them to do so. It's clear what the copy constructor should do, but the case of assignment is less clear. Should assigning a String of one size to a String of a different size

•   be an error?

•   change the size of the target String?

•   copy only the smaller of the sizes of the source and target Strings?

•   pad out the source to the size of the target?

A case can surely be made for each of these alternatives. To keep things simple, I'll pick one: changing the size of the target. That's the alternative that makes assignment behave the most like the copy constructor. That is, it seems to make sense that after we execute

```
String x = y;
x = z;
```

x will have the same value as it would after we execute

```
String x = z;
```

Let's think for a moment about the relationship between the copy constructor, assignment operator, and destructor, because this relationship shows up while designing many kinds of classes. The assignment operator and the copy constructor are superficially similar to each other. In this particular class, each of them will take a String as an argument; each one's job is to copy that argument String into the current String. The main difference between the copy constructor and the assignment operator is that the assignment operator must get rid of the old value first, before it copies the new value in. This suggests that the copying part can be handled by a common subroutine; let's call that subroutine assign, and write it first. By giving it a bit of thought, we'll also be able to use this function for the constructor that takes a char* argument:

```
class String {
private:
        void assign(const char* s, unsigned len) {
                data = new char[len + 1];
                if (data == 0)
                        throw std::bad_alloc();
                sz = len;
                strcpy(data, s);
        }
        // ...
};
```

The copy constructor is now just a call to `assign`:

```
class String {
public:
        String(const String& s) {
                assign(s.data, s.sz);
        }
        // ...
};
```

The assignment operator is a tiny bit trickier; we can't delete our data and then call `assign`, because that would fail when we assign a `String` to itself! The easiest way to forestall that problem is to check for it as a special case:

```
class String {
public:
        String& operator=(const String& s) {
                if (this != &s) {
                        delete [] data;
                        assign(s.data, s.sz);
                }
                return *this;
        }
        // ...
};
```

Our class definition now looks like this:

```
class String {
public:
        String(char* p) {
                assign(p, strlen(p));
        }

        String(const String& s) {
                assign(s.data, s.sz);
        }

        ~String() {
                delete[] data;
        }
```

```
String& operator=(const String& s) {
        if (this != &s) {
                delete [] data;
                assign(s.data, s.sz);
        }
        return *this;
}

operator char*() {
        return data;
}

private:
        int sz;
        char* data;

        void assign(const char* s, unsigned len) {
                data = new char[len + 1];
                if (data == 0)
                        throw std::bad_alloc();
                sz = len;
                strcpy(data, s);
        }
};
```

25.4 Hiding the implementation

Properly shielding the implementation is an important part of the class designer's responsibility. We usually think of data hiding as protecting the class author. Hiding the implementation gives us the flexibility to *change* the implementation in response to future needs. However, properly hiding the implementation is also important to help prevent user errors.

The String class looks like it is properly shielding its implementation. After all, there are no public data. But what about operator char*()? By returning a pointer to data, it opens up three loopholes:

1. The user can obtain a pointer, and then use it to change the characters stored in data. This means that the class doesn't really control its own resources.
2. When a String is freed, the memory occupied by it also is freed. Thus, any pointers to the String become invalid. We might argue, of course, that any pointer has the same problem and users must simply be aware these problems.
3. We decided to implement assignment of one String to another by freeing and reallocating the memory used by the target String. That means that such an assignment will also invalidate any pointers into the String.

We can deal with the first problem by defining a conversion to const char* instead of to char*. This also will let us declare the function const:

```
class String {
public:
        operator const char*() const {
                return data;
        }
        // ...
};
```

This protects the class author from the user changing the stored string, but does nothing to help prevent user errors that will result if the pointer is used after the String goes away or is changed.

Perhaps we should drop the conversion altogether. After all, we're going to provide a wonderful String class, so why should the user ever need to get the actual characters stored in the String? We can provide input and output operations, and we could even provide all the standard string functions, such as those in string.h. What we won't be able to duplicate, though, are the myriad nonstandard functions that we don't even know about that operate on char* values. Character strings are such a common data structure, and their representation as a pointer to a null-terminated array of char is so firmly embedded in C, that there will be zillions of such functions. We can avoid converting our Strings to char* only at the cost of eliminating all these uses.

So it appears that we will need to let the user get at a C string. But, at least, we can make the operation explicit rather than implicit. As it stands, users may be obtaining character pointers without even being aware of that they are doing so, because the conversion to char* can happen implicitly. This implies that we should replace operator const char*() by a nonoperator function, such as

```
class String {
public:
        const char* make_cstring() const {
                return data;
        }
        // ...
};
```

This should at least make it easier for users to find out where they got a pointer that went bad.

We could go even further and eliminate the possibility of dangling pointers. To do so, we'll have to deal with memory management of the string that we give back to the user. The make_cstring function could allocate memory and copy data into that memory. But the String class can't know when to free this memory. Freeing the memory will have to be the user's responsibility. But users tend to forget to free resources that they didn't explicitly obtain, so a better strategy might be to have the user provide the space into which to copy data. If we expect our users to provide the space for the copy, we'll have to give them a way to determine the length of the data.

```
class String {
public:
        int length() const {
                return sz;
        }

        void make_cstring(char* p, int len) const {
                if (sz <= len)
                        strcpy(p, data);
                else
                        throw("Not enough memory supplied");
        }
        // ...
};
```

Because the user might have provided the wrong amount of space to store a copy of data, we check. Here, we arbitrarily decided to allow the user to give us too much space, but to treat allocating too little space as an error. Alternatively, we could have copied len characters from data. It's not clear which strategy is right; we know only that the decision has to be made, and documented.

25.5 Default constructor

Another problem with our class is that we cannot create a String without saying what its initial value is. In other words, it is a compile-time error to write

```
String s;
```

because we haven't said what initial value to give s. This means that it is impossible to have an array of Strings:

```
String s_arr[20];
```

We would be asking to create an array of 20 objects, each of which is a String. This is an error, because we haven't said what initial value to give each String, and there's no default.

Is this problem serious? It's hard to say. We could easily circumvent the problem by establishing a default value for Strings, but what should that value be?

In practice, a String class designer would probably spend a fair amount of time in devising fast allocation strategies for storing Strings, and these strategies would govern how to handle empty strings. But our concern here is limited to decisions about class behavior as seen by the user, so we'll take a simple approach. There seem to be two easy ways to deal with an empty String: We could set data to 0, or we could make data point to a null string. If we give the empty String a data pointer of 0, then we'll have to check every dereference of `data`. In the interests of keeping the presentation simple, we will have the default constructor point at a `null` string:

```
class String {
public:
        String(): data(new char[1]) {
                sz = 0;
                *data = '\0';
        }
        // ...
};
```

25.6 Other operations

So far, our class is still pretty primitive. We can create, copy, and destroy objects of type `String`, and we can get a `char*` from a `String`. What other operations should we support?

In practice, probably quite a few. For example, there are 20 functions declared in the `string.h` header file that comes with the C compiler on my system. Among them are operations to concatenate two strings, and to compare two strings, as well as lots of functions that examine or change substrings of the string. Because string handling is not one of C's strong points, we'll want to think a bit about how we can improve on these operations.

The first observation is that operator overloading will let us provide a more natural interface to comparison and concatenation. For example, we could let our users write

```
String s1("hello"), s2("world");
String s3 = s1 + " " + s2;
```

as opposed to

```
char s1[] = "hello", s2[] = "world";
char* p = (char*) malloc(strlen(s1) + strlen(s2) + 2);
strcpy(p, s1);
strcat(p, " ");
strcat(p, s2);
```

As the example shows, we'll want to be able to "add" two `String`s or a `String` and a `char*`. Also, given that we provide `operator+`, it's probably a good idea to provide the compound assignment operator as well. Because += modifies the `String` on its left-hand side, we'll need to make it a member of class `String`:

```
String& String::operator+=(const String& s)
{
        char* odata = data;

        assign(data, sz + s.sz + 1);
        strcat(data, s.data);
        delete [] odata;
        return *this;
}
```

As with assignment, it's important to protect against attempts to concatenate a `String` onto itself; we do so by keeping a pointer to the old values before calling `assign` to allocate new memory. After `assign`, we'll still have to remember to concatenate the right-hand side into the newly allocated space. Only then is it safe to `delete` the original characters.

But what about `operator+`? Should it be a member? In general, it's best to define the binary operators as nonmembers. Doing so will allow conversions on either operand. If we make `operator+` a member of `String`, then its first operand must always be of type `String`. Thus, we could write

```
String s;
char* p;

s + p;
```

but we couldn't write

```
p + s;
```

and that seems unduly restrictive. So we'll define

```
String operator+(const String& op1, const String& op2)
{
        String ret(op1);
        ret += op2;
        return ret;
}
```

This function uses only the `public` interface of `String`, so there is no need to declare it as a `friend`. Also, note that we return a `String` rather than a `String&`. What `String` might we return a reference to? Concatenation shouldn't change either of its operands (and indeed couldn't, because they are declared `const`), and we certainly don't want to return a reference to `ret`. More important, returning a value, instead of a reference, is in keeping with how addition on built-in types operates. When we add two `int`s, we get a new `int`, not a reference to some previously existing `int`.

We still have to implement the six relational operators. Each can be written in terms of `strcmp`:

```
int
operator==(const String& op1, const String& op2)
{
        return (strcmp(op1.data, op2.data) == 0);
}
```

Clearly, these functions need to be friends of String.

We'll probably want to define input and output operators. We could use either the standard iostream library or the technique described in Chapter 30 to provide I/O library independence. As usual, which approach we should take will depend on how we think users will want to use our class. The output operator that depends on iostreams is easy:

```
ostream&
operator<<(ostream& os, const String& s)
{
        return os << s.data;
}
```

We define the output operator simply to print the characters and *nothing* more. It might be tempting to provide some kind of formatting, such as a newline, after we print data. But had we done so, then users would have a hard time using our output operator to chain together several Strings to make a single line of output. In general, it's best to let the user control all formatting, and to define the output operator to print only the unadorned contents of the class.

The input operator is not particularly hard, either. It has to allocate memory and read characters until the end of the String is encountered. The only interesting decision is what the end of the String is. Often, reading characters up to the first whitespace character is the right decision. Implementation is left as an exercise for the reader.

25.7 Substrings

There are surely many more operations that we might consider providing on Strings. But as we look at likely candidates from string.h, for example, it becomes apparent that many of these operations deal with substrings. Some extract substrings from the string, and others set substrings of the string to some new value. Perhaps we should think about how to implement substrings.

The kinds of operations that we'd like to support include:
- Return the first, next, or last occurrence of some substring.
- Change the first, or every, occurrence of a character to some other character.
- Change the first, or all, occurrences of some substring to some other substring, where the lengths of the substrings need not be the same.

Given these operations, it will be useful to return substrings from functions and take them as arguments. Presumably, therefore, we'll want to make a Substring class. Substrings act like values, so we'll need to be able to create, copy, assign, and destroy them.

But what is a Substring? We can think of it as a pointer to the String of which it is a substring and a length; or as two pointers into the String—one to the beginning, and the other to the end, of the substring.

So a Substring evidently is a pointer to a String and a range of character positions in that String. Among the operations that a Substring should provide is the ability to go through the String, returning the "next" Substring that matches some criteria. These data and operations make it appear that a Substring will act a lot like an iterator (Chapter 14). Evidently, we'll need to think about the issues presented there when we design the Substring class.

Indeed, the question of how (and whether) to provide access to substrings is one about which library authors can argue as much as can language designers. If s and t are Strings, and we want s(i, j) to be the Substring of s that starts at character i and is j characters long, we may wish to allow

```
t = s(i, j);
```

or

```
s(i, j) = t;
```

What implementation strategy will allow the latter example? Suppose that we write

```
s(i, j) = s(k, l);
```

and the two ranges overlap? What if we somehow save the value of s(i, j) and use it later, after we have deleted s? Questions such as these affect not only library designers but language designers as well.

25.8 Conclusion

I hope that I've gone on long enough to provide convincing evidence that even a simple general-purpose class presents numerous design issues. The C++ class mechanism gives library designers an extraordinary amount of power, in effect turning them into potential language designers. It is important to use that power with judgment, skill, and taste.

26

Language design is library design

Chapter 25 looked at how the design of a library involved problems similar to those involved in designing a programming language. This chapter looks at the opposite relationship: Parts of C++ exist to make it easier to design libraries. Understanding how various features of C++ support library construction will make it easier to understand and remember how to use those features.

It is particularly important for people who wish to use a library to be able to do so without understanding the library's internal workings. For example, if your library provides a string class, it should be unnecessary to know, or even to care, whether strings are represented internally as pointers to null-terminated arrays of characters, as (*count, address*) pairs, or in some other way entirely. In other words, one thing that makes a good library is a clean separation between interface and implementation.

26.1 Abstract data types

Obviously, if we're to provide a clean separation between the interface and the implementation, then we'll want the language to support data abstraction. A couple of aspects of how C++ provides for abstract data types are worth looking at in some detail.

26.1.1 Constructors and destructors

One of the most fundamental ways in which the C++ language makes it possible to separate interface from implementation is through constructors and destructors. They are what allow the author of a class to say, "An object of this class uses information beyond the mere contents of the object itself." A constructor gives a recipe for building an object of a given class; a destructor gives a recipe for undoing whatever the constructor did.

For example, consider a class that represents a screen location in a graphics system:

```
class Point {
public:
            // stuff

private:
        int x, y;
};
```

Why should a user of this class care, or even know, that x was declared before y in the class' definition? Perhaps there is a machine out there with magic display hardware that runs faster if the coordinates are stored in reverse order in an array, so that they can both be sent at once. It would be nice if catering to such hardware involved no more than merely changing the library and recompiling the programs that use it.

Constructors provide a fundamental way of decoupling how users view an object from how the object is represented. Even though a Point class will probably have a constructor that looks something like

```
Point(int p, int q): x(p), y(q) { }
```

the mere existence of this seemingly pointless constructor makes it possible to change the representation later, without the user having to know about the change. Thus, for example, we could turn the coordinates into an array, and reverse their order:

```
class Point {
public:
        Point(int p, int q) { points[1] = p; points[0] = q; }
        // other stuff

private:
        int points[2];
};
```

The users would never need to know.

Just as constructors conceal the details of building up an object, destructors conceal the details of tearing it down. For some classes, it is not enough to say that destroying an object is equivalent to destroying that object's members. It is important that users of such classes be able to ignore the details of destruction, for exactly the same reasons that they need to be able to ignore the details of construction.

Thus, destructors are a second key to making effective libraries possible.

26.1.2 Member functions and visibility control

Another important idea is the ability to prevent users from looking at parts of classes that they shouldn't see. What good is it to conceal the structure of our `Point` class with constructors and destructors if users can refer directly to x and y anyway? By making these members private, we further strengthen the distinction between behavior and implementation.

26.2 Libraries and abstract data types

What we have seen so far are, of course, some of the ways that C++ supports data abstraction. Is library support any different? That is, what should a language do to support library design that is different from what it would do anyway to support data abstraction?

The key to the difference is that the notion of a library carries with it the connotation of classes being written by people who are different from the ones who use them. Thus, for example, one person may combine classes written by two other people for use by a fourth person. This possibility leads to language support for libraries that goes beyond mere data abstraction.

26.2.1 Type-safe linkage

As an example, C++ once required the programmer to say explicitly when a global function was to be overloaded:

```
extern double sqrt(double);
extern float sqrt(float);      // was once an error
```

This was intended to make it as easy as possible for C and C++ functions to coexist in a single program. Because C does not allow two functions to share a common name, C++ must impose a similar restriction to be able to coexist with the C world.

Of course, programmers who wanted the convenience of function overloading needed a way to express overloading; they got it by writing an explicit `overload` declaration:

```
overload sqrt;                     // was once required
extern double sqrt(double);
extern float sqrt(float);
```

By saying `overload sqrt`, the programmer was saying, "Yes, I know I can't have two C functions named `sqrt`, but I'm not going to insist that these functions must both be the same as their C counterparts." Instead, the implementation would pick the first function declared with a given name—here `sqrt(double)` —and say that that function would be equivalent to the C `sqrt` function.

This turned out to make it much harder to combine libraries, because of declarations in header files. To see why, assume first that there is a header file called `math.h` that contains a declaration of `sqrt(double)`, and, for the moment, that there is no `sqrt(float)`. Now consider what happens when someone writes a library for complex numbers, and wants to include a `sqrt` function that acts on complex arguments. That library presumably has a `Complex.h` file that includes a declaration like this:

```
extern Complex sqrt(Complex);
```

Should `Complex.h` contain an `overload` declaration for `sqrt` or not?

It turned out that either answer caused trouble, because the library author wouldn't know whether a user who included `Complex.h` would include `math.h` first or not. That meant that it was impossible to tell whether or not `sqrt(Complex)` would be the first `sqrt` function to be declared. The library author couldn't control whether or not the version defined in the library would be treated as equivalent to the C version of `sqrt`. The problem became even more acute when a user tried to combine two independently written libraries, each with a function named `sqrt`.

C++ solved that problem in 1989 by abolishing `overload` declarations outright. Instead, all functions became implicitly overloaded. That made it much easier to combine C++ libraries. Of course, there was still the problem of communicating with C programs; introducing a new declaration syntax solved that problem:

```
extern "C" double sqrt(double);
```

Here, the phrase `extern "C"` means that `sqrt(double)` should be treated, for linkage purposes, as though it is a C function. The precise nature of this treatment, of course, depends on how the particular system treats C functions.

Many people considered this a radical change at the time. If nothing else, it meant that all C++ programs had to be recompiled. But it did something important: In most cases, it freed library authors from worrying whether the names of their functions would collide with the names of functions in other libraries. It turned out also to have the useful side effect of strengthening type checking between separately compiled modules.

26.2.2 Namespaces

Namespaces provide a solution to a problem that was already significant in C and is even more so in C++: What can the language do to keep library authors from using the same names for their components?

To appreciate the problem, try the following on your favorite C compiler:

```
#include <stdio.h>

void write()
{
        printf("Hello world\n");
}

int main()
{
        write();
        return 0;
}
```

This is a strictly conforming C program. On the surface, there is nothing unusual about it. Nevertheless, it will fail in strange ways on many systems, because the printf library function uses a system function called write to do its work. By defining a function with the same name, we have preempted that system function, with unpredictable results. The ISO C standard says that implementations are not allowed to use hidden functions in this manner, but, in practice, many C implementations don't follow that part of the standard accurately.

When you're done experimenting with your C compiler, you can try the C++ version of it:

```
#include <stdio.h>

extern "C" void write()
{
        printf("Hello world\n");
}

int main()
{
        write();
}
```

Here, the definition of the function write as extern "C" may conflict with the function of the same name that happens to be part of the operating-system library. Indeed, in the case of C++, where libraries of all kinds are becoming available, it is hard to see how to avoid conflicts among libraries from different vendors. After all, doesn't each library have a class named string or String?

In principle, such a problem is easy to solve: Let every library vendor prefix every external name with a string that is unique to that particular vendor. Therefore, instead of releasing a class named String, the Little Purple Software Company should define a class named

```
LittlePurpleSoftwareCompany_String
```

The company can guarantee that that name is unique by registering its prefix as a trademark.

Of course, this causes minor problems for users who, instead of saying

```
String s;
```

must now say

```
LittlePurpleSoftwareCompany_String s;
```

This practice lends a whole new dimension to the concept of strong typing. Moreover, what happens if the company's Board of Directors decides that purple is too crude a color, and changes the corporate name to the Little Violet Software Company? Must all that company's users change all their programs?

Namespaces were added to the language to solve such problems. Essentially, namespaces allow the library author to designate a wrapper around all the names that that library would otherwise inject into the global scope. Users have two options. They can access those names by using the name qualified with the namespace name:

```
LittlePurpleSoftwareCompany::String s;
```

Alternatively, they can adopt all the names from a namespace into the program:

```
using namespace LittlePurpleSoftwareCompany;

String s;
```

Either way, the library author and library user can cooperate to avoid name collisions.

26.3 Memory allocation

C++ programmers are often concerned with special-purpose memory allocation, either to tune allocation strategies for a particular application or to make use of memory with particular characteristics. Just as C++ has ways to allow library authors to control the construction and destruction of objects of their classes, it also allows them to control the allocation of the memory in which those objects will reside.

This control takes several forms, reflecting several different ways in which class authors may want to manipulate memory.

For example, the author of a class Foo can say that objects of that class should be allocated and freed by a particular pair of functions. The way that they do so is to name the functions operator new and operator delete, and to make the functions members of the class:

```
class Foo {
public:
        void* operator new(size_t);
        void operator delete(void*);
        // ...
};
```

Now, whenever someone tries to allocate a `Foo` object in dynamic storage, `Foo::operator new` will be called to allocate memory; whenever someone tries to deallocate a dynamically allocated `foo` object, `Foo::operator delete` will be called to free the memory.

Another common form of memory allocation is in the construction of container classes. Here, the container author may wish to allocate a big chunk of memory, and to place individual objects in known locations in that memory. The syntax for that is

```
void* p = /* get a bunch of space */;
T* tp = new(p) T;
```

The second line in this example is a request to allocate an object of type `T` in the memory addressed by the pointer `p`. More precisely, it is a call to the function `operator new(size_t, void*)`, which is defined in the standard library to look like this:

```
void* operator new(size_t, void* p)
{
        return p;
}
```

Unless the user redefines it, `new(p) T` is a request to allocate a `T` object in the memory addressed by `p`.

You may have noticed that these two forms of memory allocation conflict. What happens, for example, if someone tries to put `Foo` objects, as defined before, into a container that wants to put its objects into the memory that it allocates itself?

The answer is that the container takes precedence: saying `new(p) Foo` allocates a `Foo` object in the memory addressed by `p`, even though class `Foo` has an allocator of its own. This choice was made after a great deal of thought and discussion, almost all of which was motivated by the things that library authors might want to do with memory allocation.

26.4 Memberwise assignment and initialization

Probably the most pervasive way in which the needs of library authors have influenced the language design is in the recursive default definitions of assignment and initialization. These rules are inherited from C, but take on new subtleties for C++.

As an example, consider a simplified version of our earlier `Point` class:

```
struct Point {
        int x, y;
};
```

Here, we have reduced the class to a C structure. Even so, the rules for C implicitly allow `Point` objects to be assigned to one another:

```
Point p1;
p1.x = 3;
p1.y = 7;
Point p2 = p1;
```

The issue is: What does the last statement, in which `p2` is initialized from `p1`, mean?

In C, there is no question as to the meaning of "copying a structure." Such an operation is probably implemented as copying the bits that constitute the machine representation of that structure, but, from the user's viewpoint, the operation is indistinguishable from what would happen if each of the members of the structure were copied independently.

In AT&T's first C++ release, the default definition of copying a class object was to copy the underlying C structure. This worked fine for simple classes such as our `Point` class, even after the class had acquired a constructor. For more complicated classes, of course, class authors could define their own copy and assignment operations.

But there was one case that always gave trouble: a simple class whose members were complicated classes. For example, imagine a general-purpose `String` library class with a constructor, destructor, assignment operation, and so on. The language was carefully tuned to ensure that the author of that class could control everything that happened to objects of that class. The one exception was the user who naively wrote code like this:

```
struct Person {
        String name, address, telno;
};
```

The members `name`, `address`, and `telno` each have an assignment operator defined, so we might expect to be able to assign `Person` objects as easily as assigning `Point` objects. That didn't work in C++ Release 1, though, because the effect was to copy the underlying C object, and completely to bypass whatever operations should have been performed to copy each of the members. Fortunately, the compiler also produced a warning message that said, in effect "I implemented this assignment as a bitwise copy; that's probably not what you wanted."

In the C++ spirit of engineering compromise, we might think that generating the warning message would be good enough. After all, the compiler would say that, for that class to work correctly, the class must include its own assignment and copy operations. Indeed, this approach persisted for quite a while.

One of the things that caused it to change was the realization that a thorough author of a class such as `Person` would have to include explicit assignment and copy operations all the time. After all, even if the definition of the `String` class turns out not to require such explicit operations at present, there is no obvious reason to believe that the author of the `String` class might not change the class in the future.

Another cause was that too many people failed to grasp all that was required. For example, to make our `Person` structure work, we would have had to say

```
struct Person {
        String name, address, telno;
        Person();
        Person(const Person& p): name(p.name),
                address(p.address), telno(p.telno) { }

        Person& operator=(const Person& p) {
                name = p.name;
                address = p.address;
                telno = p.telno;
                return *this;
        }
};
```

Note that it was not necessary to give the `Person` class an explicit destructor; the compiler would correctly derive the destructor from the `String` class destructor. If it could do that, why couldn't it do the same for assignment and copying?

It was questions such as these that ultimately caused assignment and copy operations to be defined by default as depending recursively on the definitions of assignment and copying for the members of the underlying class, instead of merely moving around the bits of the corresponding C structure.

26.5 Exception handling

Error handling is messy. Consider

```
template<class T> class Vector {
public:
        Vector(int size): data(new T[size]) { }
        ~Vector() { delete [] data; }
        T& operator[](int n) { return data[n]; }

private:
        // ...
}
```

In this small example, lots of things can go wrong:
- Creating a vector with a negative size
- Not enough memory to hold a big vector
- Subscript out of range
- Something going wrong inside an element constructor

Not only can lots of things go wrong, but also it's not obvious how we can deal with errors. Our choices would seem to be either to terminate the program or to set some error state. Neither of these works well in practice.

People writing interactive or other long-lived applications insist on being able to continue executing even after their users have done stupid things such as asking for zillion-element arrays. This implies that any class used by such an application had better not give up and terminate after something bad happens.

But returning an error indication doesn't work either: People don't check them—in part, because if they check all such errors, that would greatly complicate many programs.

What we need is a way of saying that something has gone wrong that should not be casually ignored, and that can be checked *if* the user desires.

The C++ exception-handling mechanism is designed to have these properties.

26.6 Summary

Library design is a kind of language design. The design of the C++ language itself has evolved to support the kinds of programs that people have wanted to write to create useful C++ libraries. We have seen several concrete examples of this. The careful student of C++ will discover many others.

Part V

Technique

Most of the classes that we've seen so far have represented some kind of data structure or family of data structures. In this part, we switch focus to look at classes that, although useful, fit no such neat categorization as data abstraction or object-oriented programming. Because these classes depart from the usual categories, our viewpoint will be unsystematic.

For example, how can we ensure that a C++ program frees exactly once each object that it allocates? One way is to define a class whose objects do no work while they exist, but log when they are constructed and destroyed. Chapter 27 shows how to define and use such a class. Another way, shown in Chapter 28, is to note, when creating each of a collection of similar objects, that the object is in that collection, and then to arrange to destroy the whole collection at once.

After discussing memory-management techniques, we will look at two techniques for creating general-purpose abstractions. These chapters date back to the early days of templates; I thought them pretty wild at the time, but the world has caught up since then. Still, the techniques have more than just historical interest.

Chapter 29 describes techniques that have since become a fundamental part of the I/O library. The basic problem is how to send an out-of-band signal such as "flush the output buffer" to a file using the same syntax that we use for writing ordinary data, so that we can write

```
cout << "Hello, world!" << endl;
```

or

```
cout << "Hello, world!" << "\n" << flush;
```

instead of having to say

```
cout << "Hello, world!" << "\n";
flush(cout);
```

After that discussion, Chapter 30 looks at a template-based strategy for designing an application not to depend on any particular I/O library.

27

Classes that keep track of themselves

A fundamental idea in C++ is that class definitions can say explicitly what should happen when objects of that class are constructed, destroyed, copied, and assigned. One implication—which may be more important than people realize—is that suitably designed classes can provide a powerful tool for understanding the dynamic behavior of programs. We touched briefly on these notions in Chapter 0, but our concern there was with the Trace class as a mechanism to explain classes per se. Here, we'll look more deeply at how classes can provide useful debugging information both about function execution and, more interesting, about class operation.

27.1 Design of a trace class

Here is a simple class that we can use to trace program execution:

```
class Trace {
public:
        Trace() { cout << "Hello\n"; }
        ~Trace() { cout << "Goodbye\n"; }
};
```

The idea is to make the program say what it is doing without significantly changing its behavior otherwise. For example, if we have a function

```
void foo()
{
        // do something here
}
```

and we want to know when this function is called, we can insert a declaration for a Trace object,

```
void foo()
{
        Trace xxx;
        // do something here
}
```

and the function will automatically print a message when it starts and another when it finishes. The reason for this, of course, is that the object xxx is constructed where it is declared, and is automatically destroyed on exit from the block that contains its declaration.

Of course, our Trace class is not terribly useful as it stands. Suppose, for example, that we use it to trace several functions. We get no clue about *which* functions are producing the Hello and Goodbye messages that are filling up our output.

Here is one way to make our tool more sensitive:

```
class Trace {
public:
        Trace(const char* p, const char* q): bye(q) {
                cout << p;
        }
        ~Trace() { cout << bye; }

private:
        const char* bye;
};
```

We now give two arguments to a Trace object when constructing it: one to be printed when the object is constructed, and another to be printed when the object is destroyed. We store the second argument in the Trace object, so that we can print it at the proper time. Using this class is only a little harder than is using the previous one:

```
void foo()
{
        Trace xxx("begin foo\n", "end foo\n");
        // do something here
}
```

We get much more useful information from this version.

However, if we use this class for a while, we are likely to discover three things:
1. The messages that we want to print have a lot in common. For example, we might discover that they all end in \n and start with either begin or end.
2. It would be useful to make the trace messages optional. We do not want to be flooded with debugging output when we are not debugging.
3. We may want our debugging information to go somewhere other than cout, so that it is not interspersed with the rest of the program's output.

We can reduce the amount of duplicated text that the user has to type by having the constructor remember the name of the function being traced, and arranging for the constructor and destructor to print the begin and end messages. Suppressing output, or redirecting it, requires a bit more thought.

Most operating systems provide a way to send output to a "file" that throws the output away. Suppressing output is identical to sending it to such a destination, or equivalently, to using a pointer to the output stream and setting the pointer to 0. Thus, it turns out that suppressing output is a special case of redirecting it.

We might add a global pointer to the output stream for use in debugging. The trouble is that one part of the program may turn on tracing by setting this global file to point to some stream, and another part of the program may turn tracing off or may redirect it to some other file. Using global data, in general, requires a great deal of care to get right.

The other extreme would be to put the output-stream pointer into each Trace object, but then we'd end up needing to say what file to print on each time we want to trace something—a tedious and error-prone strategy.

A third possibility is to recognize that trace requests are frequently bunched up. There will be some section of code that relates to some feature or subsystem that is misbehaving. Logically, we'll want a whole set of Trace objects to send output to a given file at the same time. This observation, coupled with the fundamental rule of C++ programming, *use classes to represent concepts*, suggests that we create a class to manage output for a set of Trace objects. We'll call this class a Channel. It will hold a pointer to an output stream, and will allow the Trace class to access its pointer. Each Trace object will say which Channel to use. Then, at a single point in the program, we can redirect tracing for all Trace objects attached to some Channel.

This leads to a Channel class such as

```
class Channel {
        friend class Trace;
        ostream* trace_file;

public:
        Channel(ostream* o = &cout): trace_file(o) { }
        void reset(ostream* o) { trace_file = o; }
};
```

We'll use this class in the Trace class to allow us to redirect output:

```
class Trace {
public:
        Trace(const char* s, Channel* c): name(s), cp(c) {
                if (cp->trace_file)
                        *cp->trace_file << "begin "
                                        << name << endl;
        }
```

```
        ~Trace() {
                if (cp->trace_file)
                        *cp->trace_file << "end "
                                         << name << endl;
        }

private:
        Channel* cp;
        const char* name;
};
```

We now first define logical groupings for tracing:

```
Channel subsystemX(&cout);
Channel subsystemY(0);
// other logical debugging groupings
```

This says that the `Trace` objects associated with `subsystemX` will print to `cout`, and those associated with `subsystemY` will generate no output. Now, in any function that we want to trace, we say

```
void foo()
{
        Trace xxx("foo", subsystemX);
        // do something here
}
```

which saves us a good deal of effort compared to the previous version. Moreover, we can turn off or redirect trace output by resetting the `Channel`:

```
subsystemX.reset(0);                    // turn off tracing
subsystemX.reset(&some_stream);  // redirect tracing
```

Calling `subsystemX.reset` will affect the output from all `Trace` objects associated with the `Channel` called `subsystemX`; if the argument to `reset` is zero, that will suppress the output entirely.

27.2 Creating dead code

One potential problem with debugging classes is that, even when the output is turned off, it takes space and time to test `trace_file` at entry and exit to every traced function. However, if our C++ implementation is reasonably clever, we may be able to eliminate almost all that overhead for production code, without rewriting user code to do so.

The trick is to make it possible for the compiler to realize that the `Trace` constructor and destructor are dead code under some circumstances. We can probably do that by *guarding* the actual constructor and destructor with a test of a global variable that, for production code, we will set to a constant zero:

```
static const int debug = 0;

class Trace {
public:
        Trace(const char* s, Channel* c) {
                if (debug) {
                        name = s;
                        cp = c;
                        if (cp->trace_file)
                                *cp->trace_file << "begin "
                                << name << endl;
                }
        }

        ~Trace() {
                if (debug) {
                        if (cp->trace_file)
                                *cp->trace_file << "end "
                                << name << endl;
                }
        }

private:
        Channel* cp;
        const char* name;
};
```

Note that name is now initialized by explicit assignment, instead of in the constructor initializer. This ensures that the initialization is skipped when debug is known to be zero; without that change, the initialization might occur even in production code.

This technique slightly complicates the code executed when tracing is being used. However, if the debug variable is a constant zero, many C++ implementations will realize that it is unnecessary to generate any of the code guarded by if (debug). As with most aspects of performance, different implementations will behave differently; programmers who care about this should conduct their own tests.

27.3 Generating audit trails for objects

We can, of course, embellish this class until we get tired. Instead, let's explore a different way of using these classes. It is easy to think about tracing a function, because that idea is common to most programming languages. It requires a little more insight to realize that it is also possible to trace objects without explicitly changing any of the associated code.

For example, suppose that we have a String class:

```
class String {
        // a whole bunch of stuff
};
```

We can almost produce a message for every `String` constructed or destroyed simply by adding a single extra member to the class:

```
class String {
        // the same stuff as before
        Trace xxx;
};
```

The only reason that this doesn't work is that we need to get arguments to the `Trace` object somehow. Instead of doing that, let's modify the `Trace` class to do something useful without explicit arguments. Because we will use this class for tracing objects, rather than for tracing functions, we will call it `Obj_trace`. Moreover, to keep the examples short, we will write directly on `cout`, knowing that it is easy to generalize this later:

```
class Obj_trace {
public:
        Obj_trace(): ct(++count) {
                cout << "Object " << ct
                        << " constructed" << endl;
        }

        ~Obj_trace() {
                cout << "Object " << ct
                        << " destroyed" << endl;
        }

        Obj_trace(const Obj_trace&): ct(++count) {
                cout << "Object " << ct
                        << " constructed" << endl;
        }

        Obj_trace& operator=(const Obj_trace&) {
                return *this;
        }
private:
        static int count;
        int ct;
};

int Obj_trace::count = 0;
```

Every time that an `Obj_trace` object is created, it gets a unique serial number, which the constructor and destructor print. That is true whether the object is created from scratch or whether it is copied from some other object; in each case, a new serial number goes with the new object. For the same reason, assigning an `Obj_trace` object does not copy its serial number.

Now, we can make our `String` class look like this:

```
class String {
            // the same stuff as before
            Obj_Trace xxx;
};
```

The presence of the `Obj_trace` member will cause every `String` object to record its presence with messages like this:

```
Object 1 constructed
Object 2 constructed
Object 3 constructed
Object 2 destroyed
Object 4 constructed
Object 1 destroyed
Object 4 destroyed
Object 3 destroyed
```

27.4 Verifying container behavior

The format of this output turns out to be remarkably useful for verifying memory management of container classes. To begin, we can check that every object that is constructed also is destroyed. For short output such as in this example, it is not hard to do that check by eye. Of course, real programs will generate much more output; is there some easy to verify the output?

One thing simplifies verification greatly: By sorting the trace output, we bring together all messages relating to a particular object. For example, sorting the output in the previous section gives us

```
Object 1 constructed
Object 1 destroyed
Object 2 constructed
Object 2 destroyed
Object 3 constructed
Object 3 destroyed
Object 4 constructed
Object 4 destroyed
```

Not only does this make it easy to check small output files, but also we can easily write programs to check larger output files.

To show how we might use such a class, here is a simple arraylike container:

```
// is this code correct?
template<class T> class Array {
public:
        Array(int n = 0): data(new T[n]) { }
        ~Array() { delete data; }
        T& operator[](unsigned n) {
                return data[n];
        }
```

```
private:
        T* data;
};
```

To keep the code small, we've made two intentional simplifications here. First, we are not checking whether the new expression succeeded; we assume that memory-allocation failure throws an exception. Second, we are not checking subscript bounds in operator[]. You may wish to see how many other bugs you can find in the code before reading on.

We can learn a lot about the behavior of this template by using it to store Obj_trace objects. For example, even this tiny program reveals some problems:

```
int main()
{
        Array<Obj_trace> x(3);
}
```

Executing the program yields the following output:

```
Object 1 constructed
Object 2 constructed
Object 3 constructed
Object 1 destroyed
```

Apparently, we are creating objects that are never destroyed. With that hint, it is not hard to see the problem: We must say explicitly that we are deleting an array by changing

```
delete data;
```

to

```
delete[] data;
```

After we make that change, the output is

```
Object 1 constructed
Object 2 constructed
Object 3 constructed
Object 3 destroyed
Object 2 destroyed
Object 1 destroyed
```

Notice that array elements are destroyed in reverse order, as they should be. Of course, we must check this before sorting the trace output.

Next, let's see what happens when we copy an array:

```
int main()
{
        Array<Obj_trace> x(3);
        Array<Obj_trace> y = x;
}
```

Surprisingly, the output remains unchanged:

```
Object 1 constructed
Object 2 constructed
Object 3 constructed
Object 3 destroyed
Object 2 destroyed
Object 1 destroyed
```

A little thought reveals the reason: The copy constructor for our class doesn't copy the array elements. Apparently, the memory allocator recognizes that they are being deleted twice, and does not run the destructors again; that's still not what we wanted to happen.

Again, once we recognize this problem, it is easy to add a copy constructor. The only trick is realizing that we will have to remember the array size, so that we know how many elements to copy:

```
// is this code correct yet?
template<class T> class Array {
public:
        Array(int n = 0): data(new T[n]), sz(n) { }
        Array(const Array&);
        ~Array() { delete [] data; }

        T& operator[](unsigned n) {
                return data[n];
        }

private:
        T* data;
        int sz;
};

template<class T> Array<T>::Array(const Array<T>& a):
        data(new T[a.sz]), sz(a.sz)
{
        for (int i = 0; i < sz; i++) {
                data[i] = a.data[i];
        }
}
```

Running the main program with this revised Array class definition gives us the output that we expect:

```
Object 1 constructed
Object 2 constructed
Object 3 constructed
Object 4 constructed
Object 5 constructed
Object 6 constructed
Object 6 destroyed
Object 5 destroyed
Object 4 destroyed
Object 3 destroyed
Object 2 destroyed
Object 1 destroyed
```

Next, we see whether assignment works correctly:

```
int main()
{
        Array<Obj_trace> x(3);
        Array<Obj_trace> y = x;
        x = y;
}
```

Of course, it doesn't: The output is now

```
Object 1 constructed
Object 2 constructed
Object 3 constructed
Object 4 constructed
Object 5 constructed
Object 6 constructed
Object 6 destroyed
Object 5 destroyed
Object 4 destroyed
```

Six objects are constructed (three when constructing x and three when initializing y from x), but only three are destroyed. A look at the Array assignment operator exposes the problem: There isn't one! In defining it, we note that it has a loop similar to the copy constructor, so we can make that loop into a separate, private member function:

```
// are we done?
template<class T> class Array {
public:
        Array(int n = 0): data(new T[n]), sz(n) { }
        Array(const Array& a) { init(a.data, a.sz); }
        ~Array() { delete [] data; }

        Array& operator=(const Array& a) {
                delete[] data;
                init(a.data, a.sz);
                return *this;
        }
```

```
        T& operator[](unsigned n) {
                return data[n];
        }

private:
        T* data;
        int sz;
        void init(T*, int);
};

template<class T> void Array<T>::init(T* p, int n)
{
        sz = n;
        data = new T[n];
        for (int i = 0; i < sz; i++)
                data[i] = p[i];
}
```

Now, when we run the same main program, we get another surprise:

```
Object 1 constructed
Object 2 constructed
Object 3 constructed
Object 4 constructed
Object 5 constructed
Object 6 constructed
Object 3 destroyed
Object 2 destroyed
Object 1 destroyed
Object 7 constructed
Object 8 constructed
Object 9 constructed
Object 6 destroyed
Object 5 destroyed
Object 4 destroyed
Object 9 destroyed
Object 8 destroyed
Object 7 destroyed
```

We are evidently constructing and destroying nine objects, instead of six. Why?

Another look at the assignment operator reveals the answer. We are assigning an array by deleting all the old elements and copying in the new ones. That is necessary because the source and destination arrays might be different sizes. But that means that the assignment

```
x = y;
```

does indeed destroy, and then construct, three more elements.

This behavior should also remind us to ask what happens when we assign an array to itself. As is so often the case, the answer is that the elements of the source array are deleted and then (illegitimately) copied. We can remove that bug by checking explicitly for self assignment:

```
Array& operator=(const Array& a)
{
        if (this != &a) {
                delete[] data;
                init(a.data, a.sz);
        }
        return *this;
}
```

27.5 Summary

We have seen two examples of classes whose only purpose is to inform the world of their existence. We often use such classes to trace function entry and exit. Indeed, we can write them in ways such that it is worthwhile, in most cases, to leave them in place even in production programs.

A less common use of such classes is to embed them in other class definitions. When appropriately written, such classes can be remarkably powerful tools for verifying that other classes—especially containers—behave as intended.

28

Allocating objects in clusters

C++ programs often have reasons to allocate collections of objects that will all be freed at the same time. One approach is to define a class to contain such a collection. Arranging for a collection to contain objects of unrelated classes turns out to be a nice way of using multiple inheritance.

28.1 The problem

Suppose that you have an assortment of C++ objects that you know are going to be freed together. Such situations occur often, especially in interactive or long-running programs.

For example, interactive programs will typically alternate between reading requests from a keyboard and processing those requests. Some of the objects created during that processing may stick around indefinitely, but others can be deleted at the end of the transaction that created them. As another example, container classes often control the memory allocation of the objects contained in them. Because this kind of allocation may be useful in a number of different contexts, let's see what we can do by considering the problem in an abstract way.

28.2 Designing the solution

The problem is to keep track of a bunch of objects to be freed together. To make progress on this problem, let's try to solve it by applying the fundamental principle of C++ design: *Use classes to represent concepts*.

This implies that we'll want a class to represent the idea of "a bunch of objects that will be freed together." Let's call that class a `Cluster`:

```
class Cluster {
        // ...
};
```

If `Cluster` is a class, we must be able to create objects of that class:

```
Cluster c;
```

Furthermore, the object c must evidently contain other objects that will be freed at some appropriate time.

What is an appropriate time? If nothing else, destroying c must free the objects in c, lest we lose our last opportunity to free those objects. Thus, the destructor for class `Cluster` must free the objects contained in the `Cluster` object being destroyed.

What can we say about these objects? Not much, except that there must be a way of allocating an object "in" a particular `Cluster`. Suppose T is the type of such an object. We need some way to say, "Allocate an object of type T in cluster c." Saying it that way immediately suggests a solution:

```
T* tp = new(c) T;
```

For this to work, class T will need a member `operator new` that accepts a `Cluster` as its argument. Because allocating an object in a `Cluster` presumably will modify the `Cluster`, that argument will have to be passed by reference. Thus, type T evidently must have a member:

```
void* T::operator new(size_t, Cluster&);
```

This requirement is less than useful. The problem is that we have just said something about the definition of class T, but restricting the definition of class T limits the usefulness of the `Cluster` class. The whole point was to be able to put objects of any user-defined classes into clusters. Is there any way to avoid having to touch T?

The solution is to use inheritance. As we'll see, by using inheritance and a level of indirection, we can arrange to put objects of any class into a `Cluster`. And, by judiciously using multiple inheritance, we will be able to do so without having to have access to the definition of class T. We begin by defining a base class from which people can derive classes to be put into clusters. Let's call that class `ClusterItem`:

```
class ClusterItem {
public:
        void* operator new(size_t, Cluster&);
        // ...
};
```

What else do we need in class `ClusterItem`? Some C++ implementations have the restriction that, if we have any `operator new` members, we must have one that takes only a `size_t`, to ensure that objects of that class can be allocated with plain new expressions. In this case, though, we *don't* want to allow that—if you want to allocate a `ClusterItem`, you had better do so only in a `Cluster`! To enforce this restriction, we'll define the plain `operator new`, but we'll make it private.

While we're at it, we'll make the copy constructor and assignment operator private too, so that we don't have to think about what it means to copy a ClusterItem.

```
class ClusterItem {
public:
        void* operator new(size_t, Cluster&);

private:
        void* operator new(size_t);
        ClusterItem(const ClusterItem&);
        ClusterItem& operator=(const ClusterItem&);
        // ...
};
```

As it stands, this class is still useless, because we can't create ClusterItem objects. To solve that problem, we need at least a default constructor. While we're thinking about that, we should decide what to do about destroying ClusterItem objects. Because ClusterItem will be used as a base class, we will need to give it a virtual destructor. Also, we need to decide how and when ClusterItem objects will be destroyed. The easiest design to implement is to assume that ClusterItem objects will be destroyed only as a side effect of destroying the corresponding Cluster, which suggests that we should not make the ClusterItem destructor public. Of course, we will have to nominate Cluster as a friend, lest we make it impossible to destroy ClusterItem objects at all!

```
class ClusterItem {
        friend class Cluster;

public:
        void* operator new(size_t, Cluster&);
        ClusterItem();

protected:
        virtual ~ClusterItem() { }

private:
        void* operator new(size_t);
        ClusterItem(const ClusterItem&);
        ClusterItem& operator=(const ClusterItem&);
        // ...
};
```

Now let's turn our attention to class Cluster. We will need a constructor and destructor, and we'll want class ClusterItem to be a friend. Moreover, we'll want to restrict copying Cluster objects, so that we don't have to think about what that operation would mean. That gives us the following definition:

```
class Cluster {
        friend class ClusterItem;
public:
        Cluster();
        ~Cluster();
private:
        Cluster(const Cluster&);
        Cluster& operator=(const Cluster&);
};
```

It's hard to decide what else might be required in these classes without first thinking about implementation, so let's do that next.

28.3 Implementation

Every `Cluster` remembers a collection of objects, and destroys them all at once. What's the easiest way to do this?

If we have a container library available, we can use a container from that library. It will be more educational, though, to write the container from scratch. Given that we're taking that route, it is simplest to maintain a singly linked list of `ClusterItems` rooted in the corresponding `Cluster`. That will result in deleting the `ClusterItems` in reverse order of creation—which indeed is what we want. That strategy will mirror the strategy for local variables, for example.

That means we will want to add to class `Cluster` a pointer that represents the head of the list, and to add to class `ClusterItem` a pointer to the next `ClusterItem` on the chain:

```
class Cluster {
        friend class ClusterItem;
public:
        Cluster();
        ~Cluster();
private:
        ClusterItem* head;        // added
        Cluster(const Cluster&);
        Cluster& operator=(const Cluster&);
};

class ClusterItem {
        friend class Cluster;
public:
        void* operator new(size_t, Cluster&);
        ClusterItem();
protected:
        virtual ~ClusterItem() { }
```

```
private:
        ClusterItem* next;         // added
        void* operator new(size_t);
        ClusterItem(const ClusterItem&);
        ClusterItem& operator=(const ClusterItem&);
};
```

These additions let us define the `Cluster` constructor immediately:

```
Cluster::Cluster(): head(0) { }
```

Similarly, we can define the destructor almost immediately:

```
Cluster::~Cluster()
{
        while (head) {
                ClusterItem* next = head->next;
                delete head;
                head = next;
        }
}
```

Notice that

```
delete head;
```

uses the virtual destructor in class `ClusterItem` to delete whatever class the user might derive from `ClusterItem`.

Now what about the members of class `ClusterItem`? We have to arrange that when we create a `ClusterItem` object, we link it into the chain of the associated `Cluster`. This turns out to be a little tricky, but we can figure it out by seeing what information is necessary and available at what point in the process.

When we say

```
new(c) T;
```

to allocate an object of some class `T` that is derived from class `ClusterItem`, member `ClusterItem::operator new` will be given the appropriate `Cluster` as its argument. That is the only time that the identity of the `Cluster` will be available. However, the job of `operator new` is to allocate raw memory, not to deal with objects already constructed. Thus, the job of linking the `ClusterItem` object into the `Cluster`'s chain should be done by the `ClusterItem` constructor, not by `operator new`. We therefore need a way for `operator new` to save the identity of the `Cluster` where the constructor can see it. There are several ways to do that; the easiest is to use a `static` (i. e., local to the source file) variable:

```
static Cluster* cp;
```

Because this variable is local to the file with the member-function definitions, we don't need to worry about its name.

Now, we can define `operator new`. It remembers the address of the `Clus-`
`ter`, and then calls the global `operator new` to allocate the memory:

```
void* ClusterItem::operator new(size_t n, Cluster& c)
{
        cp = &c;
        return ::operator new(n);
}
```

The constructor will pick up the `Cluster` address from `cp`, and will link the
address of the object being constructed into the chain of the appropriate `Clus-`
`ter`. We could do it this way:

```
ClusterItem::ClusterItem()
{
        next = cp->head;
        cp->head = this;
}
```

The cautious programmer, however, might wish to defend against the possibility
that `cp` wasn't set, even though there's evidently no way that that could happen:

```
ClusterItem::ClusterItem()
{
        assert(cp != 0);
        next = cp->head;
        cp->head = this;
        cp = 0;
}
```

Finally, some C++ implementations might require us to define the default
`operator new` that we had declared, even though we don't intend for it ever to
be used. Here's one way:

```
void* ClusterItem::operator new(size_t)
{
        abort();
        return 0;
}
```

The `return 0;` is necessary because the compiler doesn't necessarily know that
`abort` does not return and might therefore complain about failure to return a
value.

28.4 Enter inheritance

We said before that we can use these classes by deriving them from
`ClusterItem`. This implies that, to arrange for clustered allocation of a class,
we must know about and use `ClusterItem` when we define our class:

```
class MyClass: public ClusterItem {
        // ...
};

int main()
{
        Cluster c;

        MyClass* p = new(c) Myclass;
        // ...
}
```

This approach has two problems. First, we might want to do clustered allocation on some class that we didn't define. Second, because ClusterItem has a private destructor, we can never declare local variables of any class that has ClusterItem as a base.

Fortunately, we can solve both problems with a slight variation:

```
class MyClass {
        // ...
};

class MyClusteredClass:
        public MyClass, public ClusterItem { };

int main()
{
        Cluster c;

        Myclass* p = new(c) MyClusteredClass;
        // ...
};
```

Look at the new expression: It allocates an object of type MyClusteredClass, and converts the object's address to type MyClass*. We can use this pointer just like any other pointer to a MyClass object (as long as we don't try to delete it). When the Cluster goes away, the virtual destructor in class ClusterItem will still ensure that the MyClass destructor is called properly.

This technique seems to solve all the problems except one minor one: If MyClass has constructors aside from the default constructor, MyClustered-Class will have to repeat those constructors as well. Fortunately, this needs to be done only once.

28.5 Summary

This chapter explored a problem where the key to the solution seems to be merely stating the problem in the right way. Once we understood the problem, we saw clearly that the solution had to take a particular form (new(c) T). That form, in turn, dictated almost the entire definition of the classes required. The implementation of these classes was almost as automatic.

It is rare that stating a problem leads so directly to its solution. What is not rare, however, is for clear understanding of a problem to simplify the solution. It's tempting to jump into implementation without giving any thought to design; we have seen here an example of why it pays to think about design first.

29

Applicators, manipulators, and function objects

It is often useful to be able to send an out-of-band signal to something like a file in a way that fits neatly into the syntax of other actions on that file. For instance, if

```
cout << value;
```

causes the value of the variable `value` to appear on the `cout` file, we should also be able to write

```
cout << flush;
```

to force any data that is waiting in the output buffer to be written immediately.

This chapter describes a neat solution to this problem, based on two kinds of functions. The first, called a *manipulator*, acts in some way on the data represented by its argument. The second, called an *applicator*, is an overloaded operator whose operands are a manipulable value and a manipulator to apply to that value.

Using this terminology, we might define `flush` as a manipulator and `<<` as an applicator to let the previous example work.

We extend this technique to applicators with multiple arguments by defining a kind of function object that contains a pointer to a function, and to that function's prospective arguments.

29.1 The problem

Every useful programming language must have some way for a program to obtain input and produce output. These operations seem to be among the harder parts of languages, and they often cut across the usual type-checking facilities.

For example, many C programs use the `printf` family to produce output. The `printf` functions violate the strict rules of the C language, in that they can be called at different times with arguments of different types. Thus, we can say

```
printf("%d\n", n);
```

at one time, and

```
printf("%d %d\n", n, m);
```

at another. The `printf` function is expected to know how to determine the number and types of its arguments by inspecting the format string given as its first argument.

The semantic transgressions by `printf` buy a great deal of convenience. It would otherwise be necessary to have a separate output-conversion function for each possible argument type, and for each call of an output function to write only one single value. The actual definition of `printf` allows us to write

```
printf("%d %d\n", n, m);
```

instead of something like

```
printint(n);
printstr(" ");
printint(m);
printstr("\n");
```

C++ provides tighter type checking than C. For that reason, C++ output routines have evolved a different style: There is a separate routine for each data type that we can write, but the C++ overloading mechanism allows these routines all to have the same name. Thus, we might write the preceding example in C++ as

```
cout << n;
cout << " ";
cout << m;
cout << "\n";
```

Here, `cout` represents an output file, and `<<` names a family of overloaded operators that write values of various types. Not only does this style stay strictly within the limits of the type system, but also we can easily define output for values of user-defined types by adding another overloaded `operator<<`.

By convention, `<<` returns its left argument. This allows us to abbreviate the example above as:

```
cout << n << " " << m << "\n";
```

which is almost as compact as the corresponding call to `printf`, but still does not involve any type cheating. Moreover, this style still makes it easy to define output of a user-defined data type. For instance, if `Complex` is a type with member functions `re` and `im` to extract its components, we can define output of a `Complex` value this way:

```
ostream&
operator<<(ostream& file, const Complex& z)
{
        return file << "(" << z.re() << "," << z.im() << ")";
}
```

This definition both uses and obeys the convention that the << function should return its file argument.

Suppose that there is a function flush that takes (and returns) an ostream, and that has the side effect of causing any pending buffered output to be written to the file. Such a function might look like this:

```
ostream&
flush(ostream& file)
{
        // magic here
        return file;
}
```

Here, magic is whatever it takes to flush the output buffer.

We might use this flush function as follows:

```
cout << "Password: ";
flush(cout);
```

More compactly, we could write:

```
flush(cout << "Password: ");
```

The idea, either way, is to use flush to ensure that Password: is actually written before it is the user's turn to type.

Clearly, there is a whole class of such functions, which take and return a reference to some type and, presumably, manipulate objects of that type in some way. We will call such a function a *manipulator*. Manipulators offer a convenient way of doing things to a file that do not fit neatly into the idea of reading and writing values.

However, manipulator notation by itself is cumbersome. Consider, for instance, what it would take to write several values and to flush the file after each one:

```
cout << x;
flush(cout);
cout << y;
flush(cout);
cout << z;
flush(cout);
```

This can be abbreviated as

```
flush(flush(flush(cout << x) << y) << z);
```

but that is hard to write and understand.

29.2 A solution

The preceding usage can be sweetened—at a cost. The idea is to define an arbitrary type called, say, FLUSHTYPE, and a variable of that type. This new type exists for the sole purpose of being used in overloading operator<<; therefore it needs no members:

```
class FLUSHTYPE { };
FLUSHTYPE FLUSH;
```

Now, we define an operator<< to act on that type, which calls the function that we wanted to invoke:

```
ostream&
operator<<(ostream& ofile, FLUSHTYPE f)
{
        return flush(ofile);
}
```

Now it is possible to "write" this variable:

```
cout << x << FLUSH << y << FLUSH << z << FLUSH;
```

FLUSH is an object of type FLUSHTYPE, so

```
cout << FLUSH
```

is a call to operator<<(ostream&, FLUSHTYPE), which, of course, calls flush(cout).

29.3 A different solution

The technique of defining both a type and an object of that type, with the sole aim of using the object for overloading, is unattractive for two reasons. First, it is necessary to define a new dummy type, such as FLUSHTYPE, for each manipulator. If there are many manipulators, there will be many such types. Second, in addition to defining these types, we must define a family of dummy objects, such as FLUSH, as well.

A single trick eliminates all this excess baggage:

```
ostream&
operator<<(ostream& ofile, ostream& (*func) (ostream&))
{
        return (*func) (ofile);
}
```

We will call this operator an *applicator*. Its right operand is a manipulator, and its left operand is something to be manipulated. The applicator applies the manipulator to its left argument. That is, it calls the manipulator that is its right-hand side with its left-hand side as argument.

One effect of this is that, for *any* function f that takes and returns a reference to an ostream,

```
cout << f;
```

means the same as

```
f(cout);
```

Thus, we can now write

```
cout << x << flush << y << flush << z << flush;
```

and can do away with the dummy types and variables.

Here is an analogous example for input. We could define a mechanism for skipping whitespace in an input file, based on adding new types and dummy objects, somewhat like that described previously.

```
class whitespace { };
whitespace WS;

istream&
operator>>(istream& ifile, whitespace& dummy)
{
        return eatwhite(ifile);
}
```

This example assumes that there is a manipulator called eatwhite that will skip over whitespace in a file. We can then write

```
cin >> WS;
```

to obtain the same effect as

```
eatwhite(cin);
```

However, as we did for output, we can simplify things by defining an applicator for input:

```
istream&
operator>>(istream& ifile, istream& (*func) (istream&))
{
        return (*func) (ifile);
}
```

Now we can write

```
cin >> eatwhite;
```

and can do away with the definitions of whitespace and WS, as well as with the definition of >> with the whitespace right argument.

29.4 Multiple arguments

Manipulators and applicators seem useful, so we would like to be able to define them for arbitrary functions that manipulate some type. In particular, we'd like to be able to define a manipulator with additional arguments. For example, our I/O library may well provide some function to set the data-transfer rate of a stream associated with a terminal. This function could be defined to manipulate some `ostream` and to take an integer argument specifying the new baud rate. Given such a function, named `speed`, we'd like to invoke it as follows:

```
cout << speed(9600);
```

Unfortunately, this extra argument complicates the problem. If `<<` is to be an applicator, then whatever value `speed` returns must encapsulate both the idea of setting the speed and the value to be set. In particular, `speed` cannot return a value that has a pure function type, because then there would be no place to put the value. (It is possible to achieve this using side effects, but discussing such techniques would violate community standards in many areas.) Thus, we need to define a type to contain (a pointer to) the manipulator and the value to give it.

So, for example, let's first define `setspeed` as a manipulator that takes an extra integer argument:

```
ostream& setspeed(ostream& ofile, int n)
{
        // magic here
        return ofile;
}
```

We will call such a function an *integer manipulator*. Now, we can define a kind of function object that contains the information that we need to call this manipulator. Its `operator()` member will call the manipulator that it has remembered, with the output stream we give it, and with the additional argument that it also remembers:

```
class int_fcn_obj {
public:
        int_fcn_obj(ostream& (*f) (ostream&, int), int v):
                func(f), val(v)   { }
        ostream& operator()(ostream&, o) const {
                return (*func)(o, val);
        }
private:
        ostream& (*func) (ostream&, int);
        int val;
};
```

Here, `func` is a pointer to an integer manipulator, and `val` is the integer to use as the manipulator's argument. The constructor `int_fcn_obj` builds one of these structures from a function and a value.

Next, we can define an applicator in terms of this integer function object that
"calls" the integer manipulator and passes the file to the manipulator as its argument:

```
ostream&
operator<<(ostream& ofile, const int_fcn_obj& im)
{
        return im(ofile);
}
```

Finally, we can define a `speed` function that returns an `int_fcn_obj` structure
built from its argument and `setspeed`:

```
int_fcn_obj
speed(int n)
{
        return int_fcn_obj(setspeed, n);
}
```

With this, our original

```
cout << speed(9600);
```

works correctly. The call to `speed` returns an `int_fcn_obj` structure initialized with `setspeed` and n. That newly created object is then passed to
`ostream& operator<<(ostream&, int_fcn_obj&)`, which, in turn, calls
`setspeed` with arguments `cout` and `9600`.

It is possible to avoid having separate names for `speed` and `setspeed` by
overloading `speed`. If we did that, we would have to change the body of
`speed`:

```
return int_fcn_obj((ostream& (*) (ostream&, int)) speed, n);
```

The cast here is necessary to select the proper definition of `speed`.

29.5 An example

Let's say that we want to provide a function that, given a number, generates a
human-readable version of that number in hexadecimal. So, for example, to
print n in hex, we'd like to be able to write

```
cout << to_hex(n);
```

What type of value should `to_hex` return, assuming that we do not wish to
depend on any string library? The obvious answer is a character pointer. That
answer runs into trouble, however, when we ask when the memory addressed
by that pointer should be freed.

The memory must stay around until after its contents have been written, so
an implementor's first impulse might be to have `to_hex` return a pointer to a

static buffer that persists only until the next call of to_hex. But consider this example:

```
cout << to_hex(n) << " " << to_hex(m);
```

There is nothing to stop the compiler from evaluating to_hex(n), saving the result, evaluating to_hex(m), saving that result, and *then* calling the various operator<< functions. If the compiler does that, the "wrong" values will be printed, because the pointers returned by the two calls to to_hex will both point to the same memory. One call will have overlaid the result of the other by the time that either is printed.

One solution is for to_hex to return a pointer to memory in a circular buffer. This works well for practical purposes, but it does mean that, if a single expression calls to_hex enough times, the results will be garbled.

Consider, instead, the following solution. First, we define a long-integer function-object class (that is, a class that represents function objects that take long integer arguments) called long_fn_obj, and a long-integer applicator <<:

```
class long_fn_obj {
public:
        long_fn_obj (ostream& (*f) (ostream&, long), long v):
                func(f), val(v)   { }
        ostream& operator<<(ostream& o) const {
                return (*func) (o, val);
        }

private:
        ostream& (*func) (ostream&, long);
        long val;
};

ostream&
operator<< (ostream& ofile, const long_fn_obj& im)
{
        return im(ofile);
}
```

Then, we define a hex-conversion manipulator:

```
ostream&
hexconv(ostream& ofile, long n)
{
        return ofile << to_hex(n);
}
```

This manipulator is safe because we are using the value of to_hex immediately after we have obtained it. Finally, we overload hexconv to generate a long function object:

```
long_fn_obj
hexconv(long n)
{
        return long_fn_obj(
                (ostream& (*) (ostream&, long)) hexconv, n);
}
```

Now, we can write

```
cout << hexconv(m) << " " << hexconv(n);
```

and be assured that the converted results will appear correctly, even if to_hex returns an ephemeral result.

29.6 Abbreviations

There may be many types of manipulators that we'd like to define and use in this way. For each one, we need a function-object type and an applicator for every combination of manipulator argument types that we intend to use. But the various function-object and applicator definitions are all similar. This implies that we can use templates to exploit that similarity.

We'll need to define two templates: one to generate the function object, and the other to create the operator<< applicator. As an example, let's redo the hexconv function object that we built in Section 29.5 (page 335).

The function-object template class will look like

```
template <class stype, class vtype>
class fcn_obj {
public:
        fcn_obj(stype& (*f) (stype&, vtype), vtype v):
                func(f), val(v)   { }
        stype& operator() (stype& s) const {
                return (*func) (s, val);
        }

private:
        stype& (*func) (stype&, vtype);
        vtype val;
};
```

The associated applicator template is

```
template <class stype, class vtype>
stype& operator<<
        (stype& ofile, const fcn_obj<stype, vtype>& im)
{
        return im(ofile);
}
```

We'll also need to rewrite our version of hexconv that returns the function object in terms of the template:

```
fcn_obj<ostream, long>
hexconv(long n)
{
        ostream& (*my_hex) (ostream&, long) = hexconv;
        return fcn_obj<ostream, long>(my_hex, n);
}
```

Using it is unchanged:

```
cout << hexconv(m) << " " << hexconv(n);
```

29.7 Musings

We have presented some ways to mold the language syntax. The simplest form effectively transforms

```
z << f
```

into

```
f(z)
```

For each type that z can have (istream, ostream, and so on), there is only one possible type for f; we need therefore to define only a single applicator << for each possible type for z.

We then considered manipulators with an extra argument, mapping

```
z << f(x)
```

into

```
f(z, x)
```

Here, we need to define an applicator << and a function object for each possible pair of types of z and x. Determining the types of z and x also determines the type of f.

We could obviously extend this, mapping

```
z << f(a1, ... , an)
```

into

```
f(z, a1, ... , an)
```

This would apparently require an applicator and function object for each combination of types of z and a1 through an. With templates, this is fairly easy to write.

Why bother? Because syntax matters! It is easier to write

```
cin >> noecho >> password >> echo;
```

than it is to write

```
noecho(cin);
cin >> password;
echo(cin);
```

or

```
echo(noecho(cin) >> password);
```

and we believe that this ease of expression is well worth the effort of bringing it about.

29.8 Historical notes, references, and acknowledgments

I first wrote up these ideas in the summer of 1986 (!) and showed them to several people who since then have developed them considerably. Three deserve particular mention.

Jerry Schwarz used applicators and manipulators in his `iostream` library. As a result, most C++ programmers have *used* these ideas, even if they were unaware of doing so. For example,

```
cout << "hello world" << endl;
```

uses the manipulator named `endl` and its associated applicator.

Alex Stepanov incorporated the notion of function objects into his library of generic algorithms (see Section 18.5 (page 217) and Chapter 21). With the adoption of that library as the Standard Template Library (STL), additional examples of these ideas will become more widespread.

Jonathan Shopiro explored ways of using function objects as placeholders in complicated data structures. Shopiro also coined the phrase *function object*.

The idea of a manipulator function comes from Algol 68's *layout procedures*. Lindsey and van der Meulen describe them well in Section 7.1.1 of their *Informal Introduction to Algol 68* (North-Holland, 1977).

30

Decoupling application libraries from input-output

The author of an application library faces a tough decision: What I/O facilities should that library use? Tying the library to a particular I/O package limits its flexibility, but so does failing to do so.

This chapter applies a well-known technique to the problem: *Use classes to represent concepts.* Designing a class to represent the interface to an arbitrary I/O library allows a much looser coupling between applications and I/O.

30.1 The problem

Consider a class that represents variable-length character strings:

```
class String {
        // various definitions
};
```

How do we design such a class? Presumably, it should allow frequent operations, such as concatenation, to be expressed compactly:

```
String fullname = firstname + " " + lastname;
```

It also seems important to be able to print a String using conventional notation:

```
cout << fullname << endl;
```

After all, what good is a String class that has no way to print it?

The traditional way for such a class to handle output is to include an output function with the String class definition:

```
ostream& operator<<(ostream& o, const String& s)
{
        // do whatever it takes to print the string s
        // on output stream o
        return o;
}
```

Indeed, this approach is traditional partly because it works reasonably well.

There are, however, two potentially serious problems in doing things this way. First, someone who wants to use the `String` class is now forced to use the `iostream` classes as well. Thus, a program that doesn't use the `iostream` classes otherwise, and uses some other I/O facility instead, has to incur the space overhead of having *two* complete I/O libraries. Second, there's no easy way to print a `String` on any other kind of I/O facility. An application program that uses a specialized library for, say, interprocess communication, cannot use that library to print the contents of `String`s.

30.2 Solution 1: Trickery and brute force

One route to a solution is to tackle each problem separately. For instance, we can decouple the `iostream` library overhead from the `String` class by separating the code that depends on the `iostream` library into individually compiled modules.

The `String.h` header file then looks like this:

```
class ostream;

class String {
        // various definitions
};

ostream& operator<<(ostream&, const String&);
```

Note that there is no definition for class `ostream`. This is acceptable as long as nothing that includes this header file tries to use any `ostream` objects without first defining the `ostream` class. Thus, to print a `String`, we would have to include `iostream.h`:

```
#include <String.h>
#include <iostream.h>

int main()
{
        String s = "hello\n";
        cout << s;
}
```

Otherwise, `cout` would be undefined.

Similarly, the definition of the operator<< declared previously has to include iostream.h:

```
#include <String.h>
#include <iostream.h>

ostream& operator<<(ostream& o, const String& s)
{
        // do whatever it takes to print the string s
        // on output stream o
        return o;
}
```

By compiling this function separately, we can avoid the overhead of the iostream class unless that class is actually used.

This trick doesn't solve the other half of the problem: How do we print a String on something that isn't an ostream? If it is possible to extract individual characters from a String, then we can solve the problem by brute force. For example, here is how we might print a String on a file represented by a C-style FILE pointer:

```
void putstring(const String& s, FILE* f)
{
        for (int i = 0; i < s.length(); i++)
                putc(s[i], f);
}
```

This approach is easy to understand, and should work without difficulty. However, it is probably slow: Getting a single character from a String is almost surely much slower than is copying a whole block of characters directly out to an I/O buffer of some kind. Might there be a more elegant solution?

30.3 Solution 2: Abstract output

It is clearly impossible for the author of the String class to know how to produce output on every possible output device. It is also impossible for the author of an I/O library to know about every possible type of object that might use that library. But suppose that we could abstract the most fundamental part of an output operation, and could represent just that. That might provide a kind of fastener that could connect the String and I/O libraries.

To make this more concrete, let's look at a particular kind of output operation: sending a block of characters to some destination. We can characterize the characters to be sent by their address and length, and the destination as an object of some, as yet unknown, class. Thus, we might write

```
dest.send(ptr, n);
```

to send n characters starting at the place addressed by `ptr` to the destination characterized by `dest`. Presumably, the type of `dest` will differ for different kinds of destinations, which suggests that we use a class hierarchy with a pure virtual definition of `send` in the base class. If it has a pure virtual function, it should have a virtual destructor as well, so that, if we want to allocate derived class objects, we can use base-class pointers and still be able to free the objects.

Let's call the base class `Writer`, and let's set down what we know so far about it:

```
class Writer {
public:
        virtual ~Writer();
        virtual void send(const char*, int) = 0;
};
```

If we put the declaration of this class in, say, `Writer.h`, then it is already possible to define a general-purpose `String` output function:

```
#include <Writer.h>

Writer& operator<<(Writer& w, const String& s)
{
        for (int i = 0; i < s.size(); i++) {
                char c = s[i];
                w.send(&c, 1);
        }
        return w;
}
```

This function has two problems. The first is that it is still slow. We can solve that problem by making our function a friend of the `String` class, and giving it special knowledge of how `Strings` are implemented. It can then write an entire `String` in one call of `send`, rather than doing so one character at a time.

The second problem is that the `String` class now has to know about how `Writers` work, so there is still more coupling than we would like. We'll come back to this problem in the next section.

For this design to be of any use, we must define specific `Writer` classes for particular kinds of destinations. Here is how we might do so for a C-style `FILE` pointer:

```
class FileWriter: public Writer {
public:
        FileWriter(FILE* f): fp(f) { }
        void send(const char* p, int n) {
                for (int i = 0; i < n; i++)
                        putc(*p++, fp);
        }

private:
        FILE* fp;
};
```

We can create a `FileWriter` from a `FILE` pointer; doing so remembers the `FILE` pointer. Sending characters to a `FileWriter` causes those characters to go to the relevant file.

It is now possible to write a `String` on, say, `stdout` this way:

```
FileWriter s(stdout);
String hello = "Hello\n";
s << hello;
```

Let's sum up this approach:

- Define an abstract base class `Writer` that represents the operation of writing an arbitrary sequence of characters to an arbitrary destination.
- Use inheritance to create a specialized `Writer` class for each I/O library that you might want to use.
- Define output operations for each application class that knows how to use any kind of `Writer` to write objects of that class.

Because the `Writer` base class does so little, it can be small. Thus, application programs need to incur space overhead for only those I/O libraries that they use.

30.4 Solution 3: Trickery without brute force

We can view the technique that we've developed so far as designing a tiny I/O library that has the sole purpose of acting as an interface to other I/O libraries. Thus, our approach still retains a disadvantage: For it to be useful, the application libraries must still know about the characteristics of the `Writer` class itself.

This disadvantage manifests itself in various ways. For example, although we've seen that we can write

```
FileWriter s(stdout);
String hello = "Hello\n";
s << hello;
```

and, indeed, we can also write

```
FileWriter s(stdout);
String hello = "Hello\n", goodbye = "Goodbye\n";
s << hello << goodbye;
```

but, we cannot write the following, which we might think should be no harder to manage:

```
String hello = "Hello\n", goodbye = "Goodbye\n";
FileWriter(stdout) << hello << goodbye;
```

The reason is that `FileWriter(stdout)` is a temporary value that may be destroyed as soon as the first `<<` operation has been completed. In other words, the compiler might do this:

```
FileWriter temp1(stdout);
Writer& temp2 = temp1 << hello;
// destroy temp1
temp2 << goodbye;
```

When the reference temp2 is created, it is bound to temp1, but, in principle, that information is not available to the compiler. When the compiler destroys temp1, that makes temp2 a dangling reference.*

One way to solve this problem is to make sure that temporary Writer objects are never created, by declaring each Writer explicitly.

Another way might be to avoid using references at all. We could create a handle class, such as that described in Chapter 5. We could add a class Writer-Surrogate that would point to some underlying class derived from class Writer. WriterSurrogates would be simple objects, capable of being copied freely. Such an approach would work with the FileWriter class that we saw in the previous section and would allow operator<< to return a WriterSurrogate, rather than a Writer&.

This route is left as an exercise for the reader. Here, instead, we'll try to make more effective use of the information that is known during compilation about what classes we are using.

The Writer class that we have seen so far encapsulates the notion of "writing something to a destination," where the kind of destination can potentially remain unknown until the actual output is done. That provides more flexibility than we usually need in practice; in consequence, it is potentially more expensive than it needs to be. Moreover, because the connection between a particular Writer and its destination is established only during execution, we have seen problems with those connections being established and broken at the wrong time.

Although the author of a String class does not know, when the String class is written, what I/O package will be used, the user of that class will certainly know. There is therefore no reason to defer binding that knowledge until execution time.

Let's look again at what a Writer is: It is a class such that, if dest is an object of that class, ptr is a pointer to some memory, and n is the number of characters there, then we can say

```
dest.send(ptr, n);
```

to send those characters to that destination.

---

* According to the ISO draft of the C++ standard, the temporaries generated here are supposed stay around until the end of the enclosing statement. An ISO-conforming compiler, therefore, will handle this code without problem. However, it will be years before current compilers, some of which which take a more aggressive stance toward destruction of temporaries, are out of use. Hence, it remains important to consider the lifetime of temporaries when writing code such as this.

Once we have decided to try to connect `Writers` to their destinations during compilation, though, there's no longer any need to use dynamic binding, and there is therefore no need to make `send` a member function. Indeed, there is a significant advantage to not doing so, as we shall see shortly.

We'll now think of *writers* (no caps) as a concept. A writer is a family of types in the same sense that the various categories of iterators are families of types, as discussed in Chapter 18. The properties of writer types that we'll need are simple: Writers provide a function `send` such that, if `dest` is a writer and `ptr` and n are as defined before, we can call

```
send(dest, ptr, n);
```

to send the relevant characters to that destination.

To connect writers to application classes, we'll use a template. Here is an example to make this idea concrete:

```
template<class W> W& operator<<(W& w, const String& s)
{
        for (int i = 0; i < s.size(); i++) {
                char c = s[i];
                send(w, &c, 1);
        }
        return w;
}
```

This is an abbreviation for an infinite family of overloaded functions—one for every possible type `W`. Thus, if

```
operator<<(FILE*, const String&)
```

is not defined explicitly, this definition will define it effectively in terms of a call to `send(FILE*,char*,int)`.

Now, of course, `send(FILE*,char*,int)` is not defined as part of the `stdio` package, because `stdio` was written long before any of our writer notions were set down on paper. However, we can easily define it without any special access to `stdio`:

```
void send(FILE* f, const char* p, int n)
{
        for (int i = 0; i < n; i++)
                putc(*p++, f);
}
```

The mere existence of this `send` function, combined with the template definition of `operator<<` as part of the `String` class, makes it possible to write

```
String hello = "Hello\n", goodbye = "Goodbye\n";
stdout << hello << goodbye;
```

So we've concluded that we can provide I/O library independence as follows:

- Application classes adopt a convention that they will use a `send` template for all their output.
- Each I/O package needs an appropriate `send` function written for it. This function need not be written by the author of the package.
- Application libraries do not need to know anything at all about the details of doing output, other than how to use the `send` function.

30.5 Remarks

This technique is admittedly somewhat sketchy. Nevertheless, this chapter shows how templates can provide a way of abstracting *actions*, much as classes provide a way of abstracting data structures.

A significant gain from using templates in this way is that knowledge of the particular I/O package to be used can be bound during compilation, rather than deferred until execution time. Thus, it is possible to expand I/O calls inline, doing away with what might be significant time and space overhead. Moreover, type checking during compilation makes it possible, as usual, to locate errors earlier during development.

Even without using templates, it is possible to achieve a much cleaner separation between class libraries than we might suppose at first. The trick is to isolate the key concept, and then to design a class that represents that concept.

Part VI

Wrapup

A common criticism offered against C++ is that the language is too complicated. Certainly, it's easy to find supporting documentation for this claim. Proponents of this viewpoint can even cite the number and size of books describing C++.

I think this criticism is valid only if we view C++ in isolation. All languages—all software, for that matter—are designed in some context. As we saw in the introduction to the Part I, the context for C++ is a specific user community. That user community takes complicated problems and writes solutions that are often expected to run for a long time, meet ambitious performance requirements, work on many different hardware and operating-system platforms, and coexist with lots of other existing systems. C++ programmers live in a complicated world.

Having watched the complaints about complexity from the early days (Bjarne worried about even C with Classes being too big), one aspect of this discussion always stands out: Amidst the complaints about complexity, there has always been a backlog of requests for new language features. Some of these requests reflected insufficient understanding of how to use the existing language to accomplish some task. Some came from a natural human desire to be able to leave one's mark on what was becoming a popular programming language. Most often, however, features were requested because some collection of users faced a real problem, and they needed support in the language to solve these problems.

So, despite the desire for a simple or "clean" language, what people wanted in practice was help in solving hard problems. Because C++ is reasonably popular, we must conclude that its users are willing to trade off simplicity in their language for the expressive power and efficiency that C++ provides. Chapter 31 explores the reasons why our tools sometimes need to be complex, especially when the problems that we want to solve keep getting more complicated. We'll conclude in Chapter 32 with some thoughts on how to go about mastering C++, so that it will not be a mysterious conglomeration of features but instead an important part of your tool kit.

Simplicity through complexity

31.1 The world is complicated

From time to time, I marvel at the complexity* of everyday life.[1]

For example, I am writing this paragraph at home with help from three general-purpose computers and several special-purpose ones, while listening to a Bach violin sonata. I would like to invite you to step back for a few moments to consider some of the technology that makes this possible.

First, there is the home. Perched on the side of a ridge in a small suburban town, it isn't particularly unusual by today's standards. To a contemporary of Columbus, however, it would offer luxuries out of reach even to royalty. It is heated in winter and cooled in summer. All I need to do is to flick a little switch to select "heat" or "cool," and to set a dial to the temperature I want.[2] The house has hot and cold running water. It also has windows of glass clear and flat enough to let me see outside clearly. Most of those windows have two sheets of glass with an air space between, so as not to let heat out (or in). I can open them, too. Think about how much effort went into making each of those things possible.

Now, consider the computers that I'm using instead of a typewriter to write this chapter.[3] The computer in my house occupies about a cubic foot, including both the processor itself and the separate cabinet that houses its disk drive and the tape-cartridge device that I use to back up the disk. Attached to it are a monitor, a keyboard, and a modem. The keyboard has a mouse[4] attached to it. This computer runs an operating system, under which runs a window system and various application programs. One of these programs is half an editor.

This half of the editor is in charge of displaying text on the monitor. It "knows" how large its window is and what text it must display, from which it

---

* This chapter is based on an article that had footnotes liberally scattered throughout. Unfortunately, all those footnotes together were complex enough to overwhelm the page-balancing software that we used to typeset this book. We therefore made an engineering decision to push some of that complexity onto our readers by collecting all the footnotes into a single section at the end of the chapter.

can figure out where each character of that text should go. It can also arrange for me to have multiple windows "looking" into the same text, so that, when I change something in one, the change instantly appears in all others showing that text.

The other half of the editor is running on a similar computer in my office, about 4 miles away. That program deals with files and their contents, independently of what is displayed. Thus, as I type, the computer here collects my keystrokes and sends them every so often to the computer there, which eventually writes them into a disk file.[5]

As it happens, the disk file that contains the text is located not in my office, but rather in a computer room elsewhere in the same building, where it shares a file server—the third computer that I mentioned—with files used by a handful of my colleagues. I won't go into the technology that connects these three computers, nor will I describe how it is possible for me to be listening to sound reproduced from a performance, given 8 years ago and 4000 miles away, of music composed more than a quarter millennium ago.

31.2 Complexity becomes hidden

I once read[6] that the workings of products of mature industries are hidden. Consider, for example, an early automobile. Many of the mechanical parts were right out in the open, presumably to make them easy to fix when they break. As the automobile industry matured, two things happened. First, automobiles became much more complicated. Engines, transmissions, suspension, steering: Everything became much more complex, as people came to expect a higher level of performance and convenience. Second, those complexities became ever more deeply hidden. It is unusual to find a car in the US today that doesn't have automatic transmission or power steering, even though those systems are so complicated that they became feasible only relatively recently.

As another example, consider recorded music. Edison cylinders were simple: Incoming sound vibrated the air in a horn, which vibrated a diaphragm, which vibrated a needle, which gouged wavy lines in a wax cylinder. That cylinder could then be used to make others, which, when played, would reproduce the sound by a similar process.

Today, the predominant sound medium is the compact disc. An amazing amount of technology goes into those things. To play one back, we must first extract the bits from the minuscule pits on the disc. Think about how precise the tracking mechanism must be to achieve that. Then, there are two layers of buffering and error correction, to allow for the possibility that the disc surface might not be perfect. Only then can the bits be converted to an analog electrical signal.

As still another example, consider the cameras that people use for snapshots of family gatherings. In 1960, such a camera typically had a simple fixed-focus plastic lens and a mechanical shutter. Its design was based on the assumption that most pictures would be taken in bright sunlight, and that the film was sensitive enough to allow pictures to be taken under such conditions with a very small lens. These assumptions allowed the lens to be manufactured cheaply, and also made it unnecessary for the camera to have a focusing mechanism.

Although such cameras still exist today, it is much more common to have a camera with a much more sophisticated lens controlled by a microprocessor that controls focusing and exposure. There will often be a built-in flash unit, as well as more electronics to trigger the flash when needed, and to match the flash intensity and exposure to the distance between subject and camera. The film is color, too, instead of black and white, and the technical[7] quality is much higher than it was then.

31.3　Computers are no different

The world is a complicated place. Industrial products become more complicated as industry matures. We should therefore expect that computers also will become more complicated with time, but that the complexity will be better hidden. Is this true?

Part of the answer depends on how we define *computer-system complexity*. For example, in 1970, the main computer at Columbia University was an IBM System/360 Model 91, one of the fastest general-purpose computers available anywhere. That machine filled a room bigger than most people's houses. It needed huge amounts of well-regulated electricity, supplied by a motor–generator in the basement.[8] It needed a river of chilled water for cooling, and a raised floor to make room for the huge cables that strung it together. In size or resource consumption, it dwarfed anything I have used since. A mechanical engineer might well say that computers have gotten less—rather than more—complicated.

But that is far from the whole story. The Columbia machine had 2 megabytes of main memory; today, it is common to find desktop machines with 64 megabytes. Reading memory took about 0.4 microseconds, more than five times as long as what is common today. The 360 had about 1 billion bytes of disk storage—an amount that today will easily fit on a single disk unit small enough to fit in a shirt pocket. It typically executed between 5 and 15 million instructions per second—a figure easily exceeded by today's workstations. So has the complexity of today's machines increased or decreased?

The answer depends on your viewpoint. A desktop workstation has far fewer physical parts than a 1970 mainframe had, despite its larger capacity. What has happened is that the complexity has migrated into things that do not need to be fabricated or assembled individually. A single memory chip may be able to store megabits of data, but that complexity is obtained automatically, during manufacturing. To obtain large memories, humans no longer need to string millions of magnetic cores on tiny wires. In other words, we have learned how to use manufacturing techniques to delegate complexity.

What makes this delegation possible is a kind of abstraction: the ability to treat a bunch of similar things interchangeably, seeing only their differences. For example, the only effective way for human programmers to deal with a computer memory that contains millions of data items is systematically to assign some kind of label (typically, a number) to each part of that memory, and to treat all memory cells the same except for their labels and their contents. That is why a program to add the elements of an n-element array requires only a fixed amount of effort to design: Although it may require order n (computer) time to run, it requires only constant (human) effort to write.

As our computer systems become more complicated, this kind of abstraction gives us hope of being able to continue to manage them.

31.4 Computers solve real problems

There is no doubt that our computer systems have become more complicated from their users' viewpoints as well. In other words, the complexity of these systems is not all being hidden from view; ever more of it is escaping. Reference manuals even for ordinary systems today are so large that most people don't try to understand them: Users learn a tiny corner by consulting their colleagues, or by experimenting; then they stick with what they know. Why should this be?

Consider that people are using computers today to solve problems that they did not attempt earlier. For example, I think that the first time I seriously tried to use a computer to process text was in 1970, and it was not until 1977 that I did so at all consistently. Today, I can't think of the last time I wrote anything substantial *without* the help of a computer.[9]

As another example, I first used a time-sharing system in 1967; even then, the system had a way for users to send messages to each other. It wasn't until 1977 that I first sent a message to someone who was using a computer different from the one I was using. Today, I take it for granted that I can pause while writing an article to answer a message from my sister in Connecticut.

In other words, computers do things today that are intrinsically more complicated than what they used to do. It is not surprising that some of that complexity leaks out where users can see it.

Another source of complexity is a by-product of mass production: Once you have a sufficiently streamlined factory, it is easier to build a whole bunch of identical items than to make several different kinds. This is especially true if the manufacturing lead time is long. Thus, we see cases where every car of a particular model has a cruise control; it is easier to put cruise control in every car than to keep track of which cars have it and which ones don't. The same phenomenon applies to widely used software:[10] It is easier to sell one package that solves several problems than it is to sell a separate component for each problem. This is what leads to word-processing programs that take up tens of megabytes of disk space, and come with 800-page reference manuals.

As computers solve more complicated problems, there is therefore pressure for some of that complexity to leak out into the solutions. Perhaps this is just a roundabout way of saying that the computing industry is not mature, so there are still new problems to solve.

31.5 Class libraries and language semantics

Every programming language is a tool to help people use computers to solve problems. As those problems become more complicated, and more people try to use a language to solve more different kinds of problems, there inevitably will be pressure to push some of that complexity into the language. Because abstraction is a major theme in C++, it is reasonable to expect that much of C++'s complexity will come from the desire to offer a choice of solutions to abstraction problems.

As a simple example, consider complex numbers. C++ does not have built into it any notion of complex arithmetic. FORTRAN does, and so do other languages. However, the C++ abstraction mechanisms allow complex numbers to be implemented, with no change to the language itself, in a form that is almost as convenient to use as the ones built into FORTRAN.

Of course, we might argue that *almost* is just a euphemistic synonym for *not*, and that the FORTRAN approach is therefore better. But what if you want to implement some other kind of arithmetic data structure—perhaps quaternions? It's hard to build such things into one's FORTRAN compiler; in C++, however, it's unnecessary. Those same abstraction mechanisms make easy in C++ abstractions that would be difficult or even impossible in other languages. Let's take a look at one of the places where C++ is more complicated than might appear necessary in order to make it easier for C++ programmers to deal with abstraction.

Virtually everyone learning C++ has trouble at first understanding the difference between assignment and initialization. Some of the trouble surely comes from outside: In most languages, it makes no difference, when giving a value to a variable, whether or not that variable had a previous value. Even in C, it is hard to see any difference between

```
int x = 17;
```

and

```
int x;
x = 17;
```

Why is that difference so important in C++?

The reason is that the value of a variable in C++ is a far more general notion than it is in C or in other languages. C++ allows for the possibility that a variable may somehow "own" some resource that must be given up when that variable changes value.

This concept is hard for C++ novices to learn, perhaps because it is unfamiliar. Moreover, knowing the concept is not necessary for writing simple C++ classes. For example, a class that represents complex numbers does not need to know the difference between assignment and initialization.

The difference becomes important when we write classes that deal with data structures allocated elsewhere. Consider a class that represents variable-length character strings:

```
class String {
private:
        char* data;
        int len;
        // ...
};
```

Here, `data` and `len` contain the address and length of dynamically allocated memory that, in turn, contains the characters of the string. Suddenly, the distinction between

```
String s = "hello";
```

and

```
String s;
s = "hello";
```

becomes crucial: By the time that we are assigning a value to `s` in the second example, `s` already has a value, and we must deallocate the memory occupied by the old value before we deal with the new value.

In principle, there is no need for the C++ language to draw this distinction. Instead, we could have designed C++ to make assignment equivalent to destruction followed by initialization.[11] That would make a number of programs simpler, but it would make certain kinds of abstractions much harder to implement.

For example, some C++ libraries offer a kind of class that I have heard people call a *slice*. If we have an object that contains some data structure, we can typically create a slice that refers to a part of that data structure. Assigning a value to the slice then affects the chosen part of the original data structure.

One string class that I have seen says that, if `s` is a `String` and `m` and `n` are integers, then `s(m,n)` represents a slice of `s` that starts at character `m` and is `n` characters long. Thus, for example, after

```
String s = "the dog";
s(4,3) = "cat";
```

the value of s is the cat,[12] and after

```
s(4,0) = "big, fluffy";
```

the value of s is now the big, fluffy cat.[13] If assignment were always
equivalent to destruction followed by initialization, this kind of abstraction
would be much harder to implement.

31.6 Making things easy is hard

Writing C++ classes is an example of doing user interface design, and doing good
user interface design is *hard*.[14] A lot of the stuff in C++ is there to help class
authors solve the user-interface metaproblem by giving them the tools they need
to make life easier for class users. For that reason, designing a good library in
C++ can be more difficult than it is in other languages. The solution space is bigger: C++ offers more strategic possibilities to library designers, thus giving them
more to think about.

In exchange for that extra effort, well-designed C++ libraries can be surprisingly easy to use. Library users can take everything they know about C++, add
the little bit that is relevant to their own particular applications, and program
almost as easily as if they had a special-purpose language tailored to their own
particular problems.

In that sense, perhaps we should consider C++ library design in a different
light. Instead of noting how hard it is to design a good class library for variable-
length character strings or complex numbers, we should note instead how much
easier it is to implement such things as class libraries than it is to add them as
new features to our compilers. Indeed, users are only rarely in a position to
change their compilers at all; it is even rarer for them to be able to move those
changes from one place to another. C++ offers an intermediate abstraction gran-
ularity: It allows us to define the behavior of abstractions in more detail than we
can with most programming languages, while staying out of the compiler's inner
workings.

31.7 Abstraction and interface

Let us now look back at the situation that I described earlier: using an editor split
over two computers 4 miles apart to edit a file located on a third computer. As it
happens, these programs were written before C++ came into widespread use.
Nevertheless, they solve their particular parts of this problem in ways that C++
was designed to facilitate.

Consider, for example, how to make the part of an operating system that knows about files into something that can deal with files located on some other machine. A typical way to do this involves looking carefully at the operating system and asking, "What file operations does this operating system support?" The answer will typically consist of half a dozen or so fundamental operations: open, close, read, write, seek, and so on.

Once those operations are defined accurately, it becomes possible to write multiple sets of subroutines, each of which implements one of these operations for a certain kind of file. This makes it possible for an operating system to support several different kinds of file systems on a single machine. We can imagine one file system tuned for maximum speed, another designed to use as little extra storage as possible for bookkeeping, a third that represents files stored on other machines on a network, and so on.

Three points are important here. First, to solve this problem, we must start with useful abstractions—here, the notions of a *file* and a *file system*. Without those notions, it is hard to see how even to ask what file operations an operating system supports—how would we distinguish file operations from other operating-system facilities?

Once we know what a file system is, the second key idea is to isolate the interface to it, keeping that interface from becoming tangled up with the implementations. It is only through that isolation that we can implement more than one kind of file system, or even know that file systems can be of different kinds.

Third, we need a data structure to keep track of several different kinds of file systems—of several different implementations of that particular interface. The operating system has to know that *this* disk has a fast file system on it, *that* disk has a space-efficient one, and *that other* disk doesn't really exist at all—it's just a way of talking to some other computer over a network connection. To make that knowledge work, we had better have a separate instance of the right data structures for each disk.

It is this kind of abstraction that C++ makes easy: Use an abstract base class to describe the interface, and define a derived class for each kind of implementation. Moreover, the whole notion of abstract interfaces supporting several different implementations gives us a fundamental way of dealing with the complexity of real-world computer systems.

31.8 Conservation of complexity

What underlies this whole discussion is that real-world computer systems are complicated, period. It is sometimes possible—even desirable—to ignore that complexity, but doing so does not make the complexity go away, and ignorance always has a price.

At best, ignoring complexity will make that complexity pop up somewhere else. If you're not convinced of this by now, consider the problem of adding three floating-point numbers. Even this simple problem is hard to solve—assuming that you want the right answer. For example, the obvious solution is

```
double add3(double x, double y, double z)
{
        return x + y + z;
}
```

But this code will not give the most accurate possible answer for all permutations of the values 10^{20}, -10^{20}, and 1. The intermediate sum $10^{20}+1$ will be so close to 10^{20} on most computers that the 1 will be completely lost. The result has therefore a good chance of being 0, instead of being 1, as it should be. Only if the addition happens to be performed in a sequence that adds 10^{20} and -10^{20} will the result be correct.

When solving this problem, then, we can either deal with the complexity or we can ignore it. If we decide to deal with it, we will do so by going to the trouble of ensuring the most accurate possible answer.[15] If we ignore the complexity, that won't make it go away; the complexity will resurface in our users' hands.[16]

Software that deals with complicated problems must cope with that complexity somewhere. Some languages deal with complexity by pretending that it doesn't exist. They offer their users a clean, neat interface, and ignore the parts of the world that don't fit into their model. Others deal with it by tossing it over the fence into their users' yard.

C++ tries to steer a middle course. It lets us write programs that know about all the details of their operating environment, while still allowing us to ignore most of those details when they're not important. It pays for this flexibility by being larger than we might wish—but that's life.

That flexibility is particularly valuable to authors of class libraries. They can offer their users the ability to deal with a wide range of application domains at different levels of abstraction. And, in the long run, abstraction is the most powerful tool that we have for dealing with our complex world.

Footnotes

1. One reason that life is complex is that it has a real part and an imaginary part.
2. If I so chose, I could buy a more sophisticated thermostat that would decide for me whether the house needed heated or cooling. I could also buy one that would remember when I usually get up in the morning, when I come home from work, what my weekend habits are, and so on. I haven't done so, because then I'd have to learn how to use it. Perhaps there's a moral in that.

3.   You may first wish to consider the implications of using a typewriter instead of using pencil and paper. Or perhaps you might think about what it takes to manufacture a pencil—or paper.

4.   My cats aren't particularly interested in the mouse. They would rather sit on top of the monitor and look out the window. Sometimes they chase the cursor around the screen. It doesn't seem to bother them that the cursor is not a three-dimensional physical object.

5.   Oops—I just had an interruption: I got electronic mail from my sister in Connecticut. No problem: Switch to another window, read the mail, answer it, then switch back to my editor window. My actions imply that the connection between the two halves of the editor have to be multiplexed, in the sense that I can be doing something else in another window while the editor continues to run. This interruption also opens a window on electronic mail—another whole area of complexity.

6.   I've forgotten where I read this. If someone has a source for this observation, I'd appreciate hearing about it.

7.   The artistic quality still depends more on the photographer than on everything else combined.

8.   I never saw that motor–generator. I was told that it was kept in a reinforced concrete room so that, if its flywheel ever broke, only the people *inside* the room would be killed.

9.   I write small pieces by hand; they don't count as substantial. I can't remember when I last used a typewriter.

10.   This is less evident for software that has only a few users, because it is less obviously difficult to solve all their problems. Of course, software with no users at all can do anything its author pleases.

11.   The point is a fine one: It would then be necessary for the compiler to detect when an object is assigned to itself. It is not acceptable for

```
x = x;
```

to be interpreted as

destroy x
initialize x *from* x

Indeed, people who define their own assignment operators must often code precisely this test themselves.

12.   This library counts characters starting from zero. Doesn't everybody?

13.   That's the cat who was sitting on the monitor in Footnote 4.

14.   I have heard that a significant fraction of people who buy VCRs never program these machines because they can't figure out how to do so.

15.   This problem in numerical analysis is left as an exercise.

16.   Of course, the users may not care—in which case, we've won the gamble. That's why so many software products are shipped with imperfections.

32

What do you do after you say Hello world?

Assume that you have decided to start using C++ in your work, but you haven't done much with it yet. Perhaps you've taken a course, or read a book or two. Of course, you've already written your first C++ program:

```
#include <iostream.h>

int main()
{
        cout << "Hello world" << endl;
}
```

Where do you go from here?

What follows is informal advice on getting to where you can feel comfortable using C++ professionally.

32.1 Find the local experts

When learning something new, it helps to find people who already understand it. It is much easier to learn C++ if you know people nearby who can answer questions for you, and can help you solve problems. Moreover, because C++ is derived from C, having a C user community nearby also will help in you learn C++.

It helps to make sure that the people who you think are experts really know what they're talking about. Fortunately, there's an easy way to tell, which works most of the time: An expert is someone who not only understands the things that you're trying to master, but also can explain them to you. Anyone who can't answer your questions clearly isn't an expert as far as you're concerned. There are people who can explain things clearly and still be completely wrong, but fortunately, such people are rare.

Similar advice applies to things outside the language. There are many C++ implementations out there, running on many operating systems. Some of the problems that come up when learning to use a particular combination of language and system will be related to the system, so it is important to have people who understand both the language and the system. Remember that any useful program must communicate with the outside world somehow.

32.2 Pick a tool kit and become comfortable with it

Whether you can consult local experts can outweigh the more objective advantages and disadvantages of a particular programming environment. In the final analysis, however, the most important variable in a programming environment is the person using it. When you've used a particular tool kit for a while, you become more comfortable with it and therefore use it more effectively. You then develop a resistance to adopting new tools.

There's nothing wrong with setting up such a barrier to change, as long as you don't pretend that it is insurmountable. If you rush to pick up every new tool as soon as it's available, you won't have time to do anything else. This situation is fine if you review tools for a living; otherwise, it's a dangerous trap. A tool is a means to an end; if you concentrate on the means and lose sight of the end, you're just wasting time.

Of course, it's also a trap to reject every new thing just because it's new. The ideal is to adopt new tools when they're useful and not otherwise. One way to approach that ideal is to demand evidence that any given tool will be worth the effort of learning to use it. If you're not convinced, don't bother with the tool. Again, we return to understanding as a measure of utility.

32.3 Some parts of C are essential ...

C++ is built on C. C has ideas that anyone intending to use C++ effectively must understand. If you've used C for a long time, and feel comfortable with it, these things may be second nature. If not, make them.

For example, C++ programs tend to have more declarations than do their C counterparts. Most of the effort in figuring out what a C program does comes from reading the functions that constitute the program. Because C++ supports data abstraction directly, much more of the effort of understanding C++ programs goes into figuring out the types of identifiers and the meanings of declarations.

Understanding declarations thus is more important in C++ than in C. It does not pay to figure out over and over the difference between declaring an array of pointers and a pointer to an array, or the difference between a pointer to a constant and a constant pointer. Learn how to do so once—thoroughly.

In addition to its unusual declaration syntax, C defines a unique relationship between arrays and pointers. In no major language other than C and C++ are arrays defined in terms of pointer operations. Virtually every C program uses this relationship; learn and understand it completely, rather than figuring it out from scratch each time.

Because of the relationship between arrays and pointers, C programmers tend to express array operations in terms of pointer arithmetic. This, combined with C's ++ and -- operations, can lead to programs that are terse indeed, and that require some practice to understand.

For example, here is a C function that, given an array of pointers to functions, calls every function pointed to by the array:

```
void call_each(void (**a)(void), int size)
{
        int n = size;

        while (--n >= 0) {
                void (*p)(void) = *a++;
                if (p)
                        (*p)();
        }
}
```

Although a is conceptually an array, it is really a pointer—in this case, a pointer to a pointer to a function. This accounts for the two *s in the declaration of a. We can easily see this by looking at the declaration and saying, "Well, if we compute **a, we can call it with no arguments and get no result." So a must be a pointer to a pointer to a function.

Next, we note the expression --n >= 0, which, when used in this context, is a common way of repeating an operation n times. Again, we can see this by stepping through the loop with n = 0 and n = 1, and seeing how many times the loop body is executed.

Then, there is the declaration of p—but if you understand the declaration of a, you should have little difficulty there. Somewhat less obvious is the meaning of *a++, which is a request to fetch the element to which a points, and then to increment a to point to the next element in sequence. There is also the usage if (p), which is shorthand for if (p != 0).

Finally, the expression (*p)() is a request to determine the function to which p points, and to call that function.

None of these things is particularly complicated by itself; they are all part of C and have all been around for years. The trouble is that, if you set out to learn C++, you need to master at least this level of C knowledge. It is worth the effort to understand these parts of C well enough that you don't constantly have to stop and look them up.

32.4 ... but others are not

Some C programming techniques translate directly into C++—but others do not. Although it is generally possible to run C programs as if they were C++ programs, with little or no change, it is also possible to extend C++ programs in ways that C does not allow. There are therefore programming techniques that, although they are legitimate in C, are wise to avoid in C++ programs—because their presence there will restrict the ability to extend those programs in ways that would be irrelevant to their C counterparts.

C has stronger type checking than does its predecessors, and C++ has stronger type checking still. For example, suppose that we want to copy an array of objects of some type T into another array. We assume that N is a suitable constant:

```
T source[N];
T dest[N];
int i;

for (i = 0; i < N; i++)
        dest[i] = source[i];
```

Alternatively, we might write this loop in terms of pointers:

```
int* p = dest;
int* q = source;

while (p != dest+N)
        *p++ = *q++;
```

Either of these loops works in both C and C++.

C programmers, however, may be prone to write the solution this way instead:

```
T source[N];
T dest[N];

memcpy(dest, source, N * sizeof(T));
```

This technique works fine in C, but it invites disaster in C++. To see why, we must look at the C and C++ notions of how values are stored.

Every value in C can be viewed as a sequence of bytes. For any type T, the expression `sizeof(T)` tells how many bytes are necessary. Moreover, calling

```
memcpy(p,q,n)
```

copies n bytes from an area that starts at the location addressed by q into the location addressed by p.

Thus, in C, for any type T, if we have a declaration like

```
T x, y;
```

we are assured that

```
x = y;
```

has precisely the same effect as does

```
memcpy(x, y, sizeof(T));
```

C programmers often use this fact to copy objects without knowing what type they are.*

This technique, in general, does not work in C++, because copying a class object does not always mean the same thing as does copying the bytes that constitute the object. Instead, the copy constructor and assignment operator for the class say how to copy objects of that class.

This may be true even if the class doesn't explicitly contain a copy constructor or assignment operator—for example

```
struct PersonnelRecord {
        String name;
        String address;
        int id;
        // ...
};
```

It is possible to define records such as this one without ever writing a constructor, because, by default, C++ defines copying an object in terms of copying the object's components. In this case, it is a good bet that class `String` has a copy constructor, so that copying a `PersonnelRecord` will *not* be the same as copying the bytes that constitute that object.

How do you know which classes are safe to copy using `memcpy` and which ones aren't? If you have to ask, you probably shouldn't be doing it. Again, there is value in sticking to what you understand.

---

* It is not quite true that `memcpy` has the same effect as assignment. Not every byte in an object is necessarily relevant to the object's value. For example, in a structure such as

```
struct A {
        int i;
        char c;
};
```

there will probably be some *padding bytes* after the value of c, to make the size of the structure a multiple of the size of an `int`. These bytes do not contribute to the formal value of the structure, so, when we assign objects of type `struct A`, we don't need to copy those bytes. When we use `memcpy` to copy such a structure, however, the padding bytes assuredly will be copied, because they are included in the total reported by `sizeof`. Therefore, it is possible in principle to distinguish between regular assignment and `memcpy`. We can make such a distinction, however, only by looking in the padding, and programs that do that should be taken out and shot.

32.5 Set yourself a series of problems

If you do only what you understand, then you must have some way of enlarging your understanding. The most effective way to increase your store of knowledge is to try new problems in a controlled way. Pick *one* aspect of C++ that you haven't understood before and write a program that, aside from using that one aspect, uses only things that you've already mastered. Then, do what it takes to make sure that you understand what your program is doing—and why.

For example, if you aren't sure that you understand the difference between a copy constructor and an assignment operator, try writing a program that proves that you do know the difference. The act of designing such a program will force you to understand the difference much more effectively than will merely reading more about copy and assignment.

How might you write such a program? One way would be to design a class with both a copy constructor and an assignment operator:

```
class Test {
public:
        Test(const Test&);
        Test& operator=(const Test&);
};
```

Then you could use objects of this class in a variety of situations to see how the class behaves. For example, if you begin with the preceding class, you will discover a problem as soon as you say

```
Test t;
```

Although this class has a copy constructor, it doesn't have a default constructor. Thus, at the least, you must give it a default constructor:

```
class Test {
public:
        Test();
        Test(const Test&);
        Test& operator=(const Test&);
};
```

Of course, you must define the assignment operator, and the two constructors that you declared:

```
Test::Test()
{
        cout << "Test default constructor" << endl;
}

Test::Test(const Test&)
{
        cout << "Test copy constructor" << endl;
}
```

```
Test& Test::operator=(const Test&)
{
        cout << "Test assignment operator" << endl;
        return *this;
}
```

At this point, you could learn quite a bit about the behavior of constructors and assignment operators by writing programs that use objects of this class and looking closely at the results.

You can learn even more if you give your class a destructor. Then you can confirm that one object is destroyed for each one created. Of course, that doesn't prove that the ones created are the same as the ones destroyed; for that we must give each object an identity somehow. Here is one possibility, patterned after the design presented in Chapter 27:

```
class Test {
public:
        Test();
        Test(const Test&);
        ~Test();
        Test& operator=(const Test&);

private:
        static int count;
        int id;
};

int Test::count = 0;

Test::Test()
{
        id = ++count;
        cout << "Test " << id
            << " default constructor" << endl;
}

Test::Test(const Test& t)
{
        id = ++count;
        cout << "Test " << id
            << " copied from " << t.id << endl;
}

Test& Test::operator=(const Test& t)
{
        cout << "Test " << id
            << " assigned from " << t.id << endl;
        return *this;
}

Test::~Test()
{
        cout << "Test " << id << " destroyed" << endl;
}
```

Your class now reports object creation, destruction, and assignment, and gives each object a unique identifying number. For example, consider this simple main program:

```
int main()
{
        Test s;
        Test t(s);
        s = t;
}
```

When it runs, it prints

```
Test 1 default constructor
Test 2 copied from 1
Test 1 assigned from 2
Test 2 destroyed
Test 1 destroyed
```

Understanding why this particular output appears is proof that you know quite a bit about constructors, destructors, and assignment operators. Constructing little classes of this kind is a useful way to confirm understanding in many areas.

32.6 Conclusion

I can sum up my advice so far in two sentences:
1. Do what you understand; understand what you do.
2. Extend your understanding one step at a time.

Some additional ideas follow that may help.

- **Pick exercises that are just relevant enough.** It is tempting to try to learn C++ by choosing a problem that is closely connected to your current work. That is a good idea—as long as you don't become tied up in the work and forget about learning.

    When learning a new language, you will gain more by writing programs in a field that you understand. If you have spent the past dozen years making widgets, by all means write programs that have something to do with making widgets. But don't get carried away and turn your first widget exercise into a full-blown widget-manufacturing-support application. You will almost surely gain more if you toss your first effort entirely, and begin again from scratch.*

- **Think operationally.** The biggest conceptual change in going from C to C++ is in learning to stop thinking about the *structure* of your program and think first about the *behavior* of the program's data. For example, the Test class

---

* Amateur telescope makers have a saying: "It is easier to make a three-inch mirror and then a six-inch mirror than to make a six-inch mirror alone."

started with only a constructor and a destructor; only later, once we knew what it would do, did it acquire any data. The operations that a class supports—its interface—are usually more important than is its structure, because we can more easily change the structure than the interface.

- **Think early about testing.** If most of your program is written as class definitions, you should be able to confirm that your classes do what you think they do. One good way to do this is to write test scaffolding as you write the classes themselves. If you check that each piece works before you try to put the pieces together, you are likely to spend less time looking for problems after you do combine the pieces.

  Don't forget to save the test programs after you're done with them. Because interface and implementation are separate in C++, you have the opportunity to come back to your classes and to reimplement them, perhaps to improve their performance. A good test structure can save much time later.

  Because you can reimplement things later, keep your first implementation simple. Do only what you understand and what you know how to test. If you run into a performance problem, you can always come back later. You might even be lucky enough to find that your first implementation is good enough.

- **Think.** All this advice is just that: advice. It is up to you to decide whether it's useful for you. You can do whatever you want with my advice: Try to follow it as accurately as you can, strive to do exactly the opposite, ignore it, or laugh at it. Whatever you do, understand why you do it. You're responsible for the results, whether you understand it or not.

Index

A

abstract
  base class, 48
  interface, 343
abstraction, 25
  data, 12, 15
  incomplete, 127
Ada, 1, 204
adaptor
  function, 255
  iterator, 233
Add_an_integer class, 253
aircraft, 47
Algol 68, Informal Introduction to, 339
algorithm
  generic, 203
  merge, 267
  reversal, sequential, 237
allocation
  cluster memory, 321
  container memory, 140, 148
amortized iterator performance, 220
analysis, numerical, 359
anonymous FTP, viii
APL, 29
applicator, 329
apply function, 217, 244
argument, default, 57
arithmetic
  iterator, 168
  sequence, 227
array
  assignment, 17
  associative, 267
Array class, 144
array
  iterator, associative, 272
  ragged, 96
  two-dimensional, 95

artisan, 25
ASD, 11, 127
assign member function, 288
assignment
  and truncation, 48
  array, 17
  backwards, 283
  container and, 138
  default, 304
  operator, 287
  operator, default, 365
  self, 41, 52, 61, 106, 159, 164, 181, 289,
    294, 319
  versus initialization, 355
assignment, const and, 43
associative array, 267
  iterator, 272
audit trail, 313, 367
automatic
  landing gear, 44
  memory management, 246
  software distribution, 11
automobile, 352
  design, 23
avoiding virtual function, 121
Awk, 266

B

Bach, J. S., 351
backward linear search, 234
backwards assignment, 283
bad_alloc exception, 302
band signal, out of, 329
base class, 322, 344
Basic, 23
Belanger, David, x
bidirectional iterator, 213, 218, 234

G

H

I